371.3
M57d

1200 **DISCARDED**

DATE DUE			

Developing Instructional Units

For the Regular and Special Teacher   Third Edition

ع

Developing Instructional Units

For the Regular and Special Teacher Third Edition

Edward L. Meyen
University of Kansas, Lawrence

wcb

Wm. C. Brown Company Publishers
Dubuque, Iowa

371.3
M57d
120027
Jan. 1982

Contents

List of Figures ix

Preface xi

Acknowledgments xv

1. Unit Teaching in Perspective 1

    Unit Teaching: Appropriate for Whom?, 5
    Prerequisites to Unit Teaching, 7
    Unit Teaching in Today's Schools, 8
    Instructional Practices and Unit Teaching, 9

2. Curriculum Development in Perspective 18

    The Curriculum Development Process, 23
    Curriculum Considerations, 27
    Sources of Curriculum Information, 30
    Instructional Models, 32
    Curriculum Development and Project Procedures, 32
    Summary, 39
    Exercise 1, 41

3. The IEP and Unit Teaching 44

    The IEP: Implications for Instructional Planning, 45
    IEP Content, 46
    IEP Conference Requirements, 47
    The IEP Process, 51
    Guidelines for Developing IEP Forms, 53
    Relationship of the IEP to Instructional Planning, 55
    Instructional Planning and Exceptional Children, 60

Implications for Unit Teaching, 61
Summary, 66
Exercise 2, 69

4. The Instructionally Different Child 73

Social Class Differences, 76
Cultural Differences, 78
Differences Caused by Handicapping Conditions, 81
Implications for Unit Teaching, 85
Summary, 85

5. A Conceptual Base for Developing Experience Units 88

Organizational Construct, 90
Summary, 96

6. Developmental Steps for Writing Experience Units 98

Preliminary Steps, 99
Summary, 109
Exercise 3, 113
Preparing Lesson Plans, 119
Requirements of a Good Unit, 132
Summary, 136
Exercises 4-6, 139

7. Instructional Objectives 144

Criticisms of Using Behaviorally Stated Objectives, 148
Advantages of Using Behaviorally Stated Objectives in
    Writing Units, 150
Prerequisites to Writing Objectives, 151
A Suggested Model for Writing Instructional Objectives
    in Behavioral Terms, 153
Summary, 156
Work Exercises 7-15, 156

8. Unit-Based Curriculum Planning 174

Implications of Unit-Based Curriculum Planning, 175
"Givens" in Unit-Based Curriculum Planning, 177
Developing Specifications for a Unit-Based Curriculum
    Planning, 180

The Specification Process, 182
Summary, 193
Exercise 16, 195

9. **Developing a Year's Plan of Work for Unit Teaching** 197

Guidelines for Planning, 200
Suggested Approaches, 201
Summary, 222
Exercises 17-18, 223

10. **Evaluation Techniques** 225

Prerequisites to Evaluation, 227
Evaluating Pupil Performance on Selected Tasks, 228
Evaluating the Composite Effects of Unit Teaching, 238
Unit Evaluation Inventory Approach, 239
Comprehensive Skill Inventory Approach, 249
Reporting Pupil Progress, 251
Summary, 256
Exercises 19-23, 259

11. **Seatwork Experiences** 270

Tips on Planning Seatwork Activities, 272
Use of Commercially Prepared Work Sheets, 273
Evaluation of Seatwork Activities, 274
Developing and Sharing Seatwork Ideas, 277
Seatwork and Unit Teaching, 278
Summary, 278
Exercises 24-27, 281

12. **Sample Units** 290

Unit Topic: Time, 290
Unit Topic: Home Safety and Maintenance, 330

Appendixes 355

Glossary 363

Bibliography 367

List of Figures

1. Example of Development-Evaluation Process 25

2. Curriculum Considerations 28

3. Procedures for Analyzing Instructional Settings 30

4. Analysis of Instructional Settings—Classrooms 31

5. The IEP Process 52

6. Organizational Model 91

7. Example of Categorizing Units by Core Area 95

8. Preliminary Steps Schemata 110

9. Suggested Lesson Format 120

10. Sample Lesson 122

11. Lesson Format Schemata 133

12. Example of Numbering System 134

13. Model for Evaluating Objectives 155

14. Skill Specification Process
    Example: Reading 184

15. Application Specification Process 190

16. Continuum Approach Schemata—Year's Plan of Work 204

17. Core Area Approach Schemata—Year's Plan of Work 216

18. Unit Evaluation Inventory (Individual Form) 242

19. Unit Evaluation Inventory (Individual Form) 243

20. Unit Evaluation Inventory (Individual Form) 244

21. Unit Evaluation Inventory (Individual Form) 245

22. Unit Evaluation Inventory (Individual Form) 246

23. Unit Evaluation Inventory (Individual Form) 247

24. Unit Evaluation Inventory (Group Form) 248

25. Comprehensive Skills Inventory (Individual Form) 252

26. Comprehensive Skills Inventory (Individual Form) 253

27. Comprehensive Skills Inventory (Individual Form) 254

28. Comprehensive Skills Inventory (Group Form) 255

Preface

Unit teaching, as a methodology, allows teachers to relate instruction on basic skills to practical application by students. This occurs through couching the teaching of skills and information on themes that are both interesting and important to students. Students then become partners in the planning process and in so doing, exert influence on the content, organization, and teaching of units. To assure appropriate involvement of students, teachers must be efficient in developing instructional units and in curriculum planning. They must also be familiar with the sequential nature of curriculum content.

Unit teaching has historically been popular as an instructional methodology in the fields of social studies and in the early evolvement of special education programs for exceptional children. It's use has been greatly enhanced by recent trends in public education. Today the public schools are being asked to place more emphasis on consumer education, basic economics, understanding of our multicultural heritage, and preparation for careers. Unit teaching becomes an effective instructional option in meeting these curriculum concerns.

The purpose of this book is to provide teachers who desire to employ th method of unit teaching with a systematic approach to constructing instructional units. The procedures presented have been extensively used by teachers and teachers in training. They have been derived by the author through his own experience and the experiences shared by fellow teachers.

History of This Edition

In developing this third edition, the author has attempted to retain the original intent of the book, that is, to provide teachers with a practical but systematic resource in developing instructional units. Because of the author's conviction that unit teaching represents a generic method applicable to all students, the earlier edition used examples related to the handicapped as a means for illustrating the use of units. The objective was to demonstrate to the reader that unit teaching can be used to meet the needs of students with severe learning problems as well as the needs of students generally.

The current edition varies somewhat from the original format. The primary emphasis is on the development of units applicable to varied settings and populations of students. More attention is given to the teacher's role in adapting units to students with "instructionally" different needs. A new chapter has been included on the implications of developing units for students whose social backgrounds may differ from those of the teacher or peers; students with different cultural heritage; and students whose instructional needs are different because of handicapping conditions. The goal of the chapter is to make teachers more conscious of the differences and similarities presented by students and to remind teachers that they themselves may bring a difference to the classroom. A related but important goal of the chapter is to encourage teachers to view unit teaching as a way of acknowledging the positive nature of differences presented by students and as a method for structuring learning experiences that offer students, regardless of their needs, an opportunity to contribute to the teaching-learning process.

An additional new chapter on the design of individualized educational programs (IEPs) has been included. IEPs must now be developed for all handicapped children and youth. Because of the emphasis on meeting the educational needs of handicapped students through regular classes, all teachers must be skilled in the development, implementation, and monitoring of IEPs. Attention has been given to the role of IEPs in unit teaching. Particular attention has been given to helping the reader understand the IEP requirements in the context of instructional planning.

To the Reader

If you are reading this book as a course assignment or as part of an in-service activity, your instructor may suggest a particular sequence. For example, you may first be asked to study Chapter 7, "Instructional Objectives," or chapter 10, "Evaluation" or possibly chapter 11, "Developing Seatwork Experiences." These are skill-related chapters that are prerequisites to unit teaching, but are also applicable to other methods. They will likely represent review for experienced teachers. An attempt has been made to provide a comprehensive resource on developing instructional units and to place unit teaching in the context of curriculum planning. Thus, the book is more than a guide on unit teaching. It includes suggestions and instruction appropriate to good teaching generally. The consequence is that the ordering of chapters is somewhat arbitrary and becomes dependent on the needs of the reader. The structured sequence of the book provides the reader with a perspective through chapters 1, 2, 3, and 4; introduces a systematic approach to constructing units in chapters 5 and 6; emphasizes the writing of instructional objectives in chapter 7; chapters 8, 9, and 10 provide the reader a frame of refrence for relating the development of units to curriculum planning and evaluation; guidelines on the design of seatwork experiences are included in chapter 11; and sample units incorporating the procedures discussed throughout the book are included in chapter 12.

At the conclusion of those chapters where skills or procedures are stressed, practice exercises are included. For selected chapters additional readings are recommended. A glossary appears in the appendices as an additional aid.

Final Comment

Most skilled teachers are instructional developers. They approach each class with an attitude of determining the needs of the students and an aim toward modifying the instructional experiences in accordance with the observed needs. For the most part this means that a teacher will have to draw on his or her own talents in adapting, modifying, or designing instructional activities. In some cases the development will involve constructing materials, in other cases arranging activities, and in some cases merely guiding the student through a set of experiences. Whatever the response, it falls in the context of development. Good developers are systematic, but they also employ techniques they have found most effective for themselves as a consequence of experience. The author recognizes that teachers vary in their development skills and in the manner through which they approach development tasks. Consequently, the author does not expect all teachers who may use this book to follow each step and suggestion as if it were a recipe. The intent is to encourage teachers to be systematic in the development of instructional units. The book is presented as a resource with the hope that as teachers use it they will apply their own experiences and ideas for improving on it as a reference for future teachers.

Acknowledgments

The purpose of a revision is to improve on previous editions and not to produce a new book. To do this means that the author must be responsive to the observations and suggestions of those who are familiar with the book. Appreciation is expressed to the reviewers who offered detailed suggestions and to the many teachers who have informally, over the life of this book, shared their ideas on unit teaching. I hope these influences are reflected in th new edition.

Special tribute is due to Donna Lehr, who is responsible for many of the revisions and who served as a constructive critic during the revision process. Her efforts were extremely helpful. Appreciation is also expressed to Judy Mantle for developing the sample unit on "Home Safety and Maintenance."

1

Unit Teaching
in Perspective

John Smith, a fourth grade teacher, leaves his classroom to answer a call from the principal's office. While he is gone instruction goes on. Four students are working at an interest center clipping articles on energy from the daily newspaper. They read each article and sort them according to their emphasis on (1) cost of energy production, (2) conservation of energy, (3) general information, or (4) relationship to governmental policy. Sarah, an obviously articulate girl, is working with two peers in recording a story on the experience chart summarizing an audio tape one student made the previous night of a television panel show on energy. One boy is using a hand calculator to compute the cost of utilities from six months of billings, obtained from the Superintendent of Schools, on the building in which the class is located. Several additional students are working independently on a glossary of terms the class had begun the day before. The classroom activities are highly interrelated, but each is varied. Students are carrying out different roles but each uniquely involved. The situation is hypothetical, but it might well be true. It was created to illustrate what many teachers achieve daily through unit teaching. They involve students in selecting topics that "make sense," and they integrate the teaching of academic skills and concepts into a familiar and useful context. Primary emphasis is placed on students applying what they learn and creating an atmosphere in which group instruction allows for individualization but also encourages peer interaction. Independent performance is reinforced, while peer cooperation is required. Teacher direction is evident, as is the influence of students.

Are the students in this fourth grade different? Is John an unusual teacher? Has he always taught units? The answers to such questions, should they be posed, would probably be no to each one. Unit teaching is an exciting method of instruction limited only by the skills of the teacher. Effective unit teaching requires planning, an understanding of learner behavior, knowledge of curricular content and sequences, and familiarity with instructional options.

The scenario of John's classroom could be carried a stage further. Should Donna's mother request a conference to discuss her daughter's progress, Mr. Smith would have access to performance data as well as curricular information. Because the unit on energy, like all of his units, was written out prior to being introduced and all student induced changes have been recorded, Mr. Smith would be able to illustrate to Donna's mother a detailed description of the energy unit being studied. The unit could be related to other instructional areas of the program. Examples of work samples would be available and Donna's own record book, compiled each day as the unit progressed, could be shared. Mr. Smith would be able to emphasize the process of how Donna was learning as well as to provide examples of skill development. Donna could enter into the conference if desired and have a ready reference to relate to in sharing experiences. This example is not to suggest that other methods are not equally effective, but to accent the advantage of unit teaching.

The scenario goes on. One more example might be in order. Assume that the building principal, Mrs. Lehr, in preparing a report for the district curriculum committee, requested that each teacher submit an accounting of the curriculum experiences covered during the year that extended beyond the experiences included in various textbooks series assigned at the different grade levels. Mr. Smith's task would not be difficult. The units themselves represent curriculum plans. Work samples would add to their comprehensiveness. Had Mr. Smith employed the techniques of developing unit specifications and a year's plan of work described in this text, he would have a sequential summary of skills taught through units that would satisfy the request. In any event, the process of preparing and teaching units provides an accounting of content and pupil performance.

Defining Units of Instruction   Some educational methodologies are more easily described than defined. This is somewhat true of unit teaching. Because students vary in their responses to the methods of teachers and teachers vary equally in their teaching styles, teaching methodologies are not uniformly applied. Even when observing two teachers professing to be using the same method, marked differences may be noted. Kelly (1979), in discussing the use of units in Social Studies, states that:

> . . . units come in several varieties, but the main types are the *resource unit* and the *teaching unit*. These two types of units are not that different in kind but are different in treatment and extent. Resource units are more likely to be produced by committees of teachers, although individuals certainly can create them also. These units tend to be pools or reservoirs of ideas in that they contain more objectives, more initiatory activities, more developmental activities, and in fact more of everything likely to be encountered or needed in a unit than is the case with the

teaching unit. The value of this abundance of ideas in the resource unit is that with a large number of and variation in suggestions, the unit can fit the needs of many different youngsters and the capabilities of many different teachers. Thus, once it has been constructed, the resource unit can be a great time saver; it can serve as a source of numerous teaching units to meet the needs of a variety of classes, pupils, and teaching styles.

The teaching unit, on the other hand, usually is made by an individual teacher with a specific group of pupils in mind. Teaching units vary in style and function. The subject matter unit serves as a vehicle for helping children acquire substantive knowledge and usually involves a problem or inquiry approach. The experience unit generally reflects a high degree of social utility and is used widely by professionals in the field of special education. Some teaching units, then, focus upon substantive knowledge, and others upon problems of immediate concern to children or in helping pupils meet life's situations.[1]

The unit model described in this text builds on the advantages of both the resource unit and teaching unit. It requires the development of comprehensive resources in the form of ideas, information, and materials. It also requires that the teacher or team of teachers have in mind a specific group of learners when designing the unit. The unit model in this text will be referred to as an integrated experience unit and includes the following features.

1. In developing and teaching a unit, the teachers will draw heavily on the experiential background of the students.
2. While the unit will emphasize information, specific steps will be followed in designing the unit to assure the teaching of academic skills.
3. The topics and themes selected should represent content familiar to the student so that teaching the unit adds to the learner's repertoire of skills and information in a meaningful manner.
4. Unit are planned in advance according to a set of procedures.
5. The use of experience charts, reports, and supplemental materials is incorporated into each unit to provide practical reading experiences.
6. The central focus is on the integrations of instruction on academic and social skills, with information structured around a common theme building on the previous experience of students.

Chapters 3 and 4 are devoted to expanding on the integrated experience unit as a model. Detailed information on procedures for development and implementation are also offered. The unit will be presented as a complete teaching methodology in that it requires content to be developed, the involvement of students in instructional decision, and the employment of eclectic teaching skills on the part of the classroom teacher.

1. Edward J. Kelly, *Elementary School Social Studies Instruction: A Basic Approach* (Denver: Love Publishing Co., 1979), p. 84.

Among the instructional methodologies that a teacher may elect to employ, unit teaching is probably unique. This method's uniqueness is not related to its complexity nor to its application to specific learner deficits. It relates instead to the method's comprehensiveness, the array of teaching skills required, and its relationship to the development of curriculum products. The method involves an instructional strategy and an emphasis on curriculum development. When unit teaching is analyzed from the perspective of skills involved, it becomes apparent that the method is eclectic. A teacher must be able to construct an instructional unit as well as implement it. The teacher is placed in the role of an instructional manager, a monitor of individual progress, and an extemporaneous developer of learning experiences. Unit teaching allows teachers to be sensitive to the needs, interests, and backgrounds of students. It also calls for on-the-spot decisions in terms of what to teach and what not to teach, when child-related events occur. Such events may include social problems experienced by a particular child or an expression of interest by a group. If one were to apply task analysis to the process of unit teaching, the following examples would represent major tasks:

The design and organization of units as written instructional plans

The making of curriculum decisions on what to teach through the units

The acquisition of group and individual instructional techniques

The selection, modification, and/or development of supplemental materials

The ability to respond to current events as a strategy for maintaining student involvement

The communication of unit content to others sharing in the instructional responsibility for students

The monitoring of skill development taught in an applied context

The list could be extended, but it is sufficient to illustrate the range of teaching tasks involved. The skill that obviously stands out pertains to development. While most teachers modify and occasionally design teaching materials, unit teaching requires independent materials development. There is no alternative.

It is not the need to develop units so much as the consequence of teacher-developed instructional material that accents the necessity for development skills. For example, when a teacher modifies a lesson, designs a work sheet, or builds a series of activities to supplement instruction, the emphasis is generally on a particular skill or concept. Units are much more inclusive. When a teacher develops a unit of instruction and subsequently teaches the unit, the content includes a variety of skills, social concepts, and considerable information. In other words, the unit represents a larger portion of the child's instructional program—the curriculum. This is particularly true if the teacher implements several units during the year. Thus, teachers should take the developmental process of constructing units seriously. If units were readily available as instructional packages, teachers would not need to be concerned with their development. As this is rarely the case, most teachers find it necessary to produce their own units to meet thir pupils' instructional needs.

Unit Teaching: Appropriate for Whom?

Unit teaching is a desirable instructional approach for any student population. Certainly, arguments can be made in favor of applying the method to groups of specific students. But in reality, unit teaching is a highly generic instructional approach that allows skills and concepts to be couched in the context of themes meaningful to students. Thus, units take on both informational and skill development missions. The question of application to varying student populations is not a question of appropriateness, since the content is teacher-pupil determined. Rather the question is twofold: the amount of emphasis to be devoted to unit teaching, and the organizational format in which unit instruction is offered. The most extensive use of units (in terms of time allocation) occurs in social studies and language arts. Use of units as a vehicle for integrating the teaching of skills and concepts from a broad range of subject matter as proposed in this text increases the application of unit teaching. While units are more likely to be included as separate instructional units, they can be used as the basis for a substantial portion of instruction. In both cases, unit teaching is important to the curriculum. The difference in the emphasis tends to be related to the student population and/or the setting and the degree to which teachers have had an opportunity to develop their skills in developing and teaching units. The organizational format question also relates to the amount of emphasis to be given to unit teaching. In situations where occasional units are taught, teachers are more likely to be less formal in their approach to constructing units. The opposite is true when a substantial portion of the curriculum is committed to unit teaching. In this situation more attention is given to the design of individual units and to a system for organizing units in order to maximize their curriculum contributions.

From one point of view, the question of who unit teaching should be used with depends more on teacher variables than on learner characteristics. Teacher skills in terms of teaching techniques and preferred teaching styles probably affect the decision to use or not to use units more than information about the target student group. This does not negate the importance

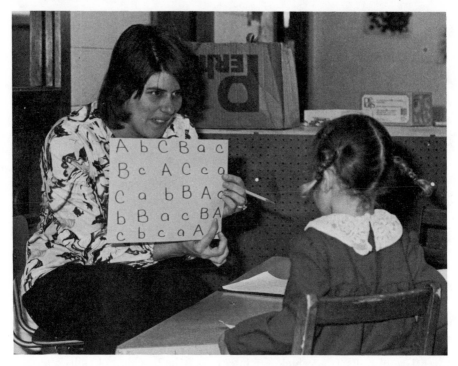

Unit teaching is generally considered a group oriented teaching method, but it also allows for individualized instruction.

of considering pupil data in selecting teaching strategies. However, it suggests that unit teaching applies to children in general, and that the primary factor relates to teacher capabilities in employing the unit technique. Circumstances in which pupils' variables dominate the decision to use units occur when the student target group has characteristics that demand serious consideration of the unit method. An example would be students whose academic skills, such as reading, are low, but because of their general ability and need for knowing concepts and information beyond their skill ability, modes of instruction that are applied in nature and not totally dependent on reading become essential. The primary learner characteristics that make units highly desirable relate to the capabilities of imbedding the teaching of skills, concepts, and information in experiences highly meaningful to the learner. Units also provide more options for students requiring concrete instructional techniques. At the same time, they allow enrichment activities and individualization sufficient to challenge the highly talented student.

Prerequisites to Unit Teaching

Although it is not reasonable to suggest that there are ten rules to good unit teaching or that there are absolute prerequisites that must be met by the teachers desiring to teach units, certain teaching behaviors do enhance the effctiveness of unit teaching. These behaviors are not unique to unit teaching. In many ways, they are essential to good teaching in general. Collectively, these teaching behaviors result in successful unit teaching.

Respect for views of students is some times assured to be an innate behavioral characteristic of people who work with children. In unit teaching, the teacher must be capable of communicating this respect to students. Unit teaching requires students to play a role in influencing content decision, instructional activities, and to a certain extent the instructional techniques used by the teacher. This is not to suggest that the teacher concede such decisions to students, or that students are asked, "What do you want to learn?" However, but it does mean that the teacher must be convincing in interacting with the students so that they recognize that their views are valued and that they have contributions to make in creating a positive teaching-learning climate.

Teacher confidence is extremely important. Unless teachers have confidence in themselves, the responsibilities of making curriculum decisions, designing units, and guiding the behavior of students may be too much. Some teachers are more comfortable in employing techniques that do not require them to construct material. Still others prefer more individualized approaches.

Knowledge of curriculum content in the subject area(s) involved in unit teaching is essential. The teacher's personal knowledge often becomes a primary resource in structuring unit content. Thus, unless the teacher is reasonably knowledgeable about curriculum skills and concepts, difficulty will be encountered in the selection and sequence of skills within units.

Sensitivity to the personal needs and behavioral patterns of students is always important, but is particularly so in unit teaching. Units allow teachers to alter instructional plans to accomodate current events and to orient units to the specific interests of students. A major advantage of the unit method is that it allows teachers to capitalize on the experiential background of students. Many students bring to the classroom a wide array of information that they probably will not be able to share unless the teacher creates circumstances that are conducive to their participation. Teacher sensitivity must be reflected in how the teacher allows students to become active participants in learning. This involves their sharing of what they have to offer.

Group teaching skills probably represent the single most important teaching skill applicable to unit teaching. Included in these skills are questioning techniques, the ability to differentiate reinforcers when working with a group, being a good listener, the ability to organize instruction and learners for participation in instruction, and being responsive to students in a convincing manner. The last skill is important. Students need attention and, above all, need to feel confident that the teacher is attending to them personally.

Flexibility becomes a virtue in unit teaching. It is not feasible to maintain a rigid time schedule. Teachers will encounter situations in which plans must be changed in order to gain closure on an experience. In other circumstances, students may not be responsive to a particular lesson, and with little notice, the teacher must shift to a relevant but contrasting activity.

These behaviors describe mature teaching behaviors. Beginning teachers will find that the challenge of developing and teaching units is a good route to developing these essential skills. Once proficient in unit teaching, the teacher can probably be successful in implementing almost any teaching technique.

Unit Teaching in Today's Schools

While there are obviously major changes occurring in the public schools that have no or little relationship to unit teaching, there are a number of changes evolving that are supportive of the kind of instruction that takes place in unit teaching. As the public expands the responsibility of education, the need to rely on an instructional technique that integrates concepts and understandings with timely events and applied content becomes essential. For example, educators are being told that young people must be informed consumers, knowledgeable of the principles that underly our nation's economy, capable of making career decisions, able to appreciate cultural differences, able to be responsive to the cultural diversity characteristic of this country, and instrumental in protecting society from the deterioration of the family structure. These societal concerns tend to be translated into educational program needs and practices for the public schools. How they are incorporated into the curriculum varies, but they initially tend to take the form of curriculum guidelines for teachers. It is not uncommon for instructional materials to be developed locally and to approximate units of instruction.

Each of the examples cited represents areas that are becoming part of the public school curriculum at the elementary to secondary levels. Because new areas of content, in reality, compete with existing curriculum commitments, they are seldom introduced into the curriculum as separate courses. Rather, they frequently become part of the curriculum via teachers attempting to integrate the new skills and concepts into an existing course or program. Over time they may emerge as course options or as a curriculum approach.

The point in mentioning the recent translations of public concerns into educational practices is that early in their development they are often introduced in the context of instructional units. They are topical in nature and focus on information related to life skills. Consumer education is an excellent example. The emphasis is not merely on making wise decisions as a consumer but also being able to apply the academic skills, often taught in isolation, to practical consumer situations. Teachers skilled in the systematic development of instructional units can greatly enhance the efforts of districts in introducing new areas to the curriculum. Because it takes time for prepared curriculum options to reach the market and in fact conceptual views on curriculum to formalize, the success of the public schools in responding to changes in the curriculum expectations of the public depend greatly on the ability of the schools to make use of the development talent represented among teachers. Thus, the role of teachers in curriculum planning is no longer primarily limited to that of selection and adaptation, and is increasingly including curriculum development in the context of construction of curriculum materials, determining content, organizing content, and implementing procedures.

The previously discussed circumstances contribute to conditions that are highly conducive to employing the unit method. Reasons exist for strengthening the development role of teachers in curriculum planning. There is a renewed emphasis on the introduction of new curriculum areas into the curriculum through a topical format. Public support for teaching applied skills is growing. Additionally, there is a developing awareness that not only do students desire to influence curriculum decisions but that they do have useful observations to share. While unit teaching continues to be popular, it is anticipated that the conditions that not only influence the popularity of unit teaching among teachers as a preferred method but that districts will begin to offer more support and in-service training for those teachers willing to strengthen their development skills.

Instructional Practices and Unit Teaching

If there is a movement in education on which some consensus can be claimed, it probably relates to the general realm of individualizing instruction. Without attempting to define individualized instruction or ascribe to a particular approach, one can examine a group of rather specific practices that, through a variety of configurations, become elements of individualized instruction. These include applying task analysis, specifying instructional objectives, the use of criterion measures, and the provision of choice through instructional options. These same practices are essential in unit teaching, even though it is frequently viewed as a group instructional approach. As previously mentioned, unit teaching draws on most teaching skills. It is, in many ways, a method requiring an eclectic teacher. In this context, teachers who use the unit method need to be sensitive to the many trends that surface and influence instructional practices. In some situations it is not the trend that is of most concern to teachers, rather it is a consequence of the trend.

Viewed from the perspective of the conditions they create, then, much can be gained by teachers' examining these trends as they relate to unit teaching. Obviously, teachers should examine educational trends regardless of their instructional orientation. However, in analyzing new approaches, trends, or ideas, it is helpful to have a frame of reference. Teachers can use their teaching style, teaching assignment, or a particular methodology, such as unit teaching, as a frame of reference. This is not to suggest that a teacher should seek to evaluate each new idea or practice only in terms of its application to his or her situation. Rather, they should be approached from the perspective of what they represent and the implications for a particular preference in teaching style or methodology.

Competency-Based Instruction   The current emphasis on competency-based instruction is impacting on teacher education as well as on elementary and secondary education. Unit instruction is directly related to the objectives and the pre- and post testing of performance against criterion measures used in competency-based instruction. Of all the trends, this probably will have the most significant influence on unit teaching, particularly on the design and construction of units, rather than the actual process of unit teaching. Most competency-based programs include the development of modules. If you examine samples of modules, it is apparent that they approximate miniunits. The emphasis on module development should yield additional insights into the improvement of unit design.

Most beginning teachers enter the field having been required in their training program to have developed at least one instructional module. Consequently, those who have not been taught how to design units will have had some experience in the design of instruction. The instructional process of preassessment, specifying objectives, preparing activities, teaching, post assessment, and revision is compatible with the process of constructing units.

Competency-Based Testing   Not to be confused with competency-based instruction is the movement toward mandating competency-based testing programs that are being legislated in most states. Such programs attempt to set minimal standards and uniform procedures for measuring student performance. The consequence of not meeting standards for the student ranges from retention or remediation at different grade levels to failure to be awarded a high school diploma at the completion of the twelfth grade. The consequence for schools is currently undetermined, but the likely impact ranges from having to reallocate resources to reexamining curriculum to strengthening the emphasis on the practical application of basic skills. In those states where the results have been made public, considerable attention has focused on curriculum offerings and their appropriateness to particular student groups.

Open School Models The movement toward the open school concept of education places considerable emphasis on pupil initiative and places the teacher in an "engineer" role. Individual learner performance is closely monitored, and the student is given considerable freedom in pursuing personal interests. Instructional approaches that allow pupil-initiated experiences to occur are encouraged. The implications for unit teaching of the open school model are twofold. First, in most open schools the climate is highly conducive to unit-related activities. Pupils are encouraged to create products and to work cooperatively on mutual projects. Thus, teachers willing to modify units for small-group efforts and capable of guiding students as participants in unit design will be able to use units effectively in the open school model. On the other hand, teachers who feel that they must control the instruction through their unit teaching will not be as successful, or they will find themselves distorting the open school concept and employing traditional methods under the guise of the open school model.

The second implication pertains to the team teaching often found in this model. Participating teachers may find it necessary to restrict the skills and concepts included in unit teaching to those instructional areas for which they are primarily responsible on the team. However, this restriction is compensated for by their having access to the experience and expertise of other team members in unit design. An additional related feature of the open school model is the frequent use of classroom interest centers, which can be capitalized on to the advantage of units. Th primary negative implication pertains to the necessity of monitoring individual student performance. This is often done at the behavioral objective level. In unit teaching, this task added to development responsibilities results in a major time commitment by the teacher.

Due Process The due process issue relating to student rights may seem far removed from unit teaching. However, it must be noted that one of the major concerns of the due process issue is the question of whether a child's educational program is appropriate and efficient. The emphasis is on accountability. Few teaching methods provide so comprehensive a course of accountability evidence as unit teaching. For example, a well-designed unit

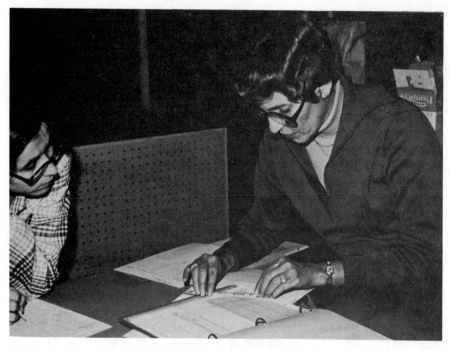

Students can and should participate in planning units.

clearly illustrates the content covered. Teachers who execute units effectively also systematically collect data on student progress. If the planning procedures described in this book are implemented, teachers will be in a position to provide complete information on the instructional program taught to the students assigned to them. This does not guarantee that the program is appropriate for every child, but it does clearly provide a source of information for making decisions on program appropriateness. This particular example is offered not as an artificial or contrived example, but to illustrate the point that a teacher need not withdraw from emphasizing unit teaching merely because of a trend towards accountability. Unit teaching provides an excellent approach to instructional accountability.

Student Participation in Curriculum Decisions   Although they are not necessarily part of a visible trend with its own identity, students are seeking and being given more of a role in influencing their curriculum. The impact goes beyond representation on planning committees at the secondary level. Teachers are being encouraged to employ more democratic procedures in selecting content and to allow students to elect options in satisfying instructional requirements. One of the strengths of unit teaching is that it allows for student participation in the planning process. Units can actually be designed so that students carry much of the instructional load through projects, interest centers, and planning activities.

Least Restrictive Environment (LRE)   For several years, the self-contained special class has been the primary instructional model for providing educational programming to exceptional children. While the special class model is still used as an instructional option for exceptional children it has been demonstrated that a variety of instructional alternatives are appropriate in meeting the educational needs of exceptional children and youth. During the late 1960s and early 1970s, a major legislative effort was made by advocacy and professional groups to assure a free and appropriate public education for all handicapped children. This resulted in passage of PL 94-142, "The Education for All Handicapped Children Act," in 1975. The law may well represent the most significant piece of educational legislation passed in decades. In addition to requiring that all handicapped children receive free and appropriate public education, it also sets forth a series of due process procedures and requires the adoption of two educational practices. These include the individual educational program (IEP) and the least restrictive concept (LRE). The IEP basically represents an instructional plan specific to the learner's needs. Although the IEP requirement is restricted to handicapped children and youth, it affects regular classroom teachers in that they must develop and implement IEPs for handicapped students assigned to their classrooms. See chapter 3 for a detailed discussion of the IEP. The least restrictive environment concept is basically a philosophical approach that has been legislated as an educational practice. It means that handicapped persons should participate in activities available to all people as much as possible in the same manner as nonhandicapped persons. In other words, the fact that a person is handicapped should not be cause to assume that they will need particular kinds of services or are destined to a specific life-style. For example, few nonhandicapped persons live in institutional surroundings except for short periods of time. Yet for many handicapped persons, this has become an accepted living environment. The least restrictive environment concept would require that living arrangements typical for nonhandicapped persons be considered first and that a priority be placed on providing whatever services may be necessary to enable a handicapped person to live in a community, that is, a normal living setting. For some handicapped persons this will mean being independent and living in a house or apartment and raising a family. For others it may mean living by oneself, but having someone available to provide assistance. Still others may live in group homes, adult foster homes, or in closely supervised living quarters. And, yes, some may need the care provided by an institution. The point is that attempts must be made to first provide for the handicapped in less restrictive settings than institutions.

Educationally, the least restrictive environment (LRE) implies the same principle, that is, meeting the educational needs in the regular class to the degree possible. This means that placement of the handicapped child outside the regular class should occur only when the nature or severity of the handicap is such that the student's needs, with support services, cannot be met in the regular class. It is clear that there is a definite trend to move away from considering the special class as the primary instructional option for exceptional children and to view it as merely one of several options.[2] Integral to the trend is a shift of responsibility for exceptional children from special educators to regular classroom teachers, with special education personnel assuming a support role. The popular term for this trend is *mainstreaming*. It implies that all children, to whatever degree possible, should remain in the mainstream of education. For exceptional children, it suggests that the focus be on assisting the regular classroom teacher, through training, consultation, and instructional resources, to meet the exceptional child's needs within their regular class. The exceptional child may, if necessary, attend a resource room or receive tutorial assistance part-time. But the child's primary identification remains with the regular class, and the regular class teacher assumes primary responsibility for his or her instruction. The self-contained special class becomes an option for those children whose learning problems are sufficiently serious to preclude their benefiting from regular class affiliation. As a result, the special class is used less frequently as an instructional option for mildly handicapped students, while it remains a viable option for children with more severe learning problems. Even in the latter situation, the special class option is viewed as tentative, and the child's placement as temporary. When appropriate, the emphasis is on shifting the child's participation from the self-contained to the regular classroom. The implications of this trend are many; it is mentioned here simply to illustrate the relationship to unit teaching.

The obvious implication is the increased instructional responsibility assumed by the regular class teacher. The range of abilities in the regular class will probably not be extended, since many exceptional children have always been assigned to regular classes. However, the number of children with severe learning problems requiring specialized instruction will increase.

---

2. A detailed bibliography of references pertaining to mainstreaming appears at the end of this chapter. The author elected not to discuss the trend fully because the subject is covered more extensively in several other sources available to most readers.

Instead of having an occasional student who is difficult to program for, regular class teachers can anticipate having many classes with students having a full range of abilities. The principles of mainstreaming call for the provision of support services to the teacher and, if necessary, directed to the child. The intent is not merely to place exceptional children in regular classes. The provision of support services necessitates the participation of additional personnel. In most cases when exceptional children are returned to the mainstream, the child's instructional program will involve at least two teachers—the regular classroom teacher and the resource teacher. This arrangement in itself does not significantly affect the application of unit teaching.

The major implication of the least restrictive environment (or mainstreaming, as LRE is popularly referred to) is for regular classroom teachers. As previously mentioned, the ability range among students in regular classes may not be changed greatly, but teachers can expect to have more students with learning problems assigned to them. The student's learning problems may relate to sensory deficits, such as vision and/or hearing, or to control of one's social behavior, to sporadic learning patterns, or to individuals who display serious developmental lags in learning. These students will probably also be receiving services from support personnel, such as resource teachers, speech pathologists, physical therapists, or school psychologists. Thus, it will be necessary for the regular class teacher to work with other personnel responsible for the handicapped student's instructional program when planning a unit.

If districts truly develop mainstreaming programs and do not merely integrate exceptional children into regular classes, sufficient resource people should be available to consult with teachers in the design of instructional units. Regular class teachers are likely to find that exceptional children will require considerable remedial instruction in the skill areas and that unit instruction will become a major vehicle for reinforcing the application of such skills. Teachers in mainstreaming situations will also find that units provide an excellent means for providing meaningful repetition. Consideration should also be given to peer teaching techniques in using units in mainstreamed classrooms.

It would be inappropriate to suggest that the trend toward placement of exceptional children in regular classes will lessen the difficulty of preparing units or create a better climate for unit teaching. It will require more planning and more emphasis on evaluating pupil performance. In the process of developing units for mainstreaming programs, teachers should experiment with planning procedures and group instructional techniques that are applicable to classes whose range of abilities and behavioral characteristics vary extensively.

Summary

Unit teaching is an instructional method requiring a wide range of teaching skills. It is generic in that the method is applicable to all students. However, it offers particular advantages for those students who profit most from being taught skills in an applied context. The intent of this chapter was to introduce unit teaching as a highly desired teaching methodology and to stress the importance of employing systmatic procedures in the development of units.

REFERENCES

KELLY, EDWARD J. *Elementary School Social Studies Instruction: A Basic Approach.* Denver: Love Publishing Co., 1979.

ADDITIONAL SELECTED REFERENCES

BARTH, Joan W., et al. *Experiences in Inquiry: HSGP and SRSS.* Boston: Allyn & Bacon, 1974.

BERRY, K. E. "Mainstreaming: A Problem and an Opportunity for General Education." *Focus on Exceptional Children* 6 (1974).

―――, et al. *The Guts to Grow.* San Rafael, Calif.: Dimensions Publishing Co., 1974.

BIRCH, J. W. *Mainstreaming: Educable Mentally Retarded Children in Regular Classes.* Minneapolis: University of Minnesota, Leadership Training Institute/Special Education, 1974.

BROOKS, B. L., and BRANSFORD, L. S. "Modification of Teachers' Attitudes Toward Exceptional Children." *Exceptional Children* 38 (1971):259-260.

CHAFFIN, J. "Will the Real 'Mainstreaming' Program Please Stand Up! (Or . . . Should Dunn Have Done It?)." *Focus on Exceptional Children* 6 (1974:1.

DENO, E. N., ed. *Instructional Alternatives for Exceptional Children.* Arlington, Va.: Council for Exceptional Children, 1973.

DE SHAW, BYRON L. *Developing Competencies for Individualizing Instruction.* Columbus, Ohio: Charles E. Merrill Publishing Co., 1973.

FOUNTAIN VALLEY SCHOOL DISTRICT. *Handicapped Children in the Regular Classroom.* Fountain Valley, Calif.: ESEA Title III Project 1232.

HANNA, LAVONE A.; POTTER, GLADYS L.; and REYNOLDS, ROBERT W. *Dynamic Elementary Social Studies: Unit Teaching.* 3rd ed. New York: Holt, Rinehart & Winston, 1973.

HARTUP, W. W. "Peer Interaction and Social Organization." *Carmichael's Manual of Child Psychology,* vol. 2, edited by P. H. Mussen. New York: John Wiley and Sons, 1970.

HILL, WILHELMINA. *Unit Planning and Teaching in Elementary Social Studies.* Washington, D. C.: U.S. Office of Education, 1963.

KING, EDITH W. *The World: Context for Teaching in the Elementary School.* Dubuque, Iowa: William C. Brown Co., 1971.

MUSGRAVE, G. RAY. *Individualized Instruction: Teaching Strategies Focusing on the Learner.* Boston: Allyn & Bacon, 1975.

PALMIERI, J. C. "Learning Problem Children in the Open Concept Class." *Academic Therapy* 13 (1973):305.

STEPHENS, LILLIAN S. *The Teacher's Guide to Open Education.* New York: Holt, Rinehart & Winston, 1974.

TALMAGE, HARRIET, ed. *Systems of Individualized Education.* Berkeley, Calif.: McCutchan Publishing Corp., 1975.

THOMAS, GEORGE I., and CRESCIMBENI, JOSEPH. *Individualizing Instruction in the Elementary School.* New York: Random House, 1967.

THOMAS, R. MURRAY, and BRUBAKER, DALE L. *Decisions in Teaching Elementary School Studies.* Belmont, Calif.: Wadsworth Publishing Co., 1971.

2

Curriculum Development in Perspective

The unit method represents an approach to organizing the content and construction of teaching activities. This is, in essence, curriculum development. Thus, it becomes very important for the teacher, in preparing units of instruction, to understand the principles of curriculum development. This chapter presents an orientation to the curriculum development process. It is not a short course in curriculum development. Throughout this book, references are made to systematic planning relative to the designing of instructional units. The intent of this chapter is to place unit teaching in a curriculum context.

Historically, teachers have served on curriculum planning committees. Numerous curriculum guides, courses of study, and, more recently, assortments of behaviorally stated objectives have been produced. Typically, the focus has been on producing a product, and insufficient attention has been given to training teachers in curriculum development skills. Consequently, teachers frequently approach participation on such committees with only a vague idea of how they are to complete the assignment, although they are fully cognizant that something will be produced. This product orientation has tended to interfere with providing teachers needed preparation in the area of development skills. Master teachers are not necessarily expert in the curriculum development process, although in general they possess the appropriate frame of reference and readiness to acquire development skills. Too often, administrators assign teachers to curriculum planning committees without considering what is required to complete the assigned tasks. This author strongly supports teacher participation in curriculum development but believes that certain skills and information should be prerequisite to their participation. To delegate curriculum development responsibility to teachers without providing them the necessary support in the form of resources, training, and leadership places them at an unwarranted disadvantage.

The cumulative effect on a child participating in several instructional units is that the experiences taught via units become a major portion of his or her curriculum. Thus, teachers must be aware of the collective impact of units on a child's curriculum. Those who employ the unit teaching method must be extremely sensitive to the overall curriculum implications of unit teaching. Readers are encouraged to pursue additional study in curriculum development. (Selected references on curriculum planning appear at the end of this chapter.)

The terms *curriculum, instructional program, courses of study,* and *curriculum guides,* to mention a few, are sometimes used interchangeably to describe what a particular student population should be taught. Although precise definitions for all processes and activities that educators engage in while carrying out curriculum development may not be necessary, it is important to differentiate between methodology and curriculum. This concern relates primarily to the confusion that surrounds instructional planning for students in situations where teachers are required to make major curriculum decisions.

Most of the educational decisions teachers are required to make are instructional in nature; they pertain to remediation of identified deficits and to techniques for enhancing the child's acquisition of particular skills and concepts. Only when a teacher encounters a child whose learning problem is serious is he or she called on to make major decisions regarding how that child is to be taught and the sequence in which the skills are to be presented. For the most part, teachers work from a base of prescribed curricula inherent in either guidelines or basal series and make their decisions to modify the program to meet the needs of individual children. This is also true in terms of teaching the majority of mildly handicapped children. For example, the child with a speech problem may receive therapy from the speech therapist and/or participate in activities aimed at speech improvement that are provided by the regular teacher. The curriculum, in terms of what will be included in the child's education, will probably not be altered by the need for speech therapy. In the case of children with sensory defects, the task becomes one of employing techniques and materials designed to maximize their learning of the regular curriculum. The sensory defect in itself will not substantially alter the curriculum content, although the rate of learning may be affected. The situation is quite different, however, when the child is limited intellectually, as in the case of the mentally retarded. Here we encounter the problem of having to make major curriculum decisions on *what* is to be taught as well as *how.*

As long as we are concerned with children whose learning problems are remedial in nature, or children who can progress in the regular curriculum with specialized instruction, the responsibilities for curriculum development are shared among regular and special teachers and curriculum consultants in general.

In situations where students are grouped for instruction because of learning characteristics that warrant special attention, additional responsibilities for curriculum decisions fall to the classroom teacher assigned to that group. As more exceptional children are placed in regular classes, teacher involvement in curriculum decisions also increases. Merely placing exceptional children in regular classes will not reduce the need for curriculum planning.

The importance of teachers' being familiar with the curriculum development process is best illustrated by the history of Special Education in planning educational programs for the mild mentally retarded. In this area, the tendency has been to establish special classes and to delegate responsibility for curriculum development to the special class teacher. Each teacher, in turn, has developed a curriculum based on what he or she felt was most appropriate to the needs of children assigned to the special class, thus producing a curriculum unique to the teacher. Other special class teachers in the same system repeated the process of planning curriculum individually. In the resulting situation, the retarded child encountered a new curriculum as he or she was transferred to other special classes or progressed through special class programs in a particular district. These circumstances should not occur. They have happened because of the general lack of investment in curriculum development and the insufficient support being provided teachers in their curriculum development efforts.

Curriculum research and, in many cases, curriculum planning relative to what specific groups of children should be taught, and in what sequence, have not received sufficient attention. Too often, the teacher has resorted to a cut-and-paste approach to curriculum development, because of a lack of direction in curriculum development literature and the absence of good local support. Although the pattern has been somewhat different in the regular classroom, in that teachers have had access to commercially prepared materials, basal series, and extensive curriculum guidelines, as the responsibility for teaching children with learning problems is extended to regular class teachers, their need for curriculum development skills will also increase. Teachers, in general, must be prepared to participate in the process of curriculum development. Such participation will take at least two forms: first, responding to children whose needs dictate the development of a modified curriculum; and second, participating in subject, school, or district-wide curriculum planning.

Defining Curriculum

The term *curriculum* is frequently and varyingly defined as the courses offered, the overall experience provided a child by the school, the program included in a particular subject field, or in some cases, the sum total of experiences afforded school-age children regardless of school sponsorship. The global nature of such definitions confounds the real differences among them. To merely talk about what occurs in an educational setting as being the curriculum implies that there is little order or planning involved. As one reads curriculum literature, it becomes apparent that while the term *curriculum* is often carelessly applied, the curriculum development process is complex, and the decision making that results in curriculum structure is by no means arbitrary.

It also becomes apparent that there are differing views on the relationship of curriculum and instruction as implemented in the classroom by the teacher. Some writers take a comprehensive perspective of curriculum and subsume instruction and teaching methods under that label, along with content specification. Others view curriculum as representing the input into the instructional program. This view suggests that given the input, teachers may select those methods that work best for them in teaching the curriculum. In other words, the curriculum may be standardized, but the instructional programs will vary by virtue of the different methods that teachers employ.

Contrasting views on curriculum are expressed in the writings of Phenix and Johnson. Phenix defines curriculum as

> simply a name for the organized pattern of the schools' educational program. A complete description of the curriculum has at least three components: (1) What is studied—the "content" or "subject matter" of instruction, (2) How the study and teaching are done—the "method" of instruction, and (3) When the various subjects are presented—the order of instruction.[1]

This comprehensive view of curriculum incorporates the instructional program along with structuring the content into a single curriculum concept.

Johnson has developed a model that conceptualizes curriculum as an output of one system and an input of another. He states:

> Accepted usage identifies curriculum with "planned learning experiences." This definition is unsatisfactory, however, if "curriculum" is to be distinguished from "instruction." Whether experiences are viewed subjectively in terms of the sensibility of the experiencing individual or objectively in terms of his actions in a particular setting, there is in either case no experience until an interaction between the individual and his environment actually occurs. Clearly, such interaction characterizes *instruction,* not curriculum. A concept of curriculum that limits it to a *post hoc* account of instruction is of little value. Surely, curriculum must play some role in *guiding* instruction. If so, it must be viewed as anticipatory, not reportorial. Curriculum implies intent.

1. Philip H. Phenix, "Curriculum," in *Contemporary Thought on Public School Curriculum,* ed. E. C. Short and G. D. Marconnit (Dubuque: Wm. C. Brown Co. Publishers, 1968), p. 9.

Surely, too, a useful concept of curriculum must leave some room for creativity and individual style in instruction. In other words, decisions regarding the learning experiences to be provided are the result of instructional planning, not of curriculum development. The curriculum, though it may limit the range of possible experiences, cannot specify them. Curriculum must be defined in other terms.

In view of the shortcomings of the currently popular definition, it is here stipulated that curriculum is as a *structured series of intended learning outcomes. Curriculum prescribes* (or at least anticipates) the *results* of instruction. It does not prescribe the *means*, i.e., the activities, materials, or even the instructional content, to be used in achieving results. In specifying outcomes to be sought curriculum is concerned with *ends*, but at the level of attainable learning products, not at the more remote level at which these ends are justified. In other words, curriculum indicates *what* is to be learned, not *why* it should be learned.[2]

This approach encourages one to think in terms of a three-dimensional construct including (1) the developmental process, (2) the composite of learning experiences delineated and ordered through the development process, and (3) the instructional program which allows students to interact in the educational milieu of their environment. The second dimension would represent the curriculum. Differentiating curriculum from instruction makes it somewhat easier for teachers to identify their role in the educational process. While they have a role to play in curriculum development, as well as in implementing the curriculum through the instructional program, they may frequently find themselves in a situation in which they are asked to carry out an instructional program compatible with a curriculum they have played a minimal role in developing.

The curriculum should provide objectives and offer a basic design for the instructional program. However, teachers should be free to employ those methods that work best for them in accommodating the curriculum. The methods they use will also entail teaching content not specified in the curriculum, especially when they plan experiences that will allow the student to learn prescribed skills, concepts, and information. Teachers will find it necessary to couch the teaching of certain curriculum aspects in content relevant to the learner but beyond the basic curriculum requirements, for example, information on sports, orientation to specific job opportunities, or experiences related to something unique to a child's development.

For the most part, teachers are responsible for the instructional program. While the curriculum specifies the outcomes they should strive for, they are generally free to use methods of their choice and to select a major portion of the supplemental instructional materials. Most likely they will also have a voice in choosing the basal series that may be used in certain subjects.

---

2. Mauritz Johnson, Jr., "Definitions and Models in Curriculum Theory," *Educational Theory* (April 1967), p. 128. Used by permission of the publisher.

The atmosphere they establish and their general teaching style are their own and are not necessarily dependent on the curriculum. Consequently, although several teachers in a school system may be implementing the same curriculum, they may vary considerably in the instructional techniques they employ. Each, of course, must be familiar with the detailed objectives and content of the curriculum.

The Curriculum Development Process

As a frame of reference, let's look at a general example of the curriculum development process. The major determinant in developing curriculum for children centers on the consequences of the child's deficits in terms of learning. For example, mentally retarded children represent a group whose primary educational problems relate to limited intelligence and social ineptness. In structuring a curriculum for them, consideration must be given to the influence these limitations will have on their curriculum needs. Figure 1 illustrates one way of looking at the relationship between the curriculum development process and instructional programs for the mentally retarded.

Curriculum Sources In Figure 1, we begin by looking at the universe of knowledge, skills, and values that could potentially be included in the school curriculum. It is apparent that if our target population is composed of retarded students, a circumscribed curriculum is required. If we are concerned with representative children in general, the content of what might be included in the curriculum would be more extensive. At the same time, it might not include some learning experiences which the representative child learns incidentally but which the retarded child must be purposefully taught.

Curriculum Decisions A number of decisions must be made in the process of circumscribing the curriculum. These decisions are not mere choices; they involve the task of giving the curriculum dimension in accordance with the educational needs of the population for whom it is being designed. These tasks include formulating objectives, delineating content in reference to the objectives, and ordering the content in a sequential manner. Each of these tasks is influenced by the known characteristics of the student population; in this case, the mentally retarded.

Curriculum Influences A number of variables exist that influence the overall development of curriculum. Many exert their influence at the point at which curriculum decisions are made, as shown in Figure 1. Among these influences are learner characteristics, situational variables, and teacher characteristics.

Learner characteristics include a number of variables necessary to consider relative to the learners for whom the materials are being developed. The selection of appropriate materials becomes a major consideration when a large discrepancy exists betwen the skill level of the students and the age of the students. The ethnic background of the student has increasingly become a consideration in the development of materials for use in instruction.

A large range of situational variables are also necessary to consider in developing curriculum, for example, the administrative arrangements of the programs, self-contained classroom versus integrated programs, and open versus traditional classes offer different possibilities. The attitudes, that is, political, religious, and philosophic beliefs, can affect the receptiveness a community to a particular curriculum product.

Characteristics that teachers bring to the learning environment influence the type of curriculum that may be appropriate. Experience, education level, knowledge of learning and development, and responsiveness to change all can become major sources of influence in the curriculum.

Curriculum   The model illustrated in Figure 1 places curriculum as the product resulting from curriculum decisions. As a product, it includes the sequentially ordered content planned as input into instructional programs designed for a particular student population. Basically, it specifies the dimensions of *what* and *when*. It may take the form of structured outcomes, which will serve as directives for teachers in carrying out their instructional programs. The curriculum places restrictions on the instructional program only to the degree that restrictions are inherent in the subject matter. These restrictions are not general, but certain subject matter areas or the nature of some skills do dictate a particular range of appropriate instructional techniques. For example, the teaching of multiplication facts would be difficult to accomplish through a discussion approach.

Instructional Programs   Operationally, the instructional program can be defined as the experience provided the learner in the educational setting. The teacher plans these experiences as a means of implementing the curriculum. Through the instructional program, learners interact with their environment. Within the learning environment, learners interact with their teachers, peers, and materials, as well as with aspects of the school's physical setting. The teacher manipulates environmental components to maximize the child's response to his or her environment. The emphasis is on facilitating the child's progress in attaining the outcomes specified in the curriculum. While teachers may extend their instructional program beyond the dictates of the curriculum, they should be sensitive to the curriculum based on goals for the student. Given the same curriculum, teachers will vary in the instructional methods they employ.

Figure 1. Example of Development—Evaluation Process

Terminal Behavior   The overall impact of the curriculum as executed through the instructional program is ultimately to influence the learner's behavior as he or she progresses through the system. This implies that there are certain accepted concepts about the general nature of learners who have completed the curriculum. These beliefs relate to what they are prepared to do in terms of additional learning, what they are capable of doing at the time they complete the curriculum, and the general social adjustment desired for the particular individual. The goals related to terminal behavior may change as new data are obtained on the group's capabilities and as more effective methods are found.

Evaluative Feedback

Curriculum development is a continuous process. Successful development relies heavily on formative evaluation. As evidence is acquired that a change should be made in sequence, content, teaching strategies, or curriculum product format, this evidence should be considered. Evaluation is an important element of the development process. The primary evaluation technique employed in curriculum development is field-testing, that is, trying out curriculum activities in situations approximating the intended application. Such evaluation allows for product improvement during the development process. This procedure is typically referred to as *formative evaluation*. As illustrated in the model (Figure 1) evaluation occurs at each step in the development process. Most developers approach curriculum design with an evaluation frame of reference. In some cases, evaluation represents a separate component in the development process.

A second and less frequently applied form of evaluation is *summative evaluation*. This term basically implies testing the effectiveness of the curriculum product once it has reached final form. This is after the benefits of formative evaluation have been applied in the design of a prototype and in the field-testing. In the area of curriculum development, summative evaluation is often delayed until the product is available commercially. Under these circumstances, the teacher as a consumer participates in the summative evaluation. As long as the developer employs good formative evaluation procedures and uses the results to improve the product during the development stages, the final product should prove effective under summative evaluation.

The model presented in Figure 1 is intended to provide teachers with a frame of reference for the ways their instructional programs relate to the curriculum development process. In essence, what they do in their instructional program is dependent on the curriculum. Although teachers should participate throughout the curriculum development process, if they are special class teachers in a small district or even regular class teachers at small attendance centers, it is possible that they will fall heir to the task of determining the curriculum as well as implementing an appropriate instructional program. Under these circumstances, they will be likely to integrate developmental aspects with instructional program planning. The other alternative is to borrow the input resulting from curriculum planning done by other districts and select materials and methods to set an instructional program in motion. The immediate concern is to prepare for teaching their classes. For this reason, additional discussion on curriculum considerations and instructional models is warranted.

Curriculum Considerations

In examining commercial versions of curriculum, it is easy to overlook the effort and complex processing that are employed in developing quality curriculum. It may be apparent that a number of persons are involved in the project and that certain evaluation strategies are employed in testing the curriculum. However, the specific development steps are not so obvious. A brief introduction to the curriculum development steps applicable to unit teaching will be presented in Chapter 8. At this point, it is important that the reader be aware of certain factors that warrant consideration in curriculum development. Although curriculum development is not as situation-specific as the instructional program for a selected child, it is not feasible to develop curriculum and then assume it can be implemented without modifications in all settings. It is incumbent on curriculum developers to be sensitive to the conditions under which the proposed curriculum will be implemented. Teachers must approach the implementation of prepared curriculum with the awareness that they will need to make adaptations to apply the curriculum in their particular classroom. Figure 2 illustrates selected variables that must be considered both in curriculum development and in teacher implementation. Too often, teachers are disappointed in curriculum products because they have assumed that the curriculum could be implemented as packaged, and not be affected by local conditions so long as the directions were followed.

Although the variables warranting consideration in curriculum development and implementation are numerous, five basic factors have been selected for discussion: pupil behavior, instructional environment, external supports, established curricula, and teaching style. Although these factors interact considerably, each has its particular influence on curriculum development. In any curriculum development project, these areas should be carefully explored as prerequisites to curriculum development. Collectively, they provide the context in which most curriculum decisions are made.

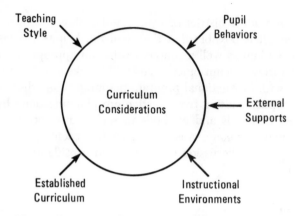

Figure 2.   Curriculum Considerations

Pupil Behavior   Except in unusual situations where instructional materials are developed around very restricted content, as in designing instructional packages about special events (for example, the 1976 Bicentennial), most curriculum development efforts are aimed at meeting the needs of a specified learner population. Thus, it is important to be maximally familiar with the target population. When classroom teachers prepare instructional units or develop curriculum specifications (see Chapter 8), they are familiar with the target population. It is incumbent on teachers who participate in curriculum development to keep the characteristics of the learner in mind as they make curriculum decisions. It is easy to be sidetracked into attending to the subject matter and focusing on creative ways of teaching while overlooking the unique needs of the target population. Even if you are familiar with the group of children for whom the curriculum is being produced, it is helpful to inventory their characteristics relative to the acquisition of cognitive, motor, and social skills. In addition to overt behavior, it is helpful to keep in mind those environmental factors in the child's history that have influenced current behaviors. These include the child's performance history in school as well as his or her home and community history.

External Supports   A serious consideration in any major curriculum development effort is the level of support offered by the administration, such as consultation, budget resources, free time for development, and general leadership. All these are included in the context of external support. A subtle but important support pertains to the reinforcement received by teachers for participating in curriculum development. It may be difficult to identify specific examples of reinforcement. However, with teachers who have previously invested energy in curriculum development projects, it is not difficult to determine their perception of the value placed on their contributions by the administration and by their colleagues.

Instructional Environment The major environment to be concerned with in curriculum development is the classroom(s) where the curriculum will be implemented. In unit teaching, many activities frequently take place outside the classroom. One can determine, in general, the degree to which the classroom and the attendance center are conducive to implementing the proposed curriculum. If experiences are to take place outside school, though, the problem is a little more complex. It is first necessary to determine whether school policy allows for community resource utilization and whether financial reserves are available. These are important considerations that take on added significance when a proposed curriculum change requires unique environmental factors, such as introducing an open school model. Because of the extensive use that unit teaching makes of group and small group techniques, it does make demands on the instructional environment. These should be considered when planning a curriculum involving unit teaching.

Established Curriculum Whenever a curriculum development activity is initiated at the school district level, the current curriculum must be examined. The emphasis is either on revision, replacement, or the addition of a new curriculum element. Thus, the departure point in development is the existing curriculum. Too often, a need for curriculum development emerges as a result of some attempt at assessment of needs. Or special interest groups observe a problem in what they consider to be the instructional program and present it as a major need. In reality the stimulus for curriculum development or revision may not relate to actual needs. A careful curriculum review will often reveal that the problem may not be the curriculum itself but insufficient skill on the part of teachers implementing it or, in some cases, lack of knowledge concerning the curriculum. In cases where the curriculum is clearly in need of revision, it is essential to know what is being revised. If the emphasis is on developing curriculum specifications for unit instruction, the task becomes one of determining which parts of the curriculum will be offered through unit teaching and which through other modes of instruction. In this case, knowledge of the existing curriculum will be a prerequisite to developing specifications for unit instruction. (See Chapter 8.)

Teaching Style Teachers vary in the techniques they employ in their classroom. Given the same curriculum guidelines, two teachers may be equally successful in bringing about appropriate pupil outcomes while using contrasting strategies. Teaching style becomes a serious consideration only when the proposed curriculum requires that specific teaching strategies be employed or makes unusual demands on the teacher in terms of learning new skills or having to create particular classroom arrangements. In general, teaching style is important when selecting a curriculum or new instructional material. Teachers know their own teaching style and can readily determine whether or not a new curriculum or material will require a major change in their teaching behavior.

Sources of Curriculum Information

The primary reason for teachers and others responsible for curriculum development to be concerned with "considerations" is to assure that the current content organization and format are most appropriate. This necessitates that all relevant variable with potential for influencing curriculum decisions be identified. Once the most significant variables have been identified, it is important to determine sources of data on the variables. For example, if past student achievement is considered important by a curriculum developer, what sources of data exist? In this case the counselor or principal would likely have records on achievement testing that would be organized by class and building. In another situation the developer might consider school policies, such as use of field trips, to be important. In this case data could be acquired via a conversation with the principal, or by referring to a Personnel Handbook, should one be available.

One approach to generating ideas on curriculum considerations is to use a grid technique. The technique merely involves first identifying variables warranting consideration (given your curriculum topic) and developing a corresponding list of sources from which data on variables can be collected. See Figure 3 for an illustration of the techniques.

Directions: 1. Define the parameters of the district (program, building, class).
2. Generate a large pool of variables that should be considered when developing a curriculum.
3. Determine sources of data for your pool of variables, that is, where will you get the information.
4. Reduce the variables to a reasonable number of variables directly related to the proposed curriculum project. Consideration should be given to the cost or time involved in obtaining data and its accuracy. If the process is either too costly, time consuming, or yields inaccurate data, the variable may not warrant consideration.
5. Record the variable and sources of data on a grid as shown in Figure 4.

Figure 3.   Procedures for Analyzing Instructional Settings

Setting: **Classroom**

Source of Data

VARIABLES	IEP	RECORDS REPORTS	CREDENTIALS	SURVEY	SELF-REPORT	OBSERVATION	PROGRAM DESCRIPTOR	INVENTORY
Student Age	X	X						
Level of Performance	X	X				X		
Ethnic Background		X						
Handicapping Condition	X							
Teacher Educational Level			X					
Teacher Attitudes			X	X				
Teacher Experience					X	X		
Teaching Strategies				X	X	X		
Management & Techniques				X	X	X		
Instructional Time						X	X	
Physical Structure						X	X	
Equipment						X		X
Materials						X		X
Budget						X		
Support Staff							X	

Figure 4. Analysis of Instructional Settings—Classrooms

Instructional Models

Because it is important for teachers to approach instructional program planning systematically, criteria are required for evaluating the various elements of such programs. The most direct method of determining relevant criteria would be to base decisions regarding the instructional program on directives inherent in the prescribed curriculum. In the absence of such a curriculum, teachers are forced to seek other alternatives.

One alternative is to employ basic criteria with general application to instructional models. Lembo states that an instructional model should meet three conditions; namely, diagnostic, prescriptive, and normative.[3] These criteria are more meaningful when stated as questions.

Diagnostic:

> Does your instructional program allow for assessing the functioning levels of individuals and/or the specification of instructional objectives appropriate to their cognitive abilities?

Prescriptive:

> Does your instructional program include procedures for individualizing instruction?

Normative:

> Do you have criteria that allow you to determine when optimal conditions for learning have not been met, as well as a means for assessing pupil growth?

These criteria are not earthshaking, nor do the results of applying them resolve our problem. But they do serve to focus the teacher's attention on elements in the instructional programs that merit close examination. They are the same elements that need to be considered during the curriculum development process.

Curriculum Development and Project Procedures

The specific steps followed by curriculum developers in the process of designing instructional materials and curriculum will vary somewhat. In general, however, they are highly similar. The basic differences are in the resources available to the developer and the settings in which the development

3. John M. Lembo, *The Psychology of Effective Classroom Instruction* (Columbus: Charles E. Merrill Publishing Co., 1969).

takes place. Most curriculum development is not done by individuals. Instead, it is carried out by project staffs which have financial support. Such projects may be established by local districts, state departments of education, universities, or autonomous curriculum development centers. Much of the curriculum development that has taken place in Special Education has resulted from funding by national or regional agencies. The setting in which the project is conducted generally influences the developer's philosophy. Thus, some curriculum development centers are oriented to hiring their own developers and centralizing the development process within their staff. Others centers may employ small development staffs and rely on writing teams selected from the field to supplement their staff expertise. This increases the manpower source and creates a direct liaison with professional representatives from the field. The central development staff approach has the advantage of tight quality control over the development process. But it has the disadvantage of having to recruit a highly expert staff. On the other hand, public school-sponsored curriculum development will most likely be based on talent available within the district or accessible to the district through universities or consulting agencies. Generally, a skilled developer will be assigned responsibility for coordination, while teachers assume much of the development responsibility. To enhance teachers' development skills, districts will frequently invest in training them in needed skills as a process of project implementation. One advantage that districts have in curriculum development is that their development efforts are aimed at their own needs. They have a broad base of available talent and, over a period of time, they benefit from the residual values of conducting several projects. Their limitations relate to financial resources and the capability to commit groups of skilled personnel full-time to the development task.

Teachers become involved in curriculum development projects at the point of specifying objectives and developing content, or when it is time to field-test products. They rarely have an opportunity to participate in conceptualizing a proposal, securing funds, or carrying out the array of activities that go into curriculum development. It is not the purpose of this book to describe curriculum development procedures fully. Teachers, however, may find it helpful to be familiar with the major tasks typically involved in carrying out curriculum development projects. The approach will be to describe briefly selected tasks in the sequence in which they are generally encountered. The discussion is based on the assumption that the project is initiated as a result of needs assessment; it describes tasks, not operational procedures on how a task should be completed. It should be noted that the degree of formal attention given to each task varies with developers and the scope of the project, but in general the tasks are evident from the procedures employed.

Needs Assessment

Most curriculum development projects undertaken by school districts result from some form of assessment of needs. This is not necessarily true of all major curriculum development efforts, most of which tend to occur when an individual (or individuals) conceptualizes a development project and seeks support. Under these circumstances, needs assessment involves confirming the priority status of the conceptualized proposal. This approach to initiate curriculum development relates more to project proposals on the national level than to locally created projects. In other situations, curriculum development projects may emerge from research on theory and again are not the result of observed needs on the part of local districts. Examples of such curriculum development efforts might include the "new math," open class curriculum, and behavioral analysis curriculum. Typically, however, locally conducted projects are derived directly from observed needs. Needs assessment studies are seldom conducted to generate a need for curriculum development. Instead, school districts attempt to monitor the curriculum program constantly to detect the need for curriculum development and/or revision. However, specific procedures can be designed to assist local districts in identifying the need for curriculum development or revision.

Conceptualizing a Design Model

Most curriculum projects and major instructional products are based on a conceptual model. Development models vary in specificity from general commitments to a teaching approach—for example, discovery learning—to very complex schemata detailing interactions among pupil, environment, teacher, and material. The *importance* of the model is not inherent in its complexity but in how effectively it conveys the beliefs of the developers and the principles employed in the project. The development of a model serves a very useful purpose for the development staff. It requires the staff to specify clearly what they believe to be essential to the curriculum product they are developing. It also allows them to design a procedure that holds them accountable. In other words, once the model is complete, their views and the principles on which they propose to develop a curriculum product are open to examination by others. Curriculum developers begin to toy with the model early in the preliminary planning but wait to formalize it until they have subjected their informal plans to review by either proposed consumers of the element product or by the development staff that will eventually be recruited for the project.

Rationale

The development of a rationale is somewhat analogous to writing a justification for the project. It involves formulating a clear statement of the project goal, a description of the target population, and an identification of the assumptions underlying the curriculum development proposal. The intent of the rationale is to relate the conceptualization of the project to the results of needs assessments, supporting literature, and the capabilities of the developer(s). The rationale is important primarily for those persons who must make judgments on the merits of the proposals, such as administrators, teachers, parents, school patrons, and possibly funding agency representatives. The rationale must be couched in a statement that communicates adequately the intent of the proposed curriculum. The emphasis should not be on formulating a complex statement, but on developing a very clear statement that can be easily understood without further clarification by the developer.

Feasibility

A curriculum proposal may pass the test of a defensible rationale and still not be a feasible project. The variables that must be explored in determining the feasibility of the curriculum proposal are directly related to the capabilities of the district or center to carry out the development task and implement the final curriculum product successfully. It is best to test the rationale and feasibility questions separately. Ideally, the rationale question should be resolved first; however, circumstances sometimes exist in which the district has created sufficient development resources to have the luxury of experimenting with high-risk projects. Most districts will require that all proposals first be subjected to a rigorous test with underlying rationale. Feasibility decisions are based on available resources and needs. Obviously, rationale and needs assessment contribute to the feasibility decision.

Organization for Development Tasks

It is at this point that decisions are made relative to putting the curriculum project into operation. Certain obvious decisions must be made, such as recruiting staff, determining the training they require, obtaining space, establishing time-lines, differentiating assignments, and establishing basic organizational procedures. There is also a more subtle task involved. It concerns establishing a commitment to the project on the part of staff members at a level equivalent to the commitment that probably is held by those who conceptualized it. Basically, the developers who conceptualize the project are dependent on staff members who are not part of the conceptualization to actually carry out development. Thus, very early in the organizational stage, orientation must take place. Somehow the staff members must feel a part of the conceptualization even though they were not actual contributors. Many times this means repeating some of the processes relative to needs assessment, conceptualization, rationale, and feasibility. For the most part, the decisions regarding organization are administrative and will take the form of the structured model.

Prototype Design

Designing a prototype involves making an example of the product; that is, curriculum that approximates the conceptualization of what the final product will be. The prototype may take different forms. For example, it may be a product, such as a kit of materials, a book, or manipulative aids. At the same time, it may be detailed curriculum for a major subject area. In the latter case, it should be noted that curriculum content takes several different forms. For example, some curriculum products are skill-oriented toward the teaching of concepts and/or information. Still others are intended to influence attitudes. Regardless of what constitutes content, the emphasis should be on designing a process to facilitate content generation and experiences in a prototype form that can be subjected to evaluation. The task becomes one of refinement and production of a prototype. Typically, a prototype is developed, tested, and produced as a final product. If the preliminary development has been sound and the developer has selected good formative evaluative procedures, then there is likely to be little substantive change between the final product and the first prototype. On the other hand, if errors have been made in terms of analyzing the target population or in predicting the skills possessed by teachers, considerable change may be necessary. The purpose of designing the prototype is to provide an operational example of the final product and to subject the prototype to field-testing. The procedures for designing and evaluating prototypes represent a major task for any curriculum development project.

Evaluation

Evaluation is obviously inherent in the processes of defining a prototype. The development of curricula and/or curriculum products (materials) not only dictates the application of evaluation procedures but also presents a set of circumstances conducive to evaluation. In the realm of curricula, a considerable number of products emerge that are intended to bring about change on the part of learners. Consequently, evaluation can focus on the development process, the status of products at particular stages, and the subsequent effect on the learner. If designed appropriately, the evaluation process can serve to initiate a cycle procedure focusing on improvement of the product, that is, correcting its deficiencies. From this perspective, the evaluation becomes an attainable curriculum goal. However, it is apparent to teachers who have engaged in applied evaluation or research in the classroom that there are many variables which are difficult to control in curriculum evaluation. For example, it is not possible to control student attitudes, distractions within a classroom, or even prior experiences of students engaged in the activity being evaluated. To the degree possible, developers attempt to design evaluation procedures that take these variables into consideration. Their goal is to design an evaluation system that improves the product relative to the setting in which it will ultimately be implemented.

Implementation and Dissemination

Local districts produce or revise curriculum with an intent to implement the results within their own programs. Depending on the scope of projects local districts carry out, they may also engage in broader dissemination efforts. Certainly major curriculum development projects are carried out by curriculum development centers with a commitment to dissemination and implementation. In general, curriculum development projects of this scope will develop dissemination procedures aimed at alerting the field to the availability of the curriculum product and to the nature of their design. Depending on the product, a project may also design procedures for training consumers (teachers) in the actual use of the curriculum to facilitate its adoption. Publishers frequently assume a major responsibility for the implementation and dissemination task. Since publishers have a commitment to marketing, it is important that potential users of the curriculum be familiar with the product and have sufficient information to make decisions on acquisitions.

The tasks previously described are representative of those encountered in the curriculum development process. They are presented solely for the purpose of adding to the reader's perspective on what constitutes curriculum development. It is not assumed that teachers will necessarily participate in all dimensions of curriculum development, but it is important that they be aware of the processes that ultimately create the products used in the classroom. It is also important that teachers recognize that development processes are very similar to the procedures they employ in designing teaching experiences and/or in actually constructing instructional units.

As has previously been pointed out, many teachers find themselves in the position of having to make decisions independently about what they are going to include in their instructional program. This is particularly true of teachers working with exceptional children. Special Education consultants or supervisory personnel may not be available. The building principal, while interested and willing to help, is likely to be overcommitted and not free to devote substantial time to assisting the teachers in organizing a curriculum that also accommodates children's needs. This, coupled with the lack of resources generally available to teachers working with exceptional children, places them in the position of having to make decisions based on personal knowledge about exceptional children. If they are oriented toward unit teaching, they may base instructional programs on the teaching of units. Since what takes place in the classroom becomes the child's curriculum, a curriculum based on the arbitrary selection of units is not a very sound approach to structuring a child's education. This is not to say that it is not feasible to develop a sound instructional program based on units. It can be done, but it must be related to a planned curriculum providing outcomes that the teacher strives to attain through unit teaching. Teachers may find it necessary to develop the curriculum as they teach units in their instructional program. This, however, does not make the practice a realistic approach. It results in the curriculum becoming what the teacher teaches, with little long-range planning involved. Another consequence is that, as children move from one special class to another, they encounter little continuity and may even encounter teachers with contrasting views about what exceptional children are capable of learning.

Because of the importance of a well-planned curriculum to the future of the exceptional child, teachers who choose to develop their instructional program around units should base their decisions about what is taught through those units on a sequentially planned curriculum. The teacher, then, is adhering to a prescribed curriculum but electing to use the unit method as the major vehicle for the instructional program. Those teachers who prefer to use units as a supplement to other methods must also be concerned with the relationship of the units they teach to the prescribed curriculum. In both cases, each unit must be well planned and executed. Teachers who base the instructional program on units have the additional task of building consistency among their units. If they are not working from a prescribed curriculum but emphasizing units in their teaching, they can reduce the risk of curriculum errors by systematic development of the units.

Summary

The emphasis in this book is on the tasks inherent in writing well-designed units. This discussion of curriculum development has been presented to provide teachers with a frame of reference concerning what is involved in curriculum development and to encourage them to look at unit teaching as one possible instructional program method.

Attention has been given to differentiating instruction from curriculum. Curriculum here is the planned series of outcomes that the child should be assisted in attaining through the instructional program. The curriculum provides directives for the instructional program, but to facilitate implementing these directives, teachers should be given considerable freedom in determining their approach. In other words, a minimum of restriction should be placed on the methods a teacher may choose to use in the classroom, and teaching units may be employed either as a primary or supplementary method. In either case, this author feels that systematically developed units will be taught most effectively. The information presented in this chapter provides a background for reading Chapter 8, which is concerned with applying curriculum development principles to the design and organization of units. Because Chapter 8 is based on the assumption that the reader is skilled in the process of developing units, the reader is encouraged to study Chapters 3 and 4 first.

Exercise 1: Complete an analysis of the variables that should be considered in designing curriculum for a district program. Include a list of critical variables and identify the sources of data available to you regarding the variables. Check cells representing sources of data per variable.

Setting: **Program**

Source of Data

VARIABLES									

REFERENCES

JOHNSON, MAURITZ, JR. "Definitions and Models in Curriculum Theory." *Educational Therapy* (April 1967).

LEMBO, JOHN M. *The Psychology of Effective Classroom Instruction.* Columbus, Ohio: Charles E. Merrill Publishing Co., 1969.

PHENIX, PHILLIP H. "Curriculum." In *Philosophy of Education.* New York: Holt, Rinehart and Winston, 1958.

ADDITIONAL SELECTED REFERENCES

BAKER, ROBERT L., and SCHUTZ, RICHARD E., eds. *Instructional Product Development.* New York: Van Nostrand Reinhold Company, 1971.

BURNS, RICHARD W., and BROOKS, GAY D., eds. *Curriculum Design in a Changing Society.* Englewood Cliffs, N. J.: Educational Technology Publications, 1970.

"Curriculum." *Review of Educational Research* 39:3. Washington, D. C.: American Educational Research Association.

"Curriculum Planning and Development." *Review of Educational Research* 33:3. Washington, D. C.: American Educational Research Association.

DRUMHELLER, SIDNEY J. *Handbook of Curriculum Design for Individualized Instruction: A Systems Approach.* Englewood Cliffs, N. J.: Educational Technology Publications, 1971.

GWYNN, J. MINOR, and CHUSE, JOHN B. *Curriculum Principles and Social Trends.* Toronto: The Macmillan Company, 1970.

HANEY, JOHN B., and ULLMER, ELDON J. *Educational Media and the Teacher.* Dubuque, Iowa: Wm. C. Brown Company Publishers, 1970.

HASSETT, JOSEPH D., and WEISBERG, ARLINE. *Open Education: Alternatives within Our Tradition.* Englewood Cliffs, N. J.: Prentice-Hall, 1972.

KAPFER, MIRIAM B. *Behavioral Objectives in Curriculum Development.* Englewood Cliffs, N. J.: Educational Technology, 1971.

KOPP, O. W., and ZUFELT, DAVID L. *Personalized Curriculum: Method and Design.* Columbus, Ohio: Charles E. Merrill Publishing Co., 1971.

LAPP, DIANE; BENDER, HILARY; ELLENWOOD, STEPHAN; and JOHN, MARTHA. *Teaching and Learning: Philosophical, Psychological, Curricular Applications.* New York: Macmillan Publishing Co., 1975.

MAYER, WILLIAM V., ed. *Planning Curriculum Development.* Boulder, Colo.: Biological Sciences Curriculum Study, 1975.

MICHAELIS, JOHN U., and KEACH, EVERETT T., JR., eds. *Teaching Strategies for Elementary School Social Studies.* Itasca, Il.: F. E. Peacock Publishers, 1972.

MORINE, HAROLD, and MORINE, GRETA. *Discovery: A Challenge to Teachers.* Englewood Cliffs, N.J.: Prentice-Hall, 1973.

SAYLOR, J. GALEN, and ALEXANDER, WILLIAM M. *Planning Curriculum for Schools.* New York: Holt, Rinehart & Winston, 1974.

VAN TIL, WILLIAM. *Curriculum: Quest for Relevance.* 2d ed. Boston: Houghton Mifflin, 1974.

WEIKART, DAVID P. "Curriculum for Early Childhood Special Education." *Focus on Exceptional Children* 6 (March 1974):1.

WHEELER, D. K. *Curriculum Process.* London: University of London Press, 1967.

3

The IEP and
Unit Teaching

Few legislated educational practices have received as much attention as the Individual Education Program (IEP) requirements of PL 94-142, the Education for All Handicapped Children Act. The impact of the IEP is evident in teacher education as well as in public and private schools. While the requirement currently applies only to handicapped children and youth, all teachers at some time participate in the design and/or implementation of IEPs. It is the intent of this chapter to clarify the guidelines that underly the development and implementation of the IEP, to relate the goals of the IEP to principles of instructional planning, and to illustrate how this new practice can be incorporated into unit teaching.

Neither individualized instruction nor the development of instructional plans for specific students is new. Teachers have historically been concerned with basing teaching on the assessed needs of their students. This has been true in regular classes and in special programs for handicapped learners. For the most part, the procedures used and the emphasis given to individualizing instruction have tended to be unique to the orientation of the teacher and/or the instructional philosophy of the faculty in a particular school. The process has been structured but informal. The primary exceptions have been in those instructional settings employing open schools or prescriptive teaching models. Many teachers in these programs individualize instruction and maintain accountability measures beyond the IEP requirements.

In order to understand why individual educational programs were mandated for handicapped children and youth, a brief discussion will be presented. The most significant source of influence was the general dissatisfaction with the impact of special instructional programs on the performance of handicapped students. The lack of data supporting the success of special programs was confounded with varied and, in some cases,

Selected sections have been adopted from Meyen, Edward L., *Exceptional Children and Youth: An Introduction*. Denver, Colo.: Love Publishing Company, 1978.

inappropriate placement decisions. During the 1960s and early 1970s, the popular practice of placing handicapped students in segregated special classes was challenged and the extensive reliance on using standardized tests for determining eligibility for placement was brought into question. While the issues were not limited to instructional decisions, what emerged among professional and advocacy groups was a common concern for focusing the attention of those responsible for educating the handicapped on instructional decisions and accountability for those decisions.

The increased emphasis on instructional planning and support for legislating the IEP can be attributed in part to the widespread growing concern among consumers. Parents and the public in general are beginning to raise questions about the reported decline in academic achievement, particularly in the basic skills. Initially, this concern tends to center on the curriculum, but eventually it focuses on decision making regarding individual students. At that level, instructional planning becomes a major issue. It would be unfair, however, to suggest that teachers are primarily responsible for the assumed failure to establish effective programs for the handicapped. The lack of progress in instructional planning has related primarily to the practical realities of the classroom teacher's role. For the most part, teachers have had to initiate, evaluate, and review student programs within the constraints of overloading schedules, minimal planning resources or directions, and limited administrative support for planning. In the past, when administrators became concerned about the need for planning or when parents sought information related to their children's programs, the teacher was the focal point of most of the pressure.

The special education teacher's role in instructional planning also has been affected by these circumstances—in spite of the obvious need for detailed planning in programming for handicapped children and youth. Too often, the evidence of instructional planning has consisted of hurriedly written lesson plans limited to general goals, detailed assignments combined with anecdotal records, and history-oriented cumulative records. Such planning gives little more than nebulous directives and does not provide the resources needed for instructional decision making. As a basis for programming for handicapped children, this process is totally insufficient.

The IEP: Implications for Instructional Planning

The current national emphasis on instructional planning for exceptional children is directly related to requirements of PL 94-142. The law does not specify the planning process to be followed, but it does set forth detailed requirements on what should be included in an Individualized Education

Program (IEP) and the conditions under which the plan should be developed. The law's intent is not to standardize instructional planning nor to promote a particular teaching methodology. The goal is to establish use of the IEP and to bring about quality education for exceptional children and youth.

The IEP concept is a major improvement over most instructional planning practices and programs of the past, when planning centered on placement decisions. The improvement comes largely from requiring a written plan that includes evaluation procedures. Too often, handicapped students have been placed in programs with attention given only to their eligibility. Now equal emphasis must be given to describing specific program components. Hopefully, the IEP requirements will stimulate districts to employ systematic instructional planning procedures.

The IEP represents the primary vehicle in PL 94-142 for assuring quality education for the handicapped. It also provides a basis for assessing student performance and program effectiveness. Teachers now have support for establishing conditions conducive to planning, but they must also exercise their own professionalism to prevent the IEP from becoming a paper process that begins and ends with the IEP conference.

IEP Content

Because requirements regulating IEP content are clearly described, certain practices are common across most districts, although the format and scope of the IEPs varies substantially. Since most districts have not had extensive experience in applying the IEP concept, validated procedures have not been designed. Very few IEP models exist. Many districts have designed their own procedures and/or adopted available systems. In all cases, the first level of concern has been the degree to which the IEP format accommodates the required content. PL 94-142 specifies that each individualized program must include the following (Federal Register, 8/23/77).

Sec. 121a.346 Content of Individualized Education Program
  The individualized education program for each child must include:
(a) A statement of the child's present levels of educational performance.
(b) A statement of annual goals, including short term instructional objectives.
(c) A statement of the specific special education and related services to be provided to the child, and the extent to which the child will be able to participate in regular educational programs.
(d) The projected dates for initiation of services and the anticipated duration of the services; and
(e) Appropriate objective criteria and evaluation procedures and schedules for determining, on at least an annual basis, whether the short term instructional objectives are being achieved.

In reviewing the content requirements, the plan clearly must be detailed; and the lack of existing resources should not be a limiting factor in recommending inclusion of a service. Teachers and support personnel should advocate for the services the student needs, even if such services are not presently available. If they don't specify the services needed, handicapped children in many districts will never receive appropriate services. But if substantial delays are likely in gaining access to these services, alternatives should be considered, with the qualification that alternative services do not substitute for nor excuse the district from developing the desired services.

The requirements viewed in the context of instructional planning are reasonable. They represent what most teachers would agree to be merely good rules to follow in instructional planning. It is important to know the student's current level of functioning, know specifically what skills or concepts to teach, to know what you want the student to be able to do following completion of your program, and to know whether or not the student profited from the instruction. The major difference between adhering to these general rules and meeting the requirements of the IEP is that the teacher's instructional decisions are public, that is, prepared in written form, and the IEP is designed in conference with parental participations.

Basically, the IEP provides a set of directions regarding specific skills or knowledge to be taught. The forms vary but contain the same general information. Some districts have designed IEP forms that are more comprehensive than the specific IEP requirements. See Appendix 1 for sample IEP forms. Teachers should keep in mind that the IEP is merely a plan. It contains a listing of the goals and objectives that were agreed to be important for the student based on an understanding of the students' current performance and needs. The performance of students will change and thus objectives must change. It is not reasonable nor desirable to specify all of the short-term objectives that constitute a student's program. This would be too detailed and probably not possible. The teacher will find it necessary to enlarge on the IEP in developing the student's program. Teachers are reminded that the intent of the IEP is to improve instruction for the handicapped through more precise instructional decisions and systematic planning.

IEP Conference Requirements

From the perspective of team decision making, the conference concept is not new. Special educators have been using the team or conference approach to make placement decisions on exceptional children for many years. The changes created by PL 94-142, however, related to the increased number of children involved, parent participation, and the requirements necessary for a written plan. In the past, conferences were held primarily in difficult cases or cases in which the child in question needed several special services. The number of conferences held by a staff depended upon program vacancies for children, the number of referrals, and the time available for staff conference participation. The result of most such conferences was a placement decision and general recommendations. Although parents may have been consulted, they rarely were invited to participate in the conference. Not uncommonly, the conference was lengthy or involved a series of sessions. Today, with the IEP requirement applying to all handicapped children, considerable attention must be given to efficiency in the use of time. It also means that careful decisions must be made regarding collection of data and organization of reports in advance of the conference. A secondary but important implication of the required conference is the public nature of instructional decisions and the increased role of the teacher in program decision makers.

School districts now are required to involve the following participants in all IEP conferences on handicapped children (Federal Register, 8/23/77):

Sec. 121a.344. Participants in meetings
(a) General. The public agency shall insure that each meeting includes the following participants:
    (1) A representative of the public agency, other than the child's teacher, who is qualified to provide, or supervise the provision of, special education.
    (2) The child's teacher.
    (3) One or both of the child's parents, subject to Sec. 121a.345.
    (4) The child, where appropriate.
    (5) Other individuals at the discretion of the parent or agency.
(b) Evaluation personnel. For a handicapped child who has been evaluated for the first time, the public agency shall insure:
    (1) That a member of the evaluation team participates in the meeting; or
    (2) That the representative of the public agency, the child's teacher, or some other person is present at the meeting who is knowledgeable about the evaluation procedures used with the child and is familiar with the results of the evaluation.

The building principal frequently is the representative of the educational agency, but in some cases it is the director of special education or other administrative personnel. Regarding teacher participation, as many as three teachers commonly are involved. If a child is referred by a regular class teacher and subsequently is to be referred for placement in a resource room, both teachers will be involved. If the child is in a depart-

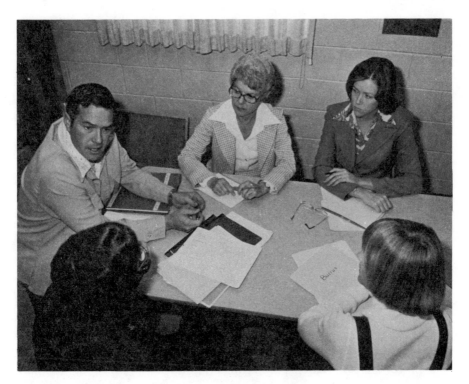

Parental participation in the IEP process is important.

mentalized program, each regular teacher may participate. This participation requirement strengthens the teacher's role and helps maintain an emphasis on instruction.

With reference to parent participation, districts must take extensive measures to encourage parents to participate. These considerations include scheduling the meetings at convenient times and maintaining effective communication with the parents. If parents refuse to participate, the conference can be held in their absence, but the district must be able to document its attempts to involve the parents and the latter's refusal to participate.

The decision on whether or not and how much to involve each student in the IEP conference is a difficult one. The intent is to have the child present by design, not arbitrarily. Of course, students should understand why changes are being made in their programs, but a discussion in the child's presence about his or her differences and needs for assistance is not always necessary. In the case of secondary-aged mildly handicapped students, valid reasons may exist for having the child present. Decisions regarding student conference participation probably are best made in consultation with the parents. "Other individuals" refers to speech therapists, psychologists, nurses, physicians, and other specialists whose expertise is related to the case being reviewed.

The conference's goal is to develop an IEP that is most appropriate for the student. But since time rarely permits involvement of all participants in more than one conference relative to a particular student, evaluative and related information must be available and effectively presented during the conference.

Each person involved must be prepared to participate. The person assigned to chair the conference is obligated to moderate the discussion in an objective manner and to encourage full participation. The emphasis, again, must be on developing an appropriate IEP for the student. One of the most difficult tasks faced by chairpersons of IEP conferences is helping the group reach agreement on the IEP. Two main strategies—staff preparation and communication with parents before the conference—will aid this decision making. Parents are expected to report their concerns and expectations for their child. It would be unfair to suggest that they will tend to be defensive, but in many cases they will need encouragement to participate, particularly in terms of their informative role. Since school personnel lack experience in working with parents in making educational decisions, the task may not be an easy one. Teachers, both regular and special, frequently will have the most difficult role. They must advocate the most appropriate IEP but at the same time may not have access to information acquired by the specialist until the time of the conference.

An important concern at this juncture is to guard against prematurely incorporating recommendations in to the IEP merely to gain support from the parent or to reach agreement on the IEP. One must remember that the law does not hold the school liable if the child fails to achieve the IEPs objectives. Also, the risk is always present that an unreasonable expectation can emerge from an IEP conference. On the one hand, the IEP may exceed the student's capabilities or, on the other hand, the short-term objectives may exist already within the student's repertoire of skills. When participating in a conference, teachers need to keep in mind that they are responsible for implementation. If they knowingly agree to an IEP that they believe is not appropriate, they are not being fair to themselves or to the student. Although changes can and should be made when needed in the IEP after it is implemented, naturally it is best to begin with the most appropriate program possible. Teachers willing to assume advocacy roles can help guard against premature decisions in an attempt to reach agreement on the IEP. Because of the large number of conferences held and the time required to monitor IEPs, the potential hazard exists that the conference will become a routine meeting, with decisions made in advance and programs designed with such a low expectation level that the child will too easily attain the objectives—or unrealistic objectives may be included to fulfill parental expectations.

The most important implication of the conference process for the classroom teacher relates to his/her ultimate responsibility for the instructional decisions made. Some IEPs will be primarily concerned with support services, such as speech or physical therapy. However, most will detail specific objectives for classroom instruction. The regular and/or special teacher becomes responsible for carrying out the educational directions of the plan. It is important that teachers play a major role in influencing the final IEP. This requires participation by teachers. Attending the conference is not enough. Teachers must be willing to share their observations and opinions. They also must be willing to voice questions when specialists make recommendations that, from their view, are not sound. Participation in IEP conferences is different from parent-teacher conferences. In the typical parent-teacher conference the outcome is generally one of sharing information. The teacher frequently exercises control over the questions asked and the information shared. For the most part such conferences include only the teacher and the parent(s). In the IEP conference, the number of participants may be large, the chairperson is often an authority figure and the outcomes are instructional decisions. Many teachers will find that they will need to develop a certain level of assertiveness in order to appropriately influence decisions on IEPs.

The IEP Process

Prior to passage of PL 94-142 the referral and placement process involved conferences and instructional recommendation. However, parental involvement centered around the placement decision and they were not routinely involved in recommending what would take place once the child was in a special program. Instructional recommendations were rarely detailed in the form of a plan with procedures for evaluation. Above all there was not a set cycle for reevaluation of the placement decisions or the instructional recommendations. The IEP requirements have not necessarily altered the sequence of referral, placement, and instructional decisions, but they have tended to give more prominence to the instructional decisions. Figure 5 illustrates a process that is typical of many local school districts. The steps are related to the suggested instructional planning steps discussed on page 56.

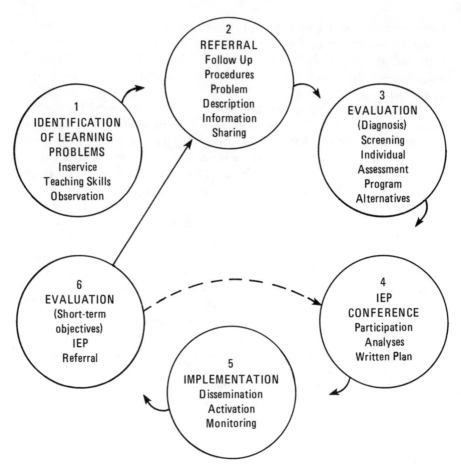

Figure 5.   The IEP Process

Step 1.   Identification of learning problems remains the initial step in determining whether or not a student's problem is brought to the attention of appropriate personnel.

Step 2.   Referral (this step remains essentially the same).

Step 3.   Evaluation is broadened to include an extensive review of the available service alternatives required to meet the student's needs.

Step 4.   The IEP conference replaces the instructional placement decision step. Previously collected data and program needs are presented. A written plan is prepared.

Step 5.   Implementation becomes a more comprehensive step in terms of the IEP, as the plan must be disseminated to all persons who will participate in the student's program. The plan is actually put into effect at this stage. Each participant is required to monitor the student's performance and to make any necessary modifications to the plan. This is the "service delivery" stage.

Step 6. Evaluation is repeated as a final step in the cycle. The intent is to determine student progress and the IEP's general effectiveness. During Step 3 the evaluation focus was on diagnosing the student's problem in preparation for recommending an IEP. During Step 5, the evaluation emphasis continues, but focuses on achieving short-term objectives. In this step a decision must be made on the IEP's overall effectiveness. The decision may be to continue the IEP with minimal modification, or to initiate a referral to obtain additional evaluation services. In the latter case, Step 2's referral process will be repeated. In other cases, procedures may call for holding another IEP conference. This generally occurs when the original IEP is considered tentative and the committee desires a report at a particular time. Primarily, Step 6 is intended to satisfy the annual evaluation requirement, but in most cases evaluation should be carried out on a more frequent basis.

Guidelines for Developing IEP Forms

For districts to monitor the effectiveness of developing, implementing, and evaluating procedures relative to IEPs, they have become aware of the necessity to rely on specially designed forms, which may be self-designed, modified, or adopted from available systems. Well-designed forms allow for efficient collection and assessment of essential information without placing undue demands on teachers. Unfortunately, special education programs have a history of creating sometimes unnecessary forms that may have been *too* comprehensive. Consequently, the use of forms often is suspect. The IEP, however, *requires* a recorded plan; thus, special forms are now necessary.

The written plan serves at least three purposes: (1) it provides a permanent source of information on the student's plan that can be shared with parents, as well as with the teacher and other personnel responsible for implementing the student's program; (2) it provides a reference regarding instructional decisions made on a particular student's program; and (3) it creates a cumulative data base for future program planning for individual students. Forms are important because districts must maintain records containing data on the IEPs—when they are developed and initiated, and evaluation data on their effectiveness. The traditional cumulative record of information ranging from test scores and anecdotal comments to attendance records is no longer sufficient or appropriate.

Designing selected forms for use in recording and monitoring the IEP necessitates an understanding of the IEP concept and the district's philosophy toward instructional planning. A system of forms can be designed that meets requirements of the law regarding IEPs, but still not have a positive influence on the student's program. If attention is given only to administrative procedures or to minimal content requirements, the consequence may be a written plan that falls short of promoting quality instruction. Following are guidelines to be considered in designing or selecting forms for use with IEPs. Particular attention has been given to suggestions that strengthen the teacher's role in the implementation stage.

1. *Accommodation of Full Service Information*   The forms must be designed to allow for the specifying of plans for the entire range of services a student may require. For example, a mildly handicapped student's plan may include objectives and evaluation data in the areas of academic skills, language skills, social behavior, and psychomotor tasks.

2. *Content Flexibility*   As objectives are specified, the IEP begins to include program content, but the forms themselves should not dictate the content. For example, some districts have designed forms that include skill checklists; skills considered appropriate for each student are checked, representing objectives. Such an approach is restrictive in that all skills cannot be listed. These forms also contribute to decisions that are not appropriate to the student's needs. Better, teachers should be allowed to develop scientific objectives based on their knowledge of each student's needs.

3. *Emphasis on Retrieval of Program Related Information*   In designing forms, the temptation may be to request information because it is interesting, of possible future use, or simply accessible. But the primary objective should be to elicit information related only to student program needs. Since IEPs for most students relate to educational services, the design should emphasize retrieval of instructionally related information.

4. *Effectiveness without Repeated Use*   Forms used in the implementation stage should not require constant use. If the teacher or specialist is required to record information on a regular, daily basis, or on every task in a therapy session, more time will be involved in recording than in instruction. Consideration of the teacher or other specialist's time is critical to the design of an effective system. Information must be recorded while the IEP is being implemented, but this should be accomplished without excessive time demands on the staff.

5. *Provision for Full Participation*   Most IEPs necessitate the involvement of two or more professionals (i.e., regular teachers, special teachers, and/or specialists). The system must encourage their full participation.

A primary requirement is that the system provide a communication basis among participants; they should be able to exchange information on the student's performance.

6. *Utilization without Extensive Training* This guideline is almost a commandment. If the system is so complicated or detailed that extensive training is required for its use, it likely will not be successful. Again, time is a factor. If a system is complicated, it probably will be difficult to implement. Because regular educators as well as special educators are involved in implementing IEPs, various persons must understand the system. The amount of training required to understand and use the form system should be minimal. This is not to suggest that the system should be so simple that it becomes of little value, but it does suggest that serious attention should be given to any training requirements for implementation. A good system need not be complicated.

7. *Cumulative and Program-Based Qualities* The form system must allow for collecting information on the student's program in those areas identified in the IEP. If this is accomplished, cumulative information will be available as a basis for making decisions on IEP changes. Too many form systems require only the recording of data regarding whether or not the IEP was implemented and its effects on student performance. If the goal is to improve as well as judge instruction, a more continuous approach to recording information is required.

8. *Sustaining Nature* A major investment of time, effort, and resources is involved when a district designs or adopts a form system. Little is gained if changes routinely are made in the system after it has been initiated. Consideration should be given to reducing the likelihood of having to make changes each year. Some modifications are almost inevitable over time, and supplementary forms may be necessary additions, but to the fullest extent possible, uniformity and continuity should be maintained after a system has been initiated.

9. *Format Considerations* Readable, understandable forms are highly desirable wherever they are used. A well-designed form is innately helpful, but someone also should be available to assist or clarify the use of the IEP system forms. (See Appendix 1 for sample IEP forms.)

Relationship of the IEP to Instructional Planning

The author feels strongly that the IEP should be viewed as integral to instructional planning and not as one of several due process safeguards. Because the IEP has evolved as a result of a legislative mandate that also sets forth a series of due process procedures, there has been a tendency for many teachers and administrators to view the IEP as a noninstructional task and to approach it as an administrative procedure. Unless its instructional value is emphasized, the IEP could become a perfunctory procedure equivalent in value to the outmoded cumulative folder or the abused lesson plan book.

No single set of planning procedures applies to all instructional settings. Teachers vary in their planning preferences, just as they prefer particular teaching methodologies. Differences in available resources also influence the instructional planning approach a teacher might follow. Certain general principles and planning concepts have broad application and, if followed, increase the opportunities for quality instruction. Instructional planning ideally results in providing effective instruction appropriate to learner needs. Within this context, at least four objectives specific to instructional planning are set forth:

1. To make use of available information on learner characteristics and instructional options in planning specific teaching activities.
2. To establish short-range objectives within a long-term plan that can be implemented as intended, often by persons other than the teacher responsible for the original planning.
3. To allow for collecting evaluative evidence that illustrates the pupil's cumulative performance.
4. To provide a base for instructional decisions regarding programs for individual pupils.

These principles are highly compatible with the IEP requirements. If one were to design a planning process based on these principals, the requirements of the IEP would be easily met. The reason for emphasizing instructional planning apart from the IEP process is that the IEP requirements are far too minimal to serve as a basis for instructional planning and tend to be too closely linked to accountability for placement decisions. The emphasis in this section is to offer guidelines on instructional planning that are applicable to teachers participating in the IEP process and who engage in unit teaching.

To be effective, instructional planning must focus on the uniqueness of the individual learner. Thus, a planning process does not substitute for the teacher's lack of knowledge about how children learn. Calder (1977) offers eleven principles for instructional decision making. These principles illustrate a range of teacher competencies that can be considered as prerequisites to effective planning. They are also compatible with developing IEPs and instructional units.

1. The learner should possess the basic readiness skills needed to ensure some degree of success in the new task.
2. The learner should be made aware of the value and meaning of the new task.

3. The task should be analyzed to determine the difficulties that may be encountered because of any special needs of the learner.
4. The task should begin with familiar experiences and skills and progress to new experiences and skills.
5. The task should be presented in a manner that will provide the learner with a degree of success and satisfaction.
6. The task should be planned and a procedure developed for presenting it to the learner. When possible, the plan should be initiated and executed by the learner.
7. The task should include options that meet the learner's learning style.
8. The task should have flexibility and provide for differentiated assignments in order to meet the individual needs of the learner.
9. The task should be planned to provide the learner with reinforced repetition and practice to ensure retention.
10. The task should provide for constant performance evaluation by the learner, teacher, paraprofessional, or peer tutor.
11. The assignment of a new task should be the result of continuous evaluation of the learner's performance on the present task.

In implementing these objectives and principles, a systematic approach to instructional planning is clearly required. To be maximally effective, instructional planning for exceptional children must encompass more than merely specifying objectives, initiating activities, and measuring their effects on pupil performance. Consideration must also be given to identifying behaviors that suggest learning problems and becoming familiar with procedures that bring the children to the attention of appropriate resource personnel. While these concerns are beyond the actual instructional process, they are critical to instructional planning that will result in the most appropriate educational placement for the exceptional child. For the nonhandicapped child, instructional placement decisions rarely are made, since the child merely progresses through the graded system; placement decisions are important, but they primarily serve to set the conditions for instructional decisions.

Planning Guidelines

Following are suggestions that can serve as guidelines in the instructional planning process. They are not rules, nor do they constitute a recipe for successful instructional planning. Rather, they derive from observation of teachers engaged in successful instructional planning for exceptional children.

Systematization The purpose of instructional planning is to assure that instructional decisions about a student's program consider all information pertaining to the learner's needs. This requires systematic planning. The relative severity of learning problems exhibited by exceptional children dictates further that planning be continuous and not occur only when the child's problem is interfering with instruction.

Detail No plan can describe all of the skills, concepts, and information that a child will or should be taught. Even if this were possible, it would not be desirable. Learners vary in their responses to tasks, and the risk is present that a teacher may adhere to a detailed plan when evidence shows that the plan should be altered to meet the child's changing needs. Planning must allow for "on-the-spot" decision making.

On the other hand, sufficient planning time on the part of the teacher is important to success of the plan. Decisions must be made on how detailed a plan should be regarding skills, activities, and materials. The more serious the learner's problem, the more precise the planning required. Another major consideration pertains to whether or not persons other than the teacher will be involved in carrying out the plan. The plan should contain sufficient information to assure appropriate interpretation and implementation.

Format The content and provisions for remediation, not the plan's organizational format, determine its appropriateness for a particular student. The organization and recording format of instructional plans, however, do influence how well planning efforts succeed. An organized plan simplifies the matching of instructional options to learner characteristics.

To ensure uniformity, districts often adopt or design a particular planning system. Some advantages accrue in having all teachers use a similar format, a uniform approach simplifies the administrator's role in evaluating the effectiveness of teacher planning, and uniformity in format enhances communication among teachers. In most cases, forms are designed to make planning more convenient and to reduce the amount of time involved.

Program Emphasis In developing instructional plans, teachers have a tendency to refer only to the child's most immediate problems. Certainly, more specific planning is required to remediate obvious serious learning problems, but a program or curriculum emphasis also must be maintained. For example, a visually impaired child who is skilled in math may be experiencing difficulty in social studies because of slowness in reading by the braille method. Planning attention must be given to the student's needs in mathematics and other subjects, even though more short-term planning may be involved in developing the student's braille reading speed and alternatives for acquiring experiences in socal studies.

Intensiveness   Once a teacher has developed a program in which a child progresses satisfactorily, the time and effort (intensity) allocated to planning can be reduced. This does not mean that the teacher stops recording plans, collecting performance data, or conferring with other teachers. It means that less detailed planning is required and more planning time can be devoted to students for whom a satisfactory plan has not yet been developed.

Because of the amount of time required in effective instructional planning, the teacher must make judgments regarding how much time to devote to planning for each student. If evidence suggests that a student is progressing satisfactorily, planning becomes less formal and the emphasis shifts to program monitoring.

Evaluation   Unless planning includes the evaluation of short- and long-term objectives, the benefits will be minimal. Because specific evaluation tasks are sometimes difficult to design and not generally available in commercial form, some teachers tend to resort to available achievement measures or other standardized tests. Although standardized tests have certain advantages, they generally are not appropriate for measuring student performance on specific tasks included in routine instructional plans.

Teachers need to carefully determine when standardized measures are appropriate and when they need to consider other options. Teachers must evaluate their instructional planning, but they must use evaluation measures that relate directly to the student's instructional program. This generally results in teachers' having to design at least part of their evaluation tasks. When incorporating evaluation tasks into instructional planning, attention must be given to the relationship of the evaluation task to the instructional activity, the time required for the teacher to design the task, the time required by the student to demonstrate task performance, and the value of the information derived in this process.

Procedures   In deciding upon instructional planning procedures, two primary factors must be considered—the impact of instructional planning on student programming, and the demands the planning process places on teachers. The previously outlined guidelines (systematization, detail, format, program emphasis, intensiveness, and evaluation) combine to influence programming for students. But they also create time demands on teachers. If the procedures are too complex and time consuming, the teacher may not be able to plan and teach effectively. If the plan is too simple, little is gained in terms of pupil benefits.

The initial goal is to design procedures that allow for efficiency on the part of the teacher and to enhance instructional decision making specific to students' needs. The ultimate goal is to employ planning procedures that result in benefits for the learner.

Teachers should assume leadership in developing planning procedures. Administrative concerns do not always contribute to teacher efficiency or pupil benefit, and administrators often answer general program questions by expanding instructional planning requirements. If program questions can be answered by an instructional planning process that does not add substantially to the teacher's work load, that process should be considered. The primary emphasis, however, should be on instructional planning for specific students, and the emphasis must on developing *workable* planning procedures.

Instructional Planning and Exceptional Children

Instructional planning for exceptional children differs from instructional planning for nonhandicapped students only in intensity and the formality of procedures inherent in the IEP requirements. It is equally important to be systematic in planning for all students. The requiring of instructional planning for exceptional children and youth, however, does require regular classroom teachers to become more sensitive to the needs of exceptional children (See chapter 4).

Some exceptional children enter school already having been identified as possessing characteristics that likely will interfere with their school performance. In general, the most serious handicapping conditions are congenital in nature and include impaired vision, defective hearing, physical problems, and multiple handicaps. For exceptional children whose problems have been identified prior to entering school, instructional planning specific to their needs can be initiated upon their enrollment. Under such circumstances, the teacher probably will have the advantage of possessing information regarding the child's preschool history.

The majority of exceptional children, however, are not identified until they encounter demands in school with which they cannot effectively cope. Although instructional planning should occur for all children, too often specific instructional planning does not occur until after a student is identified as having a problem. If the child is fortunate, a teacher will notice the child's difficulty before it becomes more serious.

Conditions resulting in the identification of a child as exceptional are numerous—social inadequacies, language skills not fully developed, academic requirements beyond the child's ability, specific learning tasks for which the child has not developed readiness, and minor vision or hearing problems that previously had been unnoticed but which do affect his/her school performance. For these kinds of students, instructional planning must be broadened to include the identification of behaviors that suggest potential learning difficulties. The planning process for exceptional children must begin *before* the child has been identified as having special needs.

Implications for Unit Teaching

Teachers oriented toward unit teaching will find developing IEPs a familiar exercise. The instructional features incorporated into the IEP process are closely related to the developmental steps for writing units suggested in chapter 4. The skills required by teachers to be effective in unit teaching, that is, writing objectives, designing activities, and structuring assessment tasks are also essential to implementing IEPs. In many ways a well-designed IEP represents the exact information the teacher needs as directives in designing units.

In developing instructional units, teachers make use of instructional resources, such as curriculum guides, texts, and supplemental material. However, such use is selective as the teacher organizes content and sequences skills within a plan of instruction designed around a useful and meaningful theme. An IEP should set forth guidelines in the form of short-term goals that can be used by the teacher in planning units. IEPs, in general, do not dictate teaching methodology, but they do identify instructional priorities for individual students. The major task for teachers using units will be to reflect in their unit plans how they will accommodate the short-term objectives for particular students. Teachers using other instructional approaches will also be faced with the same demand. In the case of unit teaching, the situation will be easier. Teachers who teach units are accustomed to individualizing within group instruction. In planning units, they must take into consideration the needs and backgrounds of individual students. Above all, they approach teaching and instructional planning from the perspective of developing instruction, making content and methodology decisions, and relating teaching activities to objectives. Because unit teaching requires that the units be written, each experience is planned by the teacher in contrast to adhering to textbooks. In unit teaching, the teacher expects to plan activities for students with similar needs or to plan independent activities.

The short-term goals appearing in IEPs are generally related to skills, acquisition of information, or the understanding of concepts. Because they are expressed in terms that describe the skill or concept, it is necessary for the teacher to further break the goal down into objectives related to "teachable" tasks. Typically the goal or the more refined objectives do not

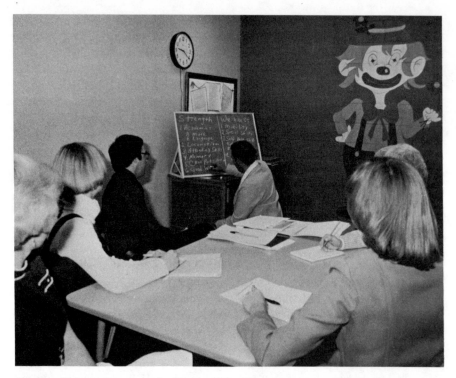

The specifying of goals and objectives should occur in the IEP conference.

indicate the context in which the skill or knowledge is to be taught. In the development of units, teachers can plan for teaching the skill or knowledge called for in the short-term goals included in the IEPs. Even in situations in which a teacher has prepared a unit and has begun instruction on the unit prior to an IEP being planned for one of his/her students, the teaching of short-term goals can be accommodated through seatwork, group activities, tutorial experiences, etc. Units provide the advantage of being able to couch the teaching of skills and concepts in a meaningful context.

Frequently, students have difficulty learning skills or concepts because they are taught in isolation and independent from an application experience. In unit teaching emphasis is placed on teaching skills and concepts in a useful manner and building on areas of knowledge possessed by the student. In planning units for groups containing students on whom IEPs have been developed, it is important to approach the breaking down of short-term goals from the perspective of task analysis. In doing so, don't worry about the unit topic. Initially only be concerned with breaking the goals down to teachable elements. Obviously, the teacher must use judgment so that the set of objectives is not too detailed and extensive. Once you have detailed the goals, you can then review the units being planned or currently being taught and structure activities aimed at teaching those particular objectives. You will likely find that other students in the class have similar needs.

Following are examples of short-term goals and how they have been detailed as a reference for preparing teaching activities. The examples have been randomly selected to illustrate different skill and subject areas.

Example A

Short-Term Objectives: To assist the student in indicating monetary amounts using the following coins of differing monetary values: pennies, nickels, dimes.

Enroute Objectives:

1. The student will be able to exchange a nickel for 5 pennies when given a nickel.
2. The student will be able to exchange a dime for 10 pennies when given a dime.
3. The student will be able to exchange a dime for two nickels when given a dime.
4. The student will be able to show the following amounts ($.08, $.11, $.15, $.23) when they are given orally by using pennies.
5. The student will be able to select coins from a given set of coins (2 dimes, 3 nickels, and 5 pennies) to total the amount when orally given the following amounts: $.07, $.13, $.19, and $.21.

Example B

Short-Term Objective: To assist the student in performing motor movements with flexibility in a standing position.
Enroute Objectives:

1. The student will be able to bend forward and extend both arms to touch his/her toes, without bouncing at the waist.
2. The student will be able to bend, from an upright standing position, to his/her left and right side at the waist, with hands placed on the hips or extended at both sides.
3. The student will be able to twist his/her upper trunk at the waist to the right, then to the left.
4. The student will be able to do a "split" to the sides, using the hands forward on the floor as support.
5. The student will be able to do a forward "split," using the hands extended to the floor on both sides as support.

Example C

Short-Term Objective: To assist the student in understanding that water is necessary for life and must be conserved.

Enroute Objectives:

1. The student, after discussion and looking at pictures of water use, will be able to state that water is used in many ways in everyday life.
2. The student, when asked, will be able to state three ways water is necessary for his/her personal use, such as drinking, cooking, washing, bathing.
3. The student, given pictures of water being used in the following situations, will be able to state how the water is being used: irrigation of a field, school drinking fountain, fire truck using water, cooking, washing hands, water used in factory.
4. The student, when asked, will be able to state how water is necessary for animal and plant life, such as drinking, washing.
5. The student, given a list of ten ways water is used, two of which are wasteful, will be able to identify the eight that are necessary.
6. The student will be able to identify three ways to conserve water, such as not leaving a faucet running, taking a shower instead of a bath, fixing a leaky faucet, not using an electric dishwasher except to do full loads.

Example D

Short-Term Objective: To assist the student in expressing multiwork sentences.

Enroute Objectives:

1. The student will be able to complete a sentence when presented with a picture stimulus, i.e., "This (is a dog)."
2. The student will be able to describe the function of an object using a four- or five-word sentence, i.e., 'Soap is for washing."
3. The student will be able to express a four-word utterance, noun-verb-adjective-noun, i.e., "I want red cup."
4. The student will be able to express a four-word utterance, noun-verb-preposition-noun, i.e., "Boy climbs up tree."
5. The student will be able to use a four-word utterance containing a negation, i.e., "I want no more."
6. The student will be able to recite sentences or simple rhymes from memory.

Example E

Short-Term Objective: To assist the student in developing meaningful two- and three-word utterances.

Enroute Objectives

1. The student will be able to use a two-word utterance containing a preposition or modifier as a relational term, i.e., "More milk."
2. The student will be able to use a two-word, verb-object, utterance to express wants, i.e., "Go school."
3. The student will be able to express two-word, subject-verb, utterances, i.e. "Boy go."
4. The student will be able to express an external negation, i.e., "No milk."
5. The student will be able to use a three-word, subject-verb-object, utterance to label action in a picture or event, i.e., "Girl ride bike."
6. The student will be able to use prepositions in two- or three-word utterances, i.e., "Throw in box."

Example F

Short-Term Objective: To assist the student in developing the ability to work independently.

Enroute Objectives:

1. The student will be able to complete assigned tasks without requesting assistance from the teacher or peers.
2. The student will be able to demonstrate consistent on-task behavior when unsupervised.
3. The student will be able to work independently on a series of assigned tasks for increasingly longer periods of time.
4. The student will be able to work independently throughout the school day.
5. The student will be able to demonstrate consistent on-task behavior when unsupervised in the work setting.

In examining these examples it is apparent that the skills or concepts involved could be taught through a variety of unit topics. Using the short-term goals as a reference it is not difficult to integrate activities into units that allow for teaching the respective skills or concepts. If a teacher develops unit specifications in accordance with the guidelines presented in chapter 8, it will be easy to determine the prerequisite skills as well as where the skills or concepts fit relative to the sequence of more complex skills and concepts.

Summary

Instructional planning for exceptional children historically has been a concern of special educators. Until recently, however, planning has focused primarily on decisions regarding where the child will be placed for service and the type of services to be provided. Attention was given to diagnosis, but little attention was given to describing how the specific remediation needs of the student were to be met.

A major change in instructional planning for exceptional children today relates to the involvement of regular educators along with special educators. In most cases, participation in instructional planning includes a regular class teacher and a special teacher; participation now is being expanded to include those teachers and specialists having responsibility for the student's program. A result of this trend is the need for systematic procedures, personnel skilled in planning, and provisions for sharing information.

Now that school districts are required to develop written, individualized programs (IEPs) for all handicapped children, instructional planning must become more systematic and specific. Instructional planning for exceptional children must be comprehensive and include data on the student's current level of performance, long- and short-term objectives, and evaluation procedures. Parental participation is an essential component.

The instructional features of the IEP are highly compatible with the principles of unit teaching. The teacher competencies required for unit teaching include those required to develop and implement IEPs. The IEP provides teachers who employ the unit teaching method with essential information needed in the process of designing and adapting units to the instructional needs of students.

While the author is a proponent of instructional planning and supports the implementation of the IEP requirements as a step toward improved instruction without time for planning and administrative support, teachers will not be able to carry out planning at the desired level of intensity.

Certain conditions essential for effective instructional planning are important to implementing the IEP process. In general, these conditions include:

1. Administrative support
   a. The emphasis administrators place on instructional planning as a priority should be clearly visible to teachers.
   b. An investment should be made in resources required for instructional planning.
   c. Administrators should view instructional planning from a cumulative perspective and not as something that occurs only at the beginning of the school year.

2. Definition of roles
   a. A comprehensive approach to instructional planning involves several different roles; these roles should be carefully defined.
   b. After roles are agreed upon, emphasis should be placed on each participant's understanding of his or her role in relation to the roles of others, including teachers, principals, parents, and support personnel.
3. Open communication
   a. Communication among all participants in the student's program is essential and communication procedures need not be formal.
   b. Parents and students *must* be included in the communication process.
4. Instructional planning model
   a. Teachers and support personnel should be oriented toward a model that emphasizes pupil needs, design of activities according to needs, trying out activities, evaluation of activities, and revision based on what has been learned.
   b. Establishment of the above condition likely will require in-service training.

Exercise 2: Using a case study provided by the instructor or using data on one of your own students, prepare an IEP. If your district does not have a recommended IEP form, use the sample form appearing in Appendix 1.

REFERENCES

CALDER, C. R. "The Curriculum-Instruction Continuum with Respect to Mainstreaming of Handicapped Children. In *Instructional technology and the education of all handicapped children,* edited by R. Heinrich and S. C. Ashcroft. Columbus, Ohio. National Center on Media and Materials for the Handicapped, 1977.

Federal Register, 42 (163) August, 1977.

Meyen, E. L. *Instructional Based Appraisal System* (IBAS). Bellevue, Wash.: Edmark Associates, 1976.

ADDITIONAL SELECTED REFERENCES

Because most literature pertaining to IEPs and instructional planning is relatively new, an extensive listing of suggested references is included. The topics include IEPs, individualized instruction, and evaluation of pupil performance.

AIELLO, B. *Mainstreaming: Teacher Training Workshops on Individualized Instruction.* Reston, Va.: Council for Exceptional Children, 1975-76.

ARENA, J. *How to Write an IEP.* Novato, Calif.: Academic Therapy Publications, 1978.

ARMSTRONG, J. R. "Individually Guided Instruction (IGE): One Model for Mainstreaming." *Focus on Exceptional Children,* 1976, Vol. 8, No. 7.

BORICH, G. D. "Program Evaluation: New Concepts, New Methods." *Focus on Exceptional Children* 9 (3) (May 1977):1-14.

BRIGGS, L. J. "An Instructional Design Theorist Examines Individualized Instruction Systems." In *Systems of Individualized Education,* edited by H. Talmage. Berkeley, Calif.: McCutchan, 1975.

CEGELKA, P. T., and PHILLIPS, M. W. "Individualized Education Programming at the Secondary Level." *Exceptional Children* 10 (1978):84-87.

CLEMENTS, J. E., and ALEXANDER, R. N. "Parent Training: Bringing It All Back Home." *Focus on Exceptional Children* 7 (1975):1-12.

CRAWFORD, D. "Parent Involvement in Instructional Planning. *Focus on Exceptional Children* (7) (1978):10, 1-5.

FANNING, P. "The New Relationship Between Parents and Schools." *Focus on Exceptional Children* 9 (1977):1-10.

FENTON, K. S.; YOSHIDA, R. K.; MAXWELL, J.; and KAUFMAN, M. *Placement team Responsibility: Do PT Members Recognize Their Duties?* Washington, D. C.: U.S.O.E., BEH, State Program Studies Branch, 1977b.

GITTINS, W. "Individualized Educational Programming." *Journal of Special Education* 2 (1) (1978):3-7.

GOFF, M., and KELLY, P. "The Special Education Paraprofessional and the Individualized Education Program Process. *Focus on Exceptional Children* 10 (9) 1979:10-13.

GORMAN, P. "IEPs: Confusion Abounds." *American Teacher* (March 1978).

HEISS, W. "Relating Education Assessment to Instructional Planning." *Focus on Exceptional Children* 9 (1) (March 1977):1-11.

HOWE, C. E., and FITZGERALD, M. E. "Evaluating Special Education Programs." *Focus on Exceptional Children* 8 (9) (February 1977):1-11.

HUDSON, F. G., and GRAHAM, S. "An Approach to Operationalizing the IEP. *Learning Disability Quarterly* 1 (1978):12-32.

"Individualized Education Plan: Questions and Answers." *Exceptional Parent* 8 1978:7-10.

KAPPELMAN, M., and ACKERMAN, P. *Between Parent and School.* New York: Dial Press, 1977.

KAYE, N. L. and ASERLAND, R. "The IEP: The Ultimate Process." *Journal of Special Education* 12 (2) (1979):137-44.

KROTH, R. L., and SIMPSON, R. L. *Parent Conferences as a Teaching Strategy.* Denver, Colo.: Love Publishing Co., 1977.

LOVETT, T. "The Who, When, and What of IEPs." *Early Years* 8 (1) (1977):49-52.

MACMILLAN, D. L., and SEMMEL, M. I. "Evaluation of Mainstreaming Programs." *Focus on Exceptional Children* 9 (4) (September 1977):1-14.

MARION, R. "Minority Parent Involvement in the IEP Process: A Systematic Model Approach. *Focus on Exceptional Children* 10 (1979):1-10.

MEYEN, E. L. *Instructional Based Appraisal System (IBAS)*, Bellevue, Wash.: Edmark Associates, 1976.

MORAN, M. R. "The Teacher's Role in Referral for Testing and Interpretation of Reports. *Focus on Exceptional Children* 8 (6) (1976):1-15.

MORRISON, P. A., and SAFER, N. "Implications for Special Education: The Individualized Education Program." *Viewpoints* 53 (1977):31-38.

NEYHUS, A. I. "Assessment for Individualized Education Programming." *Volta Review* 80 (1978):286-95.

SAFER, N.; MORRISSEY, P. A.; KAUFMAN, M., and LEWIS, L. "Implementation of IEPs: New Teacher Roles and Requisite Support Systems." *Focus on Exceptional Children* 10 (1) (1978):1-20.

SIRVIS, B. "Developing IEPs for Physically Handicapped Students: A Transdisciplinary Viewpoint." *Teaching Exceptional Children* 10 (1978):78-82.

TORRES, S., ed. *A Primer on Individualized Education Programs for Handicapped Children.* Reston, Va.: Council for Exceptional Children, 1977.

TURNBULL, A. P. "Training Professionals and Parents in Developing and Implementing the IEP." *Education and Training of the Mentally Retarded* 13 (1978):414423.

TURNBULL, A. P.; STRICKLAND, B.; and HAMMER, S. E. "The Individualized Education Program—Part I: Procedural Guidelines. *Journal of Learning Disabilities* 11 (1978):52-58.

TURNER, R. M., and MACY, D. J. *A Five Year Longitudinal Study of IEP Implementation.* Dallas: Dallas Independent School District. Paper presented at Council for Exceptional Children Topical Conference on IEP Planning, Albuquerque, New Mexico, February 1978.

WESSEL, J. A., ed. *Planning Individualized Education Programs in Special Education.* Northbrook, Ill.: Hubbard, 1977.

YOSHIDA, R. K.; FENTON, K. S.; and KAUFMAN, M. J. "Evaluation of Education for the Handicapped." *Phi Delta Kappan* (September 1977).

YOSHIDA, R. K.; FENTON, K. S.; MAXWELL, J. P.; and KAUFMAN, M. J. "Group Decision Making in the Planning Team Process: Myth or Reality?" Hartford, Conn.: State Department of Education, 1977.

YOSHIDA, R. K., and GOTTLIEB, J. "A Model of Parental Participation in the Pupil Planning Process." *Mental Retardation* 15 (1977):17-20.

4

The Instructionally
Different Child

What constitutes a difference? Is a difference determined by teachers using their own standard as a reference? Is a difference the contrast of sameness? Can a difference be good? Are some children different in school but like their peers when at home? What difference makes a difference instructionally? These questions may appear to be insignificant and created only for the purpose of acknowledging that few children are alike. This author believes that these are significant questions and must be addressed by each teacher independently and in the privacy of what one might call conscience searching. Teachers are human. They vary in their attitudes toward children, and they vary in their values about life. Teachers come to school having been influenced by their childhood experiences, their families, peers, what they have been taught in college, and their previous teaching experiences. To say that all teachers are capable of viewing each child in an objective manner would be unrealistic. On the other hand, teachers who are willing to periodically examine their own values and to purposefully assess the total needs of their students against their perceptions of student participation and performance will likely approach objectivity in their instructional decisions.

The value placed on being different is determined by the perceptions held by others. Johnny, who excells in math, is different. For some teachers, who lack confidence in their ability to provide challenging instruction in math, Johnny's difference may take on a negative value. The same may be true of a student who lags far behind others in class in a particular subject. Differences are real and must be responded to by teachers, but they need not be given a value nor made obvious to others.

Not all "differences" have instructional meaning, but many do. At least the manner in which teachers respond to these differences can produce significant consequences for those students perceived as different. Teachers are reminded that too often the most significant difference is not observable, that is, the cultural background of the student, the student's perception of school, the student's previous relationships with teachers and peers, and the impact of prior experiences with school-related learning. While it is important for teachers to understand normal patterns of growth and development, this knowledge is not sufficient as a base for identifying instructionally significant differences.

It would be both presumptious and inappropriate to present a list of characteristics which, if presented by a student, would classify the student as being different. Children vary from each other and also vary in their own behavior over time. Within variance of children is most difficult to interpret and is often the reason for a teacher perceiving a child as being different. This is a child who is responsive one day and inattentive the following day, or a student who demonstrates high achievement for a period of time, then begins to fall behind in school work. Instructionally, this "within" variance is as important to some students as a serious hearing loss is to others. Both require the special attention of a teacher in structuring appropriate instructional responses. To provide a definition of instructional difference that is highly generalizable would require at least describing the (1) instructional setting including student characteristics, (2) teacher style and expectations, and (3) anticipated instructional outcomes. Depending on how these variables interact, a student may or may not be perceived as being instructionally different. Some teachers do prefer particular teaching styles, and their repertoire of teaching options will accommodate the student needs through routine instructional planning. Others will find it necessary to seek assistance or to devote time specifically planning for those particular students.

Teachers, through their own resources, such as personal values, teaching skills, and general responsiveness, can minimize most differences initially presented by students. The important thing is for teachers to accept responsibility for those differences that have instructional implications and in responding to those differences do what is necessary to avoid making such differences visible.

The discussion thus far has focused on instructionally significant differences. It is apparent to experienced teachers that students are also highly similar in their development. It is also obvious that patterns of growth and development are subject to considerable influence at different times in life. Such influence might include nutrition, family relationships, nature of early experiences, and quality of previous experience. Williams and Stith summarize principles of development as follows.

1. Development is similar for all, following genetic sequences yet influenced by environment; each child is unique.
2. Development is continuous, occurring in stages; children normally pass through each stage, often at different rates. Each stage has characteristic traits.

Differences presented by students vary in the type of instructional response required in order to meet their needs.

3. There is correlation among the rates and phases of the various structures and functions, the maturity of one facet affecting others, resulting in uneven growth tempo.
4. The rate of development is usually highest at the onset closely associated with the principle of indigenous motivation which may cause a child's use of emerging developmental abilities to appear exaggerated and intense.
5. Behavior is largely controlled by human needs and is a function of developmental status.[1]

Understanding normal patterns of growth and development increases the sensitivity of teachers to variances in rate or sequence of development displayed by particular students. Caution should be exercised by teachers

1. Joyce W. Williams and Marjorie Stith, *Middle Childhood Behavior and Development* (New York: MacMillan Publishing Co., 1974), p. 28.

to consider such observations and as reason for concern and not necessarily cause for alarm. Children do vary. Determining why a child appears to be lagging behind the anticipated pattern of development is as important as noting the descrepancy.

The purpose of this chapter is to remind teachers that while there are expected patterns of normal growth and development, some children do vary from such patterns and present to teachers differences that are instructionally different. It also tries to emphasize that there are students who, as a group, present differences that are instructionally significant. These group differences may be in addition to the individual differences of group members. Space does not permit a comprehensive discussion of group differences, however, a detailed bibliography of suggested references is included at the end of this chapter. The following discussion will elaborate on social class differences, cultural differences, and differences related to handicapping conditions.

Social Class Differences

While there appears to be a tendency to avoid reference to social class differences in the United States, sociologists and other researchers who examine communities consistently report that differences related to social class do exist. Whatever the cause, be it economic, lack of opportunities for upward mobility, or, as has been true in the past, ethnic segregation, a number of factors interact to create social class differences. These factors are often reflected in differences and attitudes toward school, values placed on education, child rearing practices, behavioral norms, vocational aspirations, levels of self-esteem, and perceptions of the larger society.

It is difficult to discuss social class differences without risking interpretations based on a hierarchy of qualitative or value-ladened inferences. Typically, social class differences are described under some variety of three general levels, that is, upper class, middle class, and lower class, with upper class referring to the financially secure and well-established; middle class including white collar workers and most professionals; and lower class being comprised of semi- and unskilled workers. The primary reason for referring to social class differences is to acknowledge that there are groups of people who share a common social history that influences their behavior, needs, and perceptions of life in general, and to point out that these social differences must be accommodated in the context of instructional planning. Although major efforts have been initiated during the past two decades to minimize social class differences, they continue to exist. Teachers are generally, as a group, considered to be primarily middle class, whereas, a major portion of their students come from working class homes, and many are from the lower class. The differences in value between these groups vary sharply.[2]

McCandless, in discussing the social class differences relative to the teachers instructional role, places considerable emphasis on communication. He states:

> "Major differences in values result in serious communications difficulties between middle-class and lower-class people; these are particularly troubling to the relations between teachers and lower-class children. Because of their failure to understand each other's behavior, standards, and goals, mutual distrust—even hostility—may result. The implications of this situation for the education of lower-class children are grave, and are made even more serious because lower-class parents typically do not support the schools' educational efforts. Middle-class parents, on the other hand, offer strong support to the schools; and teachers present about the same image to middle-class children as their parents do.
>
> Lower-class children appear to be less well-accepted by their peers (as well as by their teachers) than middle-class children are. Boys may be more fortunate in this respect than girls, since they may be able to break the class barrier by means of athletic proficiency. For both boys and girls, social acceptance seems to be positively (although only moderately) related to good personal adjustment; middle-class youngsters appear to be better adjusted than those of lower social status.
>
> Lower-class children seem to respond well to teacher techniques that combine fairness and warmth with strength. Their education might also be furthered by providing them with textbooks (particularly early in their school career) that have more in common with their way of life than the rather pallid reading fare ordinarily offered them. Compensatory education, if it can permeate regular education and extend downward to nursery school, offers great hope. Children strongly desire "training for competence."
>
> Appreciation and respect for the individual can help bridge the gap between teachers and lower-class children. Specifically, teachers should strive to know these children and their families better, and to develop a more realistic understanding of their needs and standards. Developing attitudes of objectivity and acceptance toward others means that teachers must examine and justify—and, where necessary, modify—their own system of values. Such steps as these, thoughtfully and sincerely taken, can go far toward improving the education of lower-class children, and of all other youngsters as well."[3]

2. B. R. McCandless, *Children Behavior and Development*, 2d ed. (New York: Holt, Rinehart and Winston, 1967), p. 611.
3. Ibid.

It is important for teachers to be conscious of their own values and sensitive to the backgrounds of others. To integrate concerns or differences in social background requires more than a cognitive understanding. Teachers should invest time and effort in examining their own belief and backgrounds as a basis for understanding the social histories that students bring to the instructional situation.

Cultural Differences

The previous discussion on social class represents, in part, a cultural difference. However, there are also cultural differences that stem from the heritage of ethnic groups. The emphasis on the neighborhood school in this country appears to make teachers more aware of the instructional implications presented by the presence of ethnic groups. In situations where only one or two students represent children from minority groups in a class, their cultural background is frequently overlooked as an important consideration in instructional planning.

It is not sufficient to merely teach a series of lessons on the cultural heritage of selected ethnic groups, though this is important. The cultural heritage of many groups operationalizes into specific instructional needs. Thus, to acknowledge their heritage without accommodating their instructional needs does little to enhance their performance in school-related tasks.

Recently attention has been given to multicultural education, that is, education that values cultural pluralism. Multicultural education does not mean that teachers should seek to melt away cultural differences or the view that teachers should merely tolerate cultural pluralism. Instead, multicultural education means that teachers should be oriented toward the cultural enrichment of all children and youth. If cultural pluralism is so basic a quality of our culture, it must become an integral part of the educational process at every level. To accomplish this requires that teachers be sensitive to the need for emphasizing cultural pluralism and capable of influencing the curriculum. Education for cultural pluralism includes: the teaching of values that support cultural diversity and individual uniqueness; the encouragement of the qualitative expansion of existing ethnic cultures. While schools must insure that all students are assisted in developing their skills to function effectively in society, such a commitment should not ignore cultural differences.

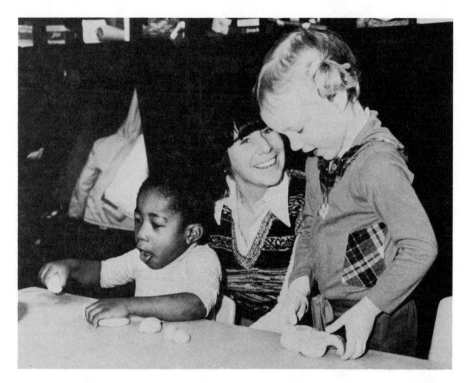

Teachers must be sensitive to the cultural heritage of all children.

Oden, in discussing the schools' responsibility to minority group children, presents the view that education

> . . . is more than reading, writing, and arithmetic, education is preparation for life. Students need more than facts and problem-solving skills; they need to know how to lead full and useful lives in a complex world. In a nation made up of a variety of races and nationalities, that means learning how to live and work with people of different skin colors and cultural backgrounds. If one accepts this broad view of education, one cannot imagine a worse way of undertaking it than in a classroom segregated by race, national origin, or handicappedness. Segregated classrooms deny millions of Americans the opportunity to become acquainted with the minority child whose future they share.[4]

4. C. W. Oden, Jr., "Desegregation and Mainstreaming: A Case of Deja Vu," in *Mainstreaming and the Minority Child*, ed. R. L. Jones. (Reston, Va.: The Council for Exceptional Children, 1976), p. 56.

Due to the lack of extensive curriculum materials for use in multicultural education, teachers fall heir to designing their own units and to modifying instructions to accommodate the many subtle instructional needs presented by students from cultures other than that of the teacher. Pepper,[5] in writing about the education of the American Indian child, provides a comparison of values using the child from the dominant society and the Indian child as references. This comparison will be presented because it illustrates the array of insights a teacher can gain from studying cultural differences and their implications for instruction.

A Comparison of Values

Indian	*Dominant Society*
Wisdom of age and experience is respected. Elders are revered by their people.	Older people are made to feel incompetent and rejected.
Excellence is related to a contribution to the group—not to personal glory.	Competition and striving to win or to gain status is emphasized.
Cooperation is necessary for group survival.	Competition is necessary for individual status and prestige.
Children participate in adult activities.	Adults participate in children's activities.
Family life includes the extended family.	Family life includes the nuclear family.
Time is present oriented—this year, this week—NOW—a resistance to planning for the future.	Time is planning and saving for the future.
Clocktime is whenever people are ready—when everyone arrives.	Clocktime is exactly that.
Work is when necessary for the common good. Whatever Indian people have, they share. What is mine is ours.	Work is 9-5 (specified time) and to obtain material possible and to save for the future. What is mine, stays mine.
Good relationships and mutual respect are emphasized.	Success, progress, possession of property and rugged individualism is valued above mutual respect and maintaining good relationships.

5. F. C. Pepper, "Teaching the American Indian Child in Mainstreaming Settings," in *Mainstreaming and the Minority Child*, ed. R. L. Jones (Reston, Va.: The Council for Exceptional Children, 1976), pp. 135-36.

People express their ideas and feelings through their actions.

People express themselves and attempt to impress others through speech.

People conform to nature.

People try to dominate and desecrate nature.

Early childhood and rearing practices are the responsibility of the kin group.

Early childhood and rearing practices are the responsibility of the nuclear family.

Native religion was never imposed or proselytized other groups.

Religious groups proselytize, coerce and impose their beliefs on others.

Land gives the Indian his identity, his religion and his life. It is not to be sold, not owned, but used by all.

Land is for speculation, for prestige, to be owned, sold, or torn up.

Going to school is necessary to gain knowledge. Excelling for fame is looked down upon by the Indian.

Going to school is necessary to gain knowledge and to compete for grades.

Indians have a shorter childhood and the male is held to be a responsible person at the age of 16.

There is an extended childhood and the male is held to be a responsible person at the age of 21.

People are usually judged by what they do.

People are usually judged by their credentials.

Differences Caused by Handicapping Conditions

To present handicapped children as being different would not be representative of the author's view. Certainly, as individual learners, their behavior and needs approximate those of most children. However, they do have needs, depending on the nature of their handicapping condition, that require special consideration in instructional planning and in the process of teaching. For the most part, the instructional needs of handicapped children, when isolated as instructional techniques and/or adaptations, do not differ from the needs of many nonhandicapped students. Most students experience learning and/or behavioral problems that at least momentarily require special attention. The handicapped student, however, is more likely to present a configuration of special needs and be less responsive to remediation techniques.

The trend toward mainstreaming was discussed in chapter 1, and the development of individual education programs (IEPs) for handicapped children were discussed in chapter 3. Both discussions emphasize the increased responsibility being assumed by regular class teachers for the education of the handicapped children and youth and for talented and gifted students. (When handicapped students and gifted students are referred to as a group, the term *exceptional* is applied as an inclusive descriptor). As the responsibility for educating exceptional children is shifted to the regular classroom setting, the need for regular classroom teachers to fully understand the needs of exceptional students becomes essential. It also becomes important for regular class teachers to be knowledgeable of available support services, referral procedures, special instructional techniques, and affective implications.

Historically, exceptional children have been defined from the perspective of ideology, with the primary emphasis being placed on a set of characteristics considered common to particular types of exceptionalities. While this approach has served a useful purpose in advocating for public support of special education programs, it has also resulted in the definitions being perceived as labels. The label then takes on a meaning suggesting limitations inherent in the learner. The use of labels continues, but there is a trend toward giving more attention to the instructional options required by exceptional children and youth and moving away from primary reliance on descriptors of handicapping conditions. The author, in an earler publication, has suggested an approach that defines exceptional children based on their instructional needs.

> Instructional Options for exceptional children are those which require:
> accurate, in-depth assessment of learner strengths and weaknesses
> intensive remediation intervention attention by specially trained teachers, support personnel, and instructional aids
> a focus on instructional needs which require more time to remediate than routinely can be accomplished in regular instructional settings
> precise instructional planning by teachers and support personnel
> the use of specially designed instructional materials and/or activities
> modifications or adaptations in the organization and/or structure of the regular curriculum
> Given that instructional options meeting the above conditions are established, children and youth whose characteristics dictate the need for such instructional options would be considered exceptional.[6]

While the author encourages teachers to give primary attention to the array of instructional techniques, materials, and resources which are appropriate and effective in accommodating specific deficiencies presented by students with handicaps, it is recognized that in the foreseeable future most

---

6. Edward L. Meyen, *Exceptional Children and Youth: An Introduction* (Denver, Colo.: Love Publishing Co., 1978), p. 60.

teachers will find it necessary to be familiar with handicapping conditions and the terms used to identify students with such handicapping conditions. Thus, in spite of their limitations and general lack of instructional meaning, the definitions of handicapped children included in P.L. 94-142 are reported. These definitions will be useful for teachers in searching for resources on instructional strategies.

Sec. 121a.5 Handicapped children.

(a) As used in this part, the term "handicapped children" means those children evaluated in accordance with Sections 121a.530-121a.534 as being mentally retarded, hard of hearing, deaf, speech impaired, visually handicapped, seriously emotionally disturbed, orthopedically impaired, other health impaired, deaf-blind, multi-handicapped, or as having specific learning disabilities, who because of those impairments need special education and related services.

(b) The terms used in this definition are defined as follows:

(1) "Deaf" means a hearing impairment which is so severe that the child is impaired in processing linguistic information through hearing, with or without amplification, which adversely affects educational performance.

(2) "Deaf-blind" means concomitant hearing and visual impairments, the combination of which causes such severe communication and other developmental and educational problems that they cannot be accomodated in special education programs solely for deaf or blind children.

(3) "Hard of hearing" means a hearing impairment, whether permanent or fluctuating, which adversely affects a child's educational performance but which is not included under the definition of "deaf" in this section.

(4) "Mentally retarded" means significantly subaverage general intellectual functioning existing concurrently with deficits in adaptive behavior and manifested during the developmental period, which adversely affects a child's educational performance.

(5) "Multihandicapped" means concomitant impairments (such as mentally retarded-blind, mentally retarded-orthopedically impaired, etc.) the combination of which causes such severe educational problems that they cannot be accommodated in special education programs solely for one of the impairments. The term does not include deaf-blind children.

(6) "Orthopedically impaired" means a severe orthopedic impairment which adversely affects a child's educational performance. The term includes impairments caused by congenital anomaly (e.g., clubfoot, absence of some member, etc.) impairments caused by congenital anomaly (e.g., clubfoot, absence of some member, etc.) impairments caused by disease (e.g., polio-myelitis, bone tuberculosis, etc.), and impairments from other causes (e.g., cerebral palsy, amputations, and fractures or burns which cause contractures).

(7) "Other health impaired" means limited strength, vitality or alterness, due to chronic or acute health problems such as a heart condition, tuberculosis, rheumatc fever, nephritis, asthma, sickle cell anemia, hemophilia, epilepsy, lead poisoning, leukemia, or diabetes, which adversely affects a child's educational performance.

(8) "Seriously emotionally disturbed" is defined as follows:
 (i) The term means a condition exhibiting one or more of the follow-ing characteristics over a long period of time and to a marked de-gree, which adversely affects educational performance.
  (A) An inability to learn which cannot be explained by intellec-tual, sensory, or health factors;
  (B) An inability to build or maintain satisfactory interpersonal relationships with peers and teachers;
  (C) Inappropriate types of behavior or feelings under normal cir-cumstances;
  (D) A general pervasive mood of unhappiness or depression; or
  (E) A tendency to develop physical symptoms or fears associated with personal or school problems.
   (ii) The term includes children who are schizophrenic or autistic. The term does not include children who are socially maladjusted, unless it is determined that they are seriously emotionally disturbed.
(9) "Specific learning disability" means a disorder in one or more of the basic psychological processes involved in understanding or in using lan-guage, spoken or written, which may manifest itself in an imperfect ability to listen, think, speak, read, write, spell or to do mathematical calculations. The term includes such conditions as perceptual handicaps, brain injury, minimal brain dysfunction, dyslexia, and developmental aphasia. The term does not include children who have learning prob-lems which are primarily the result of visual, hearing, or motor handi-caps, of mental retardation, or of environmental, cultural, or economic disadvantage.
(10) "Speech impaired" means a communication disorder, such as stuttering, impaired articulation, a language impairment, or a voice impairment, which adversely affects a child's educational performance.
(11) "Visually handicapped" means a visual impairment which, even with correction, adversely affects a child's educational performance. The term includes both partially seeing and blind children.[7]

Except for teachers at the primary level, children will likely be iden-tified as handicapped prior to enrollment in regular classrooms. Consider-able information will be available on the student's history, and an IEP will either be available or in the process of being developed. Regular class teachers should be prepared to ask questions about the student's instruc-tional needs, and if the student is already placed in his or her class, teachers should be prepared to offer instructionally related information.

7. *Federal Register*, Part IV (Washington, D. C.: Department of Health, Education and Welfare, August 1977), 42, (163).

Much of the information accumulated on handicapped students emphasizes deficits and needs. Care must be exercised to also focus on the student's strengths. Frequently this will not occur unless the discussion is initiated by teachers. Understanding information about the student's handicapping condition will be helpful but the most useful information will center on the instructional implications. Merely knowing that a student has a hearing loss, is mentally retarded, or has a physical handicap will not be helpful.

Implications for Unit Teaching

Unit teaching offers many advantages over other methodologies in accommodating the needs of instructionally different students. These advantages are related to the control the teacher exercises over the content to be included in units of instruction, the manner in which students can be involved, and the flexibility offered the teacher in employing varied instructional strategies and techniques. If teachers know their student's background and needs, units can be designed that are tailored to the individual and collective needs of students in the class. Unit teaching allows the teacher to engineer experiences that capitalize on the strengths and backgrounds of each student. It is also possible, when appropriate, to develop units on types of differences, such as cultural, ethnic background, and/or the handicapped. The latter option is not suggested as a substitute for attending to instructional differences presented by students routinely, but circumstances will arise when such information will benefit the total class. The unit method offers the teacher a structure for teaching such information.

Beyond the content control characteristic of instructional units, the opportunity to involve students in planning and implementing units represents a major advantage. Unit teaching provides teachers opportunities to communicate to students respect for their heritage, understanding of their specific instructional needs, and above all respect for them as individuals.

Summary

While most children follow a common pattern of growth and development, they also vary. Most individual differences are normal and do not call for instructional modifications. Some students, however, come to school with a cultural background greatly different from their peers and teachers. Others have different needs because of handicapping conditions. The intent of this chapter has been to remind teachers that all students have needs that are similar, but some students, because of their backgrounds and/or learning characteristics, require special attention. The challenge to teachers is to determine when a characteristic or background makes a difference instructionally.

REFERENCES

Federal Register (Part IV). Washington, D. C.: Department of Health, Education, & Welfare, August 1977, 42, (163).

McCANDLESS, B. R. *Children Behavior and Development.* 2d ed. New York: Holt, Rinehart and Winston, 1967.

MEYEN, EDWARD L. *Exceptional Children and Youth: An Introduction.* Denver, Colo.: Love Publishing Co., 1978.

ODEN, C. W. JR. "Desegregation and Mainstreaming: A Case of Deja Vu." *In Mainstreaming and the Minority Child,* edited by R. L. Jones. Reston, Va.: The Council for Exceptional Children, 1976.

PEPPER, F. C. "Teaching the American Indian Child in Mainstreaming Settings." *In Mainstreaming and the Minority Child,* edited by R. L. Jones. Reston, Va.: The Council for Exceptional Children, 1976.

Williams, W. J., and Stith, M. *Middle Childhood Behavior Development.* New York MacMillan Publishing Co., 1974.

ADDITIONAL SELECTED REFERENCES

ALLEY, G. and FOSTER, C. "Nondiscriminatory Testing of Minority and Exceptional Children. In *Instructional planning for exceptional children,* edited by E. L. Meyer; G. A. Vergason; and R. J. Whelan. Denver, Colo.: Love Publishing Co., 1979.

FANNING, P. "The New Relationship Between Parents and Schools. In *Instructional planning for exceptional children,* edited by E. L. Meyen; G. A. Vergason; and R. J. Whelan. Denver, Colo.: Love Publishing Co., 1979.

GARDNER, W. I. *Learning and Behavior Characteristics of Exceptional Children and Youth.* Boston: Allyn & Bacon, 1977.

GEARHEART, B. R., and WEISHAHN, M. W. *The Handicapped Child in the Regular Classroom.* St. Louis: The C. V. Mosby Co., 1976.

HARING, N. G., ed. *Behavior of Exceptional Children.* Columbus, Ohio: Charles E. Merrill Publishing Co., 1974.

HEISS, W. "Relating Educational Assessment to Instructional Planning. In *Instructional planning for exceptional children,* edited by E. L. Meyen, G. A. Vergason and R. J. Whelan. Denver, Colo.: Love Publishing Co., 1979.

HENRY, JEANNETTE. *Textbooks and the American Indian.* San Francisco: Indian Historian Press, 1970.

HOBBS, N. *The Futures of Children.* San Francisco: Jossey-Bass Publishers, 1975.

ITZKOFF, SEYMOUR W. *Cultural Pluralism and American Education.* Scranton, Penn.: International Textbook Co., 1969.

JONES, R. L., ed. *Mainstreaming and the Minority Child.* Reston, Va.: Council for Exceptional Children, 1976.

JORDAN, J. B., ed. *Teacher, Please Don't Close the Door.* Reston, Va.: Council for Exceptional Children, 1976.

KOBLER, ROBERT J.; CEGALA, DONALD J.; BARKER, LARRY L.; and MILES, DAVID T. *Objectives for Instruction and Evaluation.* Boston: Allyn & Bacon, 1974.

MACHT, J. *Teaching Our Children.* New York: John Wiley and Sons, 1975.

METCALF, LAWRENCE E., ed. *Values Education: Rationale, Strategies, and Procedures.* 41st Yearbook. Washington, D. C.: National Council for the Social Studies, 1971.

MERCER, J. R. "Cross-Cultural Evaluation of Exceptionality. In *Alternatives for Exceptional Children,* edited by E. L. Meyen, G. A. Vergason, and R. J. Whelan. Denver, Colo.: Love Publishing Co., 1975.

MEYEN, EDWARD L. *Exceptional Children and Youth: An Introduction.* Denver, Colo.: Love Publishing Co., 1978.

MEYEN, E. L.; VERGASON, G. A.; and WHELAN, R. J., eds. *Alternatives for Teaching Exceptional Children.* Denver, Colo.: Love Publishing Co., 1975.

MORAN, M. "Nine Steps to the Diagnostic Process." In *Instructional Planning for Exceptional Children,* edited by E. L. Meyen; G. A. Vergason; and R. J. Whelan. Denver, Colo.: Love Publishing Co., 1979.

RATHS, LOUIS E.; HARMIN, MERRILL; and SIMON, SIDNEY B. *Values and Teaching: Working with Values in the Classroom.* Columbus, Ohio: Charles E. Merrill Publishing Co., 1966.

SILBERBERG, N. E., and SILBERBERG, M. C. *Who Speaks for the Child?* Springfield, Ill.: Charles C. Thomas, 1974.

5

A Conceptual Base
for Developing
Experience Units

This chapter presents a point of view on how teachers can conceptually approach the design of experience units. The ideas discussed can be generalized to teachers in a variety of settings. However, the approach described is most appropriate for teachers who are assigned to the same group of children for large blocks of time and who are oriented toward experience-type units rather than units that may be rather narrow and restricted to a specific subject matter area.

Units take different forms; consequently, when the term "unit" is mentioned, teachers vary in their interpretation of its implications. Some teachers associate resource units with those used in regular social studies programs, while others are oriented towards activity-centered units. Still others may view units primarily as a vehicle for allowing students to apply previously learned skills. Each perspective on unit teaching is accurate. No single structure for developing units is applicable to all situations.

There are, however, some features of unit teaching that are appropriate for use with pupils of average ability that are not applicable for use with children of limited intellectual ability. For example, in teaching resource units, the teacher typically plans the experiences around a central theme, introduces certain concepts, and involves the pupils in experiences that encourage them to seek information independently. Frequently, once the resource unit is operational, the pupils assume much of the responsibility for searching out information, reporting, and decision making. The teacher remains in control but accomplishes this through guidance, observation, and questioning. The pupil's role in the resource unit requires reasonable competence in reading and work-study habits. Children with limited intellectual ability are capable of considerable involvement in decision making regarding unit direction, but they do not possess the academic skills to work independently to the same degree as the average regular class pupil. At the same time, the activity-centered unit is not totally appropriate for those students. Most activity-centered units are of short duration and geared to holidays or special events; they are seldom coordinated with other aspects of the curriculum. In general, they are designed to involve the children in projects. The main objective of such units is frequently the teaching of information and social skills with a minimum emphasis on academic skills. Although this type of unit has merit, particularly as a change of pace, it fails to take full advantage of the opportunity to integrate the teaching of academic skills with social and activity-oriented experiences. Considering the shortness of the instructional day for many special classes and their slow rate of learning, the instructional program must make maximum use of each learning opportunity.

In contrast to an information-type unit, teachers are encouraged to consider an experience-type unit that is oriented toward the teaching of academic skills. The informational and social aspects of units will not be played down; rather the unit's potential as a vehicle for teaching skills and concepts will be stressed. The emphasis on skill development does not take unit teaching out of the realm of practical instruction. What it does is to capitalize on the relevance of unit teaching in making the teaching of academic skills meaningful. This approach to developing experience units will be developed more fully in the remainder of this chapter.

The emphasis on a "practical" approach to teaching academic skills and social skills to the mildly mentally retarded has resulted in unit teaching becoming a popular technique among special class teachers. In spite of its popularity, though, attempts to design and experiment with guidelines to assist teachers in writing and teaching units have been minimal. Suggested formats appear in a variety of publications. Because these are so general, teachers tend to develop their own unique procedures, and the units are of little value to other teachers. This is reflected in many units that have been published, as well as in the large number of curriculum guides developed by local school districts. They tend to be more informational than skill-oriented. Relevant information on a particular theme serves as the vehicle for most unit teaching in special classes for the mildly mentally retarded. The dimensions of such units are determined more by what the teacher knows about the topic than by the theme's potential for teaching or applying academic skills. The attention given to the systematic teaching of specific academic skills within the framework of the informational aspects has been minimized.

Administrators, researchers, and informed observers have been quick to point out the inadequacies of unit teaching as typically applied by many teachers. Criticism centers on the lack of internal consistency and sequencing of skills within units and on the failure of most teachers to formulate a structure for teaching units. These views are realistic concerns and warrant the attention of teachers and teacher educators who espouse the unit method of teaching. Unit teaching can be made more systematic if unit development is approached from a more structured orientation.

A conceptual construct will be presented along with specific steps for writing experience units. This material is not intended to suggest that unit teaching is a new concept in methodology. Rather, the emphasis is on the systematic development of experience units. The suggested approach is based on the premise that the development of units should be more than the organization of information around topics.

Any discussion of unit teaching must acknowledge the significance of decisions made by teachers in the formulation of their instructional programs. Inherent in these decisions should be a clarification of the emphasis given to unit teaching in the instructional program. An equally important decision relates to the structuring of units that reflect both scope and sequence in the presentation of information and the teaching of basic skills. Prior to committing their energies to developing and teaching units, teachers must cope philosophically with the role they are going to give to unit teaching in their instructional program. This decision has implications for teaching style as well as for the overall organization of the instructional program.

The more emphasis given to unit teaching, the more important it is that each unit be planned in accordance with the content of previously taught units or units to be taught later in the program. It also becomes extremely important that the content covered in units be coordinated with other aspects of the instructional program.

Organizational Construct

The experience unit approach discussed in this book is based on the integration of skills and concepts from six core areas of learning into each unit taught. The core areas are communication, arithmetic, social competency, safety, health, and vocation. The emphasis is on integrating skills and concepts from all core areas into each unit, which requires considerable planning on the part of the teacher. The reason for the integrated approach is to capitalize on units' informational aspects to make the teaching of skills and concepts relevant to the learner. This does not necessarily deemphasize the informational aspects of units; rather, the information is made a more viable part of the unit. Frequently, in teaching units, teachers devote a major portion of the time spent on units to teaching information on the unit topic. For example, at the secondary level, a teacher might teach a unit on applying for a job. In doing so, he or she might center most of the activities on how to apply for a job. While this fulfills the need for information about applying for a job, a number of arithmetic and language skills can also be developed as part of the unit, if the teacher approaches the unit with a set toward using it in teaching specific skills.

Units are often developed with a concern only for teaching information relevant to the topic. The potential of units for teaching and reinforcing academic skills is too great to be ignored. If teachers merely select a topic and proceed to outline what they know about it into some teachable form, it is likely that the end product will be an informational-type unit with only minimal attention given to skill development. This is not to say that academic-type experiences will not be included. However, it is relatively safe to say that the academic emphasis will be secondary.

The approach suggested in this book gives attention to the informational aspects from two perspectives. First, it acknowledges the value of information about places, situations, and interpersonal relationships in unit teaching. Secondly, it places value on utilizing the informational content as a vehicle for teaching academic skills. Unit teaching allows the teacher to build on the student's repertoire of experience. The student is able to keep the content within a familiar realm. Consequently, it is logical for the teacher to capitalize on the student's interest in the unit subject matter to teach academic skills.

The six core areas collectively represent most curriculum areas. Figure 6 illustrates the relationship of the core areas to unit topics.

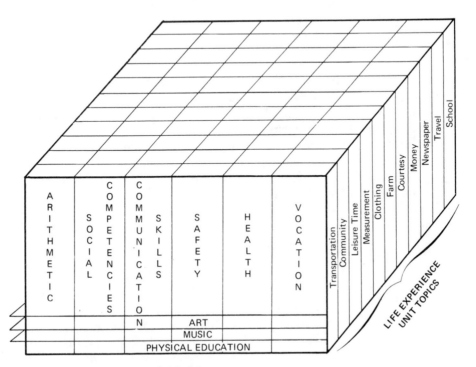

Figure 6.   Organizational Model

Experiences in each of the six core areas are incorporated into each unit taught, as illustrated in Figure 6. The unit topics listed on the right side of the model are for illustrative purposes only and may not be the particular topics a teacher would choose. Regardless of the topics selected, experiences in each core area can be developed that are relevant to the unit topic. Unless teachers consider the core areas when they are planning the unit, they will probably emphasize only the core area most logically related to the topic. For example, if they select the unit topic "measurement," the unit will probably be heavily oriented in arithmetic skills. At the same time, however, if they explore the topic's potential, they will find that there are many opportunities to build into the unit experiences in each of the other core areas. It becomes almost impossible to select a unit topic that does not allow for teaching experiences related to each core area.

Instructional areas such as art, music, and physical education are not considered core areas. In many programs, these areas are taught by the regular art, music, or physical education teacher; or exceptional children are grouped with children from regular classes for instruction. It may be that teachers will develop a unit around the topic of music, art, or physical education. In this situation, they could just apply the core concept as they would with any other unit topic. The limited reference to art, music, and physical education in this model does not imply relative importance. The areas are listed on a plane that permeates each core area as well as each unit topic. Teachers should incorporate experiences in art, music, and physical education into each unit when such activities are appropriate to the unit topic. In contrast to the core areas, these three areas represent experiences that are also technique-related. That is, art activities may be developed as a means of teaching a particular arithmetic skill. From this perspective, these areas are generic as applied to unit teaching.

Although learning experiences in the six core areas can be developed for each unit, the relative emphasis on the individual core areas will vary. For example, a unit on money lends itself more readily to the development of arithmetic skills than to skills in other core areas. But meaningful experiences in the other core areas can also be developed. The outcome is a unit with a major strength in one core area, with relevant content allowing for teaching of skills in other core areas. For purposes of clarification, each core area will be briefly discussed.

Communication

The communication core area is probably the least difficult to integrate into an experience unit. Reading, writing, speaking, and listening are its major elements. Although reading and writing experiences cannot be overstressed, speaking or the use of conversational speech should not be neglected. Oral communication will probably be used much more by most students than reading or writing. The ultimate aim of this core is the teaching of a functional vocabulary for speaking, listening, and recognition. A secondary but important aim is the provision of opportunities for the retarded to apply their communication skills. Too often the emphasis on individual instruction detracts from encouraging spontaneous speech. The students with learning problems need opportunities to participate in discussions within a group setting. Through such experiences, they also develop their listening skills.

Arithmetic Concepts

This core should be geared to the teaching of basic arithmetic skills including number facts and an understanding of their uses. Consideration should also be given to teaching concepts of measurement, time, money, comparisons, and so forth. When arithmetic is viewed in terms of its practical use in daily life, arithmetic experiences can be related to almost any unit topic.

Social

This core warrants considerable emphasis. Regardless of the student's achievement in learning other skills, the success of some children in becoming socially and occupationally acceptable depends, to a large extent, on their possession of good attitudes and social traits. Most units offer unlimited opportunities for the introduction of this core. Children need to be taught how to get along with others, the social graces of having and being a guest, desirable social habits expected by employers, plus many more of sufficient importance to be included in curriculum. It is the lack of acceptable social skills that often sets some students apart from their peer group. They become stereotyped because of social incompetencies. It is difficult to separate social performance from success on the job, family relations, or interpersonal interaction. Most unit topics involve subject matter of a social nature. However, particular attention must be given to developing socially acceptable attitudes and traits if the student's overall adjustment is to be fostered. This model calls for teachers to relate the teaching of social information and skills to every unit they teach.

Health

There is obviously a strong tie between the core areas of health, safety, and social competencies. This core area includes experiences involving cleanliness, good grooming, dental care, food, growth, preparation of meals, and overall self-concept. Relating the teaching of health to topics that have practical significance for the retarded makes the subject more meaningful than teaching health as a separate aspect of the program.

Safety

The need for emphasis on safety can be observed through the student's mobility, participation in school, use of leisure time, and occupational pursuits. The acquisition of adequate safety consciousness necessitates continued emphasis on this core. When selecting units applicable to a specific level, consideration must be given to those topics having potential for teaching safety habits consistent with students' present needs.

Vocational Skills

At the primary level, vocational skills will take the form of such abilities as following directions, being punctual, and working cooperatively. At the junior-senior high level, they will be more directly related to work experience. As the pupil enters actual vocational training, the emphasis shifts to job acquisition, work habits, and personal responsibility.

In reviewing the model illustrated in Figure 6, it is obvious that some unit topics lend themselves to teaching one core area more readily than others. This means that any one unit will vary in the emphasis given to the core areas. If teachers are committing considerable time to unit teaching, they may teach fifteen to twenty units during the course of the school year. Under these circumstances, the variability of emphasis given to the core areas in individual units becomes an important consideration. It is possible to select unit topics over the school year to balance the emphasis in core areas. At the same time, teachers who feel that their pupils have a greater need for more experience in social development can select unit topics accordingly. Figure 7 illustrates the pattern of unit topics selected by an intermediate level teacher who felt that the students needed additional work on social development. Although experiences were included from the other five core areas in each unit taught, the teacher selected more units that were strong in social skills. Considering that the teacher plans to teach six units that are basically strong in social competencies and will also emphasize social competencies in all other units, he or she is giving considerable attention to this core in the instructional program.

It should be pointed out that teachers will differ on how they interpret a unit topic. One teacher may view a unit on the community at the primary

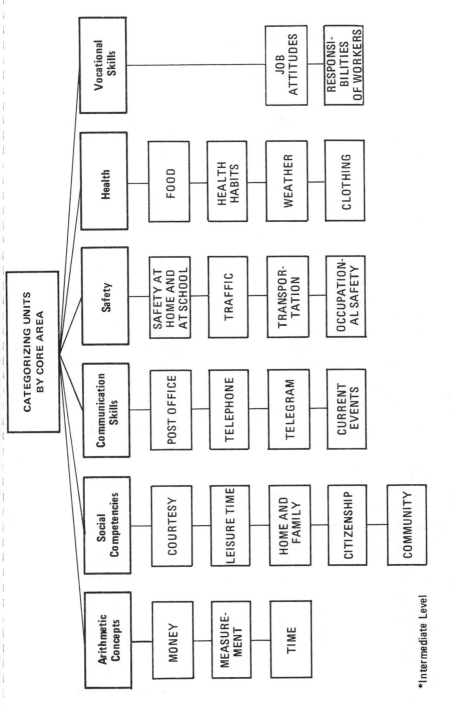

*Intermediate Level

Figure 7. Example of Categorizing Units by Core Area*

level as basically a social-oriented unit, while another may think in terms of an emphasis on safety. This presents no problem, since the individual teacher selects the unit topic and determines its relationship to the instructional program. Additional discussion on organizing units into a year's plan of work will appear in Chapter 9.

Utilizing the informational content of units as a means of integrating the teaching of academic skills with a practical frame of reference makes the teacher's knowledge of basic skills crucial. This is particularly true if considerable emphasis is given to unit teaching in the instructional program. The discussion on the core areas in general is offered from a descriptive perspective. If teachers are to implement this model, they must be familiar with the skills, concepts, and attitudes within each core area and strive to include these sequentially in the units they teach. This is not a new requirement, for teachers should be competent in basic skills regardless of the approach they take in their instructional program. But when teachers plan a unit, following the approach in this book, they must continue to place the emphasis on skill development, in contrast to using units primarily to teach information. In this model, the major concern is to maximize the benefits derived from unit teaching. Basically, it encourages making full use of the unit's potential rather than being content with the method as a dispenser of information.

The focus on skill development through units will not necessarily detract from the instruction offered in basic skills through other aspects of the program. Even teachers who devote a significant portion of the school day to units will probably structure separate periods for basic skills. This approach to unit teaching actually extends the opportunities for teaching skills. It also enhances opportunities for students to apply the skills they are learning.

Summary

The model presented in this chapter was designed primarily for teachers who devote a substantial portion of their instructional time to unit teaching and who are oriented to a comprehensive experiential-type unit instead of a subject matter-related unit. Adherence to the model illustrated in Figure 6 and discussed in this chapter requires systematic planning by teachers. If they merely acknowledge the importance of stressing skills and proceed to write units in a global manner, the model is not being applied. To develop a unit as proposed in this book involves an investment in planning. Some teachers will feel that they haven't the time to plan their units methodically. Certainly, the task will be time-consuming. But, as is true of most tasks, once you become proficient the amount of time required is greatly reduced. Chapter 6 will deal with a systematic approach to writing units, emphasizing preliminary planning and the actual writing of teaching strategies or lesson plans.

The intent of the following procedures is to encourage teachers to explore fully the potential of the unit topic as a vehicle for teaching skills as well as information. Each step has an evaluative function and an exploratory function. The evaluative function is aimed at assessing the merits of both the unit topic and the specific activities being considered. The exploratory function is concerned with assisting teachers to expand their perspectives of what skills, concepts, and information might be included in the unit. The preliminary steps are designed to prepare teachers for the task of writing specific teaching strategies in the form of lesson plans. Throughout the preliminary steps, the emphasis is on extending the teacher's thinking about what should go into the unit and how the unit should relate to curriculum and other aspects of the instructional program.

ADDITIONAL SELECTED REFERENCES TO THE UNIT APPROACH

CHAPPEL, B. M. "Are You Using Pupil-Made Charts?" *Grade Teacher,* April 1956.

HERRICK, VIRGIL E., and NERBOVIG, MARCELLA. *Using Experience Charts With Children.* Columbus: Charles E. Merrill Publishers, 1964.

LAMOREAUX, LILLIAN A., and LEE, DORRIS M. *Learning to Read Through Experience.* New York: Appleton-Century-Crofts, 1963.

LAZAR, MAY, et al. *Experience Charts: A Guide to Their Use in Grades 1-3,* Educational Research Bulletin No. 18. New York: Board of Education of the City of New York, May 1952.

LEE, DORRIS M., and ALLEN, R. V. *Learning to Read Through Experience.* New York: Appleton-Century-Crofts, 1963.

LIECHTI, A. O., and CHAPPEL, J. R. *Making and Using Charts.* Palo Alto: Fearon Publishers, 1957, 1960.

STAUFFER, RUSSELL G. *The Language-Experience Approach to the Teaching of Reading.* New York: Harper and Row, Publishers, 1970.

6

Developmental Steps for Writing Experience Units

This chapter is organized as a work exercise. Specific steps for writing units will be discussed and followed by an example. Work sheets are included after information or preliminary steps have been presented and again after the steps for preparing teaching strategies. The intent of the work exercises is to provide readers with an opportunity to test their understanding of the various steps. In the section on developing teaching strategies, the reader is referred to Chapter 7 on instructional objectives. A separate chapter has been devoted to this topic because of its importance to unit teaching and to the evaluation process. The reader will want to refer to this chapter before proceeding with the developmental tasks.

Many teachers approach the writing of units by briefly noting the major points to be covered. Others develop an outline of content and resources relevant to a particular topic. Although some teachers may teach a successful unit in spite of minimal planning, there is considerable room for error. It is also likely that the unit will be less comprehensive than if a major planning investment had been made. Coupled with these disadvantages, poorly planned units have little meaning for other teachers and contribute little to the development of a well-designed curriculum.

In view of the paucity of instructional materials designed for use with exceptional children by regular and special teachers, it is important that teacher-made materials be structured carefully so that they can be shared. This must be accomplished without adding to the teacher's burden. Units represent one of the most popular types of teacher-made material. If a conceptual framework for developing units can be agreed on, and if teachers are willing to write out their units, then the plans they teach from can also be exchanged with their colleagues. The cumulative effect of this approach will result in a resource of teaching units. If each unit is written in an organized format, units can be used as a reference by other teachers who will subsequently teach the same children. They also can serve as a means for accounting for subject matter covered over a period of time.

If experience units constitute a substantial portion of the instructional program, the teacher is obligated to plan them in detail. While the process of systematically developing units may be time-consuming, it becomes less difficult as the teacher acquires skill in the development process. The approach proposed here is not unique; it does, however, require the teacher to complete prescribed steps. The process is divided into two areas: preliminary steps and lesson plans. The preliminary steps are designed to facilitate the writing of lesson plans, which become the body of the unit and represent the teaching strategies from which the teacher teaches.

Preliminary Steps

Keep in mind that the purpose of the preliminary steps is to evaluate the unit's potential and, in the process, to generate a resource of ideas on content, materials, and techniques relative to the unit topic. To facilitate this effort, questions are used to introduce each step. It should also be noted that in the preliminary steps the teacher is not attempting to write in a final form. Rather, the steps are merely intended as an introductory planning process prior to the actual writing of lesson plans. The preliminary steps can be written in an informal style. The teacher does not teach from the preliminary steps, but rather goes through this process to prepare for the process of writing lesson plans. The body of the unit is comprised of lesson plans and will be discussed following this section. For purposes of clarification, examples are included from a unit developed for *elementary level students*. The unit on "Likenesses and Differences" is viewed by the teacher who developed the unit as being strong in the social competency core. The examples included illustrate format and do not suggest content.

Step I. RATIONALE. Select the unit you plan to teach. (What are the reasons for teaching this particular unit at the present time?)

   A. When selecting a unit, you should consider the contributions that the unit can make to implementing your curriculum.

   1. Review the units that you have previously taught.

   2. Concern yourself with the needs of the class with respect to strengths and weaknesses in different core areas.

   3. Unless past experience with the class indicates a definite need for concentrated work in one core area, refrain from teaching more than one unit with major emphasis on the same core.

   4. Your personal interest in a unit topic is a poor criterion for teaching it.

   B. State your rationale in the form of a broad descriptive statement.

1. It should reflect the basic reasons for teaching the unit.
2. The statement should also suggest the major results expected from that unit.

EXAMPLE

STEP I. RATIONALE

The junior high mentally retarded student in a regular class may be aware of likenesses and differences among people only in a general sense. Because of an inability to understand and evaluate observed similarities and differences, the student may develop damaging stereotypes that will further limit adjustment to the environment. The purpose for including this topic in the instructional program is to help mentally retarded students recognize the roles of likenesses and differences in their lives and in the lives of others.

Step II. SUB-UNITS. A sub-unit as used in this approach is a fairly specific topic which is closely related to the basic theme. (What are the possible related themes on which lessons can be grouped within the context of the unit topic?)

A. At this stage the actual generation of ideas about the content and direction of your unit begins to take place. These sub-units will later represent collections of possible lessons. It is also quite probable that many sub-unit topics will be deleted as planning progresses.

1. This is the first test of the unit topic's potential as a teaching unit. If it is difficult to develop a list of more than five sub-unit topics, then the basic theme is probably too narrow.

2. This is the *key* step in reducing later efforts. Two or three lessons can easily be developed on each sub-unit. If the teacher does a good job of identifying sub-units relevant to the basic theme, then the lessons suggested by the sub-units will be interrelated.

B. Determining sub-units.

1. The sub-units should reinforce the basic unit.

2. Sub-units can be utilized to strengthen core areas in which the basic unit shows evidence of weakness.

3. Listing possible sub-units will facilitate the organization of learning experiences and activities pertaining to the unit.

4. What appear to be logical sub-units should first be listed in random order.

5. After listing possible sub-units in random order, organize them into what you consider a logical sequence.

EXAMPLE

STEP II. SUB-UNITS

Unit Topic: Likenesses and Differences

A. Art	F. Occupations
B. Clothing	G. Physical Fitness and Recreation
C. Cleanliness	H. Grooming
D. Heredity	I. Social Skills
E. Interviewing	J. Family

Step III. GENERAL OBJECTIVES. The general objectives should suggest areas in which lessons will be developed, but they should not be as specific as the instructional objectives that will appear in the lesson plans. The purpose of this step is to ascertain the comprehensiveness of the unit through the development of general objectives related to the unit topic. (What are the major goals of the unit?)

A. Follow an outline form in stating objectives.

1. State the objectives in general terms. At this stage in your planning you are basically concerned with establishing broad expectations regarding what you anticipate your students to gain from the unit.

2. Following the objectives, you may find it helpful to list briefly information that helps convey the intent of the objectives.

B. Keep the ability level of the class members in mind when writing the objectives.

C. The objectives will later serve as a guide for lesson selection and development.

D. Organize the objectives into a sequence that you feel represents the pattern in which the unit will be taught.

EXAMPLE

STEP III. GENERAL OBJECTIVES

A. To provide students with a realistic understanding of likenesses and differences among people.

B. To develop students' ability to appraise the relative importance of differences observed in others.

C. To enhance students' feelings of self-worth by pointing out advantageous differences they might possess.

D. To help students understand their own abilities and develop a realistic perspective of themselves in society.

Step IV. CORE ACTIVITIES. It is important that the core areas be well represented in each unit. The intent of this step is to encourage teachers to identify actual activities that can be utilized to teach each of the core areas. In other words, they are asked to list specific activities they might use to teach arithmetic, social, communication, safety, health, and vocational skills. Later, when writing lesson plans, they can refer to the list of core area activities in selecting activities for individual lessons. (What activities can be used to teach the core area skills related to the unit topic?)

A. This is an important step in the development of a well-balanced unit. If it is effectively done, the task of writing actual lessons is easier.

B. This step is also a "test" to determine the unit's strength in the different core areas. It may be easy to generate ideas on activities related to one or two core areas but difficult or impossible to come up with many for the other areas.

C. Organizing activities.
   1. Sometimes it is helpful to list at random activities that are related to your basic unit and then categorize them according to basic core areas.
   2. Arrange activities in a convenient order. Review each core area and weed out duplications. Also, check to be sure they are properly categorized by core areas. Compare the activities with the pattern of sub-units developed in Step II. Again, the purpose is to generate ideas for activities and

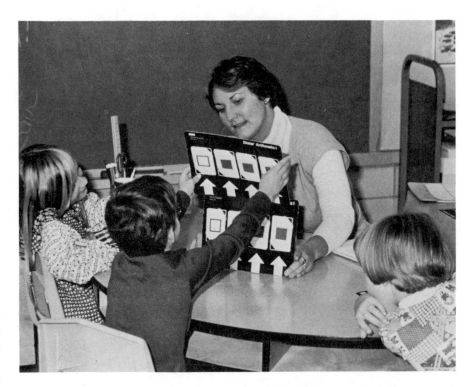

Unit teaching may also involve the use of activities from commercially prepared instructional materials.

techniques so that a resource is available to draw on when writing lesson plans.

3. The final point involves organizing activities by core areas. Be sure that they are listed as activities, not as concepts or ideas.

EXAMPLE

STEP IV.   CORE ACTIVITIES

A. Arithmetic Activities

1. Measure height, weight, and length.
2. Compute changes in height and weight from student's own health record.
3. Compare wages of different jobs requiring different skills and personal characteristics.

       4. Observe and compare money denominations.

       5. Compare prices when grocery shopping.

B. Social Competence Activities

       1. Practice asking questions of a resource person.

       2. List proper behavior to exhibit on field trip.

       3. Role-play by dramatizing behavior desired during a job interview.

       4. Form a committee to plan a presentation to be given in front of the class.

       5. Develop a checklist to evaluate own behavior and appearance.

C. Communicative Activities

       1. Retell stories that were used to teach.

       2. Use stories for practice of language skills (developing sentences, alphabetizing, spelling, punctuation).

       3. Participate in developing and writing experience charts.

       4. Use of tape-recorded lessons to develop listening.

       5. Use of tape recorder by students to evaluate speech.

       6. Present puppet shows reflecting understanding of likenesses and differences.

       7. Use telephone to request a visit by a resource person.

       8. Write letters of thanks to resource persons or hosts for field trips.

       9. Read newspapers to find jobs suited to specific types of people.

      10. Read biographies or magazine articles about famous people who had physical differences yet managed to overcome them or use them to their advantage. Select books with high interest and low reading level.

D. Health Activities

       1. Use a microscope to determine similar and/or different characteristics of small objects.

       2. Discover how heredity determines our similarities to our parents. Complete a bulletin board with snapshots of students' families and try to match students with their families on the basis of physical similarities.

3. Show how nutrition affects our appearance and causes apparent differences (acne).

4. Discover how good grooming minimizes unwanted differences.

5. Read newspaper and magazine articles that explain the effects of some diseases (German measles, mumps) and stress the importance of immunization to prevent unwanted differences in babies.

6. Read newspaper articles about transplants of human organs.

7. Feed two rats on different diets and record physical differences that develop in appearance, disposition, weight, and so forth.

E. Safety Activities
1. Develop a bulletin board based on safety during field trips.
2. Develop bus safety rules for students.
3. Discuss pedestrian safety practices to employ on field trip.
4. Read pamphlets and books relating to home accidents.

F. Vocational Activities (The formation of attitudes conducive to realistic employment goals underlies much of this unit)
1. Study want ads to determine how differences apply to job seeking.
2. Have a resource person from the Employment Security Commission discuss the opportunities for people with individual differences.
3. Arrange a field trip to a business that hires handicapped people to see how they perform their jobs. (Do not discuss the people until after the trip.)
4. Visit Goodwill Industries or a job training school to discover avenues of employment.

Step V. RESOURCES. (What resource materials and/or people would be appropriate in teaching the unit?)

A. Compile a list of resource materials and people for possible utilization in teaching the unit.

B. There is generally an unlimited supply of materials for any given unit topic. These materials are available in many forms and from various sources.

    1. Free and inexpensive materials from commercial companies, chambers of commerce, various civic departments, and the like are one source.

    2. Field trips should be utilized to supplement units.

    3. There is a wealth of material in the form of visual aids, films, records, magazines, newspapers, and disposable items that can also be used to advantage.

    4. The construction of model stores, banks, and post offices may be used when these facilitate the understanding of a concept.

C. Resource people may be brought into the classroom for demonstration, discussion, evaluation, or stimulation purposes.

    1. Resource people may be used to advantage prior to and immediately following a field trip.

    2. This occasion provides an opportunity to evaluate the students' oral discussion, as well as their social attitudes toward having a guest in the classroom.

    3. Use of resource people:

        a) They should understand the nature of their audience.

        b) The assignment should be clear to them. It may be helpful to provide them in advance with a list of questions that could be discussed with the students.

        c) The students should be prepared for the visit.

        d) The students' evaluation of the activity should be elicited through a follow-up session.

EXAMPLE

STEP V. RESOURCE MATERIALS

A. Books for Pupils

    Amram, Schienfeld. *Why You Are You.* New York: Abelard-Schuman, 1959 (*child and teacher resource*).

    Benedict, Ruth, and Gelfish, Gene. *In Henry's Backyard: the Races of Mankind.* Henry Schuman, Inc. Also film: *Brotherhood of Man* (animated and in color).

The selection of available resources is an important task in the process of developing units.

Cohen, Robert and Heymoniken. *The Color of Man.* New York: Random House, 1968.

B. Other Resources
1. Newspaper want ads
2. Driver's license forms
3. Magazine and catalog pictures
4. Cameras and color films
5. Resource persons
    a) police artist to demonstrate the method of developing a composite sketch
    b) employment office personnel
6. Trips by class members
    a) police station where you may have to go to see the composite sketches
    b) store or business with a handicapped worker

7. Art supplies: butcher paper, colors or paints
8. Film and filmstrip projector
9. Microscope
10. Overhead projector and transparencies
11. Assorted objects for comparison (leaves, snowflakes, and so forth.)

Step VI. VOCABULARY. (What crucial words can most easily be taught in relation to this unit topic?)

A. One of the principal contributions an experience unit should make to the retarded child's education is to help in developing a useful vocabulary. This vocabulary should include words that are relevant for speaking, writing, listening, and reading.

B. Compile a basic list of words that are particularly relevant to the unit topic. Concern yourself with reading, speaking, and listening.

C. You are in essence trying to identify the words that can best be taught in conjunction with the unit topic you have selected. The same words may also appear in other units.

D. In listing the vocabulary words considered crucial to the unit topic, the teacher should keep in mind that the students will undoubtedly come up with additional words that should be included in the vocabulary list.

EXAMPLE

STEP VI. VOCABULARY WORDS

abilities		shape
advertise	features	shortest
alike	heaviest	silhouette
color	lightest	size
differences	likenesses	tallest
employers	prove	traits
expression		transplant

Although the preliminary steps are presented as an informal process, they are considered integral to the systematic procedures for developing units stressed in this book. The suggested informality pertains to the manner in which information is recorded at each step. Teachers are encouraged to adopt an efficient writing style for the preliminary steps. The suggested format will become much more structured in the subsequent discussion on preparing lesson plans.

Figure 8 (p. 110) illustrates the modified task analysis approach to the preliminary steps.

Summary

If the preliminary steps have been well developed, the teacher will have a resource of ideas regarding the unit's content and scope from which to draw in writing lessons. The preliminary steps were designed to require the teacher to test the theme's potential while in the process of preparing the unit. At this point, each step should be reviewed in terms of its contribution to the lessons that need to be developed. The cumulative effect of completing the various steps should be kept in mind as each step is reviewed individually.

Having completed the preliminary steps, the next procedure is to review your notes for each step and to formulate an overall plan for the organization of the unit. This plan will then serve as a guide for developing individual lesson plans.

Steps II and III—sub-units and general objectives—are the major steps in terms of structuring your unit plan. The sub-units give you an indication of the potential scope of the unit, while the general objectives indicate the emphasis you plan to give to its different aspects. You will find that for each sub-unit, you will be likely to teach four or five lessons. Thus, by looking at your sub-units, you can estimate the approximate length of your unit. Most teachers find it is easiest to work from a sequential listing of sub-units in developing a plan to follow in writing lesson plans.

Step I. Rationale—should have helped to bring into focus the overall purposes of the unit and its relationship to your instructional program.

Step II. Sub-Units—will be helpful in determining the scope of the unit. If the list of sub-units contains six or fewer items, the unit theme may be too narrow.

Step III. Objectives—will serve as a basis for organizing individual lessons. The listing of objectives compiled in this step will provide direction for the development of instructional objectives to be included in the lesson plans.

Step IV. Core Activities—were designed to aid in generating ideas about activities and techniques for teaching core area skills.

Figure 8.   Preliminary Steps Schemata

Step V.   Resource Material—should have resulted in the selection of resources relevant to the unit theme. Some units may make considerable use of field trips and resource people while other units will rely more on resource materials. The more a teacher knows about the community the more meaningful this step will be.

Step VI. Vocabulary—was placed last so that the teacher would have the general scope of the unit well in mind before attempting to build a vocabulary list. Teachers will want to make frequent additions to this list as the unit is taught.

An extended exercise is included at this point to help you in understanding the preliminary steps.

Exercise 3.   *Preliminary Steps.* Select a unit topic and complete the preliminary steps. Don't be concerned with sentence structure, and so forth.

Unit Topic _____

Step I.   Rationale

See page 99.

Step II.   Sub-Units

See page 100.

Step III. General Objectives
See page 101.

Step IV.   Core Activities

See page 102.

Arithmetic   Communication

Social   Health

Safety   Vocational

Step V.   Resource Material
            See page 105.

Step VI. Vocabulary

See page 108.

Preparing Lesson Plans

When the preliminary steps have been completed, the task of writing the lessons should be greatly facilitated. Teachers now have a basic plan relative to the direction, scope, and general construct of the unit. They should also have a resource of ideas inherent in the preliminary steps from which to choose as they write the lessons. Teachers will want to make frequent reference to various preliminary steps as they enter the lesson-writing phase. The major purpose thus far has been to maximize their knowledge of the content and methodology most relevant to the unit topic selected.

The approach proposed for developing units places considerable emphasis on lesson design. Teachers are encouraged to write out the lessons carefully in advance. Each lesson does not need to be written exactly as the teacher anticipates teaching it, but the lessons should be sufficiently descriptive to be meaningful to other teachers. They should also be written so that a teacher can review a unit a year or more later and be able to determine the basic information, concepts, and skills emphasized. This is important for the development of other units as well as for communicating the instructional program to other staff members.

If the unit being planned is likely to require four to six weeks to teach, it may be advisable to write the first ten to fifteen lessons in detail and merely outline the remaining lessons. Once the unit is under way and it is possible to anticipate whether you have overlooked any major area of content in your preliminary planning, the remaining lessons can be developed. As they are developed, they should be completed in the same detail and format as the initial lessons. The composite of all lessons will represent the unit.

There is nothing sacred about a particular format for writing unit lesson plans. Certain risks prevail whenever a format is suggested. Some teachers prefer to use an outline form; others are less formal and merely record descriptive statements about the intent of the lessons and the activities they plan to use. If a teacher is part of a staff in which there is an interest in sharing units, then there will be considerable merit in adopting a uniform format. The suggested format, shown in Figure 9, differs from the typical outline format, since it is designed as a plan from which the teacher teaches. It allows the teacher to organize the lesson plan in a logical sequence that progresses from a statement of objectives to teaching activities and resources to be used. While teachers may prefer to develop their own format, it is vital to establish uniformity within a district. Through a uniform format, units become meaningful to other teachers. They are not dependent on the unit's author to explain the unit if they understand the format and if it has been carefully developed. An additional advantage of a uniform format is that as more teachers use a particular format, they become more proficient and are in a better position to refine its design.

Scope of Lesson Statement: _____

Instructional Objective	Activities	Resource Materials	Experience Chart

Figure 9.   Suggested Lesson Format

Scope of Lesson Statement

The purpose of stating the "Scope of Lesson" is to require the teacher to decide the lesson's general content prior to stating specific instructional objectives or selecting activities. Once the scope of the lesson has been decided, the alternatives relative to objectives, activities, and resources have been narrowed. In reviewing Steps II and III of the preliminary steps, pertaining to sub-units and general objectives, the teacher has an immediate resource of ideas from which to select meaningful lessons. When the general objectives from Step III have been organized into a logical sequence, the task becomes one of formulating a statement that reflects the intent of the lesson. It should be noted that you may need to develop a number of lessons that were not initially shown in the preliminary general objectives. Thus, in developing lessons, don't restrict yourself to the topics implied by the general objectives in Step III; situations will frequently occur that will cause your unit to move in a direction you had not anticipated.

In stating the scope of the lesson, you are actually writing a reminder to yourself as to its content. You will note in Figure 10 that the "scope of lesson" resembles an objective. It differs from an instructional objective in that it relates to the total lesson and does not focus on the individual student. Instead, it is placed in the context of teacher behavior.

Although the statements should be kept brief, they should cover the major content, concepts, and/or skills you anticipate teaching through the lesson. For many classes, a lesson will be brief and focus on only a single concept. With more advanced students, their attention span will be longer and their comprehension better. Thus, the scope of the lesson may comprise three or four major statements.

The advantage of identifying the scope of the lesson is that it helps you keep the lessons relevant to the unit theme. You can review the scope of lesson statements for ten or fifteen lessons and have an immediate check on whether or not you are keeping within the realm of your unit theme. This, of course, assumes that you teach what you imply in the scope of lesson statements.

In writing the scope of lesson statements, write them as notes to yourself. Say to yourself, "I am going to . . . teach, introduce, review, present, orient, establish, stimulate, and so forth," and then proceed to indicate the information, concept, or skill involved. Complete sentences are not necessary if you consistently begin with a verb. This type of phrasing implies you are referring to yourself, the teacher, as the subject. See Figure 8 for an example.

Column I. *Instructional Objectives*

Readers are advised to read first the following discussion on the use of instructional objectives in writing units. They should then refer to Chapter 7 for additional information and practice in writing instructional objectives.

In Step III of the preliminary steps, it was suggested that you identify the general or major objectives for the unit. While you were encouraged to focus on student behavior, the point was made that in the preliminary planning you were concerned primarily with the overall unit and not individual lessons; it was permissible to be general in stating the objectives. However, in stating instructional objectives for particular lessons, the circumstances change considerably. It now becomes necessary to be very specific.

The scope of lesson statements are a basis for setting the dimensions of the lessons. However, the major emphasis in instructional objectives is on student behavior rather than teacher behavior. They provide the basis for structuring activities and evaluating pupil performance, as well as for selecting resources. They also influence the content of the experience charts. Unless the objectives are well stated, the teacher will probably enter the teaching of a lesson with only a vague idea of what the students should gain as a result of the lesson. Well-designed objectives are necessary for every lesson. The cumulative effect of stating instructional objectives for each lesson throughout a unit has its greatest impact in the realm of evaluation. In essence, the instructional objectives serve as criteria for assessing pupil progress.

Instructional objectives have three main functions; namely, descriptive, conditional, and evaluative. The descriptive function pertains to the behavior you are attempting to influence; in other words, what you want the students to be able to do following instruction. The conditional refers to the condition under which you want the students to perform a task. Will they be asked to recall an example or will they be given a concrete situation in which to perform? The evaluative function relates to the kind of performance you will accept as successful. These three functions, specifically describing the process of developing instructional objectives, require the teacher to closely examine the pupils' strengths and weaknesses.

SCOPE OF LESSON: 1. To establish the concepts of likenesses and differences by comparing a variety of everyday objects.

COLUMN I INSTRUCTIONAL OBJECTIVES	COLUMN II ACTIVITIES	COLUMN III RESOURCE MATERIALS	COLUMN IV EXPERIENCE CHART
1. To be able to compare two or more objects provided by the teacher and: a. Identify at least two similarities. b. Identify at least two differences. c. Verbally state the trait compared (that is, color, shape, size, weight).	1. Initiate students' thinking by making a statement such as: "All these leaves came from the same tree, therefore, they are all exactly the same." Allow discussion and ask for proof of differing opinions. 2. As a group, quantify the likenesses and differences: a. Compare color. b. Trace two leaves on separate transparency sheets and place one over the other to compare shape (or trace around two leaves on blackboard with different colors of chalk). c. Use ruler to measure length and width. 3. Formulate statements about the two leaves in the form the	Objects for comparison: 1. Leaves from the same tree. 2. Snowflakes 3. Printed letters from the same newspaper. 4. Two hairs from one person's head. 5. Seeds from the same apple or two peach pits. 6. Flowers of the same kind. 7. Two stones or gems. 8. Two coins of same denomination. Overhead projector	Today we studied ways in which things are the same and different. We had to compare many things. The characteristics or traits we looked for were color, size, shape, length, width, and weight. Since our eyes did not always tell us likenesses and differences correctly, we had to be careful and prove them.

pupils will be expected to use in Activities 4. "The leaves are the same color (green). They have the same number of points (5). They are different in shape and size."	Transparencies Chalk Tape measure Ruler Microscope Scale or balance
4. Have the students form committees or groups to study the objects listed under resources. Each group is to use the necessary equipment to prove the likenesses and differences of the leaves and to formulate a summary sentence listing two likenesses and two differences.	
5. After the reports, conclude by writing an experience chart of general findings.	
6. Vocabulary: color, shape, size, compare, characteristics, traits, prove, likenesses, differences.	

Reprinted with permission from unit material prepared by the Special Education Curriculum Development Center, University of Iowa.

Figure 10. Sample Lesson

Teaching is aimed at changing the behavior of the student. Behavior means the student's performance. If you have been successful in teaching a particular concept, then there should be some change in what the student is now able to do. This change may be reflected in the performance of selected overt tasks, in verbal responses, or through some form of affective behavior. The objective may involve the ability to count five objects without error. You must, therefore, structure a situation in which the pupil is called upon to count five objects. Then you can determine whether or not the objective has been met.

Teachers have found the following suggestions helpful in writing instructional objectives for experience units:

1. Use the scope of lesson statements and the ability level of your students as a frame of reference. The objective should directly relate to the content suggested in the scope of lesson statement. Knowledge of student performance level is necessary if the objectives are to reflect reasonable expectations for your students.

2. Identify the specific behavior you wish to establish and determine the level of performance that you will accept as successful attainment of the objective. For example, if you are teaching the use of the telephone to a primary age group, the desired behavior may be to have the students successfully dial their home phone numbers.

3. The instructional objectives should suggest the conditions under which the desired behavior should occur. For example, if you write John's phone number on the chalkboard and then ask him to dial the number, this is a less difficult task than asking him to recall his phone number and dial it accurately. An additional task would be involved if you merely gave John someone's name and asked him to call that person. In this case the student must also be able to use a phone directory. The student who is capable of handling the latter situation is performing at a level higher than one who can only manage to complete the first example. Therefore, the teacher needs to make the instructional objective explicit so that the conditions under which the task is to be performed are also obvious.

4. In stating the instructional objectives, use phrases such as "to be able to . . . write, recall, identify, contrast, solve, create, and so forth."

Examples of instructional objectives:
   a. To be able to choose appropriate clothing, given an example of a social situation and weather conditions.
   b. To be able to identify cities, towns, highways, and rivers on a specific road map.

    c. To demonstrate competence in check writing and bankbook balancing by performing the assorted operations satisfactorily in a testing situation.

    d. To be able to demonstrate understanding of the concepts of *tallest, shortest, middle-sized* by choosing appropriate objects.

    e. To be able to name a body part from its description.

    f. To be able to read and verbalize the correct time, given various positions on a demonstration clock.

5. Keep in mind that if you are to ascertain whether the students have attained the objective, it will be necessary to evaluate their performance. See Chapter 10. Be alert for techniques you can employ in your evaluation. In many cases, the evaluation can take place through observation and other informal techniques. There will be times, however, when it will be necessary to develop test items, role-playing situations, or other formal means of evaluation. See Figure 10.

Column II.   Activities

The instructional objectives specify the content of the lesson and identify the student behavior you hope will change as a result of the student's participating in the lesson. Thus, the direction of the lesson has been determined, and the task is now one of designing activities that can be used to carry out its objectives. In Step IV of the preliminary steps, activities were identified that both pertain to the unit theme and are applicable in teaching information and/or skills relative to the six core areas. Consequently, you have a resource of relevant activities from which to select in developing the experiences for each lesson in the unit.

    Prior to deciding on activities for particular lessons, review Steps IV and V of the preliminary steps. These will remind you of the array of activities and resources relevant to the unit theme. The following conditions should be consulted when selecting activities.

1. The selected activities must allow for the teaching of specified instructional objectives. This does not mean that additional information or skills cannot be taught. Rather, it is to reinforce the point that the objectives determine what is to be accomplished through the lesson, while the activities represent how the material is to be taught.

2. The activities must be commensurate with the abilities of the pupils. Many activities are not successful because they are too difficult or because the tasks involved are foreign to them. The teacher must know the ability level and experiential background of their pupils, as well as the subject matter of the unit theme, prior to selecting activities for a given lesson.

3. As previously discussed, certain unit topics lend themselves to teaching information and skills in one core area, whereas they contribute fewer opportunities to present learning tasks related to other core areas. The teacher must take advantage of this situation. For example, if a unit on measurement is being planned, the teacher will want to select a number of arithmetic-type activities because the teaching of certain measurement concepts relates closely to arithmetic. The selection of activities must also be geared to the needs of the pupils in the different core areas.

4. Keep the activities meaningful. It is particularly important for students of limited ability to see some application of what you ask them to do. It is difficult for them to understand that they may later have a need for something you want to teach now. So, emphasis should be given to practical application.

5. Plan for evaluation. Since the activities column is used in this book for recording how the lesson is to be taught, reference should be made to evaluating what is taught. Some activities in a teaching sequence are evaluative in nature—for example, asking pupils to list specific information. In other cases, teachers may not record evaluation techniques for each lesson, but they should make a practice of noting appropriate means of assessing pupil performance.

6. Plan for use of experience charts. This book's approach to teaching units makes considerable use of them. A separate column is included for recording information to be developed on the experience chart. However, the content of the chart will relate directly to the activities you incorporate into the lesson.

Guidelines to Describing Activities in the Lesson Plan Format

1. Sufficient narrative information should be included so that another teacher reading the lesson plan will be able to relate the suggested activities to the instructional objectives.

2. List the activities in the order you anticipate using them in your teaching procedures. Of course, the sequence should remain flexible. However, ordering the activities in a logical sequence will add meaning for other persons who may read the lesson plans.

3. Resource materials or persons should be identified in Column III in close proximity to the activity in which they are to be used. Complete bibliographical data should be listed for books and other printed matter used.

4. If seatwork is to be used, it should be identified in the activities column but placed in the unit's appendix or attached to the page on which the activity is described. The important thing is to identify the exercise sufficiently so that there is no question about which particular seatwork exer-

cise is being referred to. Seatwork can and should involve things in addition to work sheets and other duplicated materials—for example, copying an experience chart story to include in a student notebook, comparing prices used in newspaper advertisements, and so forth.

5. Plan for teaching the vocabulary words identified in Step VI of the preliminary steps.

Column III: Resource Materials

Column III should be used to identify the resources you plan to use in your lesson. The selection of resources will depend on the activities that have been planned. In Step V of the preliminary steps, an inventory of resource materials, persons, and field trips was developed. These suggestions should be reviewed when choosing resources for each lesson. In the lesson plan, it is important that the resources appear alongside the activity in which they are to be used. They should also be well documented. Documentation includes all necessary information for ordering a film, book, or other instructional material. In the case of field trips, the place, address, and key contact person should be specified. Resource people should be listed by name and address, or if you are mainly interested in using a representative of a particular occupation, merely listing the occupation would be sufficient. (See Figure 10)

Column IV. Experience Charts

The use of experience charts has long been a popular tool for teachers of language arts, particularly in beginning reading. Although the technique has retained its popularity, its application in the classroom varies considerably from teacher to teacher. Some teachers use experience charts merely to record information, daily weather reports, student jobs for the week, and special events; others use them as the focal point in the development of teaching stories. However, the use of experience charts with the mildly mentally retarded can serve a more significant purpose. They can provide a means for teaching subject matter and are an effective tool for teaching academic skills. This expanded use of experience charts is central to the process of unit teaching presented in this book.

In regular classes, we find a wide array of printed material used to convey the subject matter of the curriculum. This is not the situation in special classes for exceptional children. For example, while there are some texts specifically written for the mentally retarded, the teacher is forced to modify regular material to their needs. Herein lies a major use of experience charts in teaching the mentally retarded—they can be effectively used in teaching subject matter. As discussed at the beginning of the book, experience charts should be used to teach content as well as to develop skills.

Experience charts typically take the form of a story or narrative state-ment developed by students and recorded on a large chart or chalkboard. They can also be used to present information or as an evaluation tool. While the use of 24-by-36-inch chart paper is recommended for unit teaching with elementary age children, the use of transparencies with an overhead projec-tor is encouraged with older pupils. Both media serve the same purpose. However, the use of chart paper with older pupils is sometimes viewed as a little juvenile. It need not be perceived this way if presented appropriately by the teacher. Transparencies, on the other hand, can also be developed through class participation. The novelty aspects of the overhead projector help to hold attention. Because teachers face the class while writing on the transparencies, they are able to observe pupil interaction and give more at-tention to involving students in developing the content being recorded.

Advantages of Experience Charts

1. They add continuity to your unit. If an experience chart is developed as part of each lesson, an accumulation of subject matter evolves through the series of experience charts. Charts from previous lessons can serve to stimulate student thinking about the unit's theme. At the completion of the unit, the experience chart represents the unit's text, with the order of experience charts representing the sequence in which the unit lessons were taught.

2. They provide a source for review. Experience charts can serve as the focal point for reviewing a particular lesson or the complete unit. As a permanent source of review, the charts can be used as much as a year later to review the basic content taught through the unit. Since the stu-dents contributed to building the charts and have read them numerous times during the teaching of the unit, the charts serve as a concrete and meaningful review technique. Without such a source, the review of units often falls into the realm of discussing scanty information on the unit topic, or reviewing student projects which, typically, are not inclusive of all the concepts or information originally covered in the unit.

3. They serve as an attention-holding device. Many teachers encounter dif-ficulty in teaching units because they persist in "talking" rather than teaching. Even in a group with good listening skills, such an approach is not very appealing. Although student participation in activities can be en-couraged and various audiovisual techniques employed, a need still exists for a center of attraction. The experience chart fulfills this need if used appropriately. It should be developed through the lesson and not merely as a culminating activity. As the children contribute to building the chart, it becomes the production of the lesson, and consequently, the focus of their attention.

Although the experience chart is placed last on the lesson plan format, teachers must begin to think about what they hope to record on the chart as they begin to specify the instructional objectives for a given lesson. When the scope of the lesson has been determined, the instructional objectives completed, and the activities described, you should have in mind the specific information you anticipate recording on the chart during the lesson. This is not to suggest that you should attempt to obtain from the students the exact wording included in your lesson plan. Rather, you should record in the experience chart column the major points you hope to gain from the students during the lesson. It then becomes the teacher's responsibility to stimulate discussion in order to obtain the desired response.

The content specified in the lesson plan, as well as the content resulting from the lesson, should reflect the scope of the lesson statements and the instructional objectives. The activities listed in the activities column may or may not be referred to on the experience chart. If a demonstration is provided or a field trip taken during the lesson, then the experience chart will probably contain information on the lesson activities. However, if the activities involve an exercise in making change or a task incidental to the theme of the unit, it may not be reflected in the experience chart. The following are some suggestions for planning experience charts in your lesson plans; they are applicable when using either chart paper or transparencies:

1. Plan at least one experience chart for each lesson.
2. In writing your experience chart as part of the lesson plan, write it as you would hope the children will develop it. Don't describe it. For example, don't say, "Identify safety rules." Instead, specify the rules in your plan. The process of writing the charts out in detail in your plan is excellent practice. It allows you an opportunity to evaluate the relevance of the content to the unit theme. It also affords you a chance to plan for the inclusion of specific vocabulary words on the experience chart.
3. Review the scope of the lesson statements and the instructional objectives prior to writing the experience chart in the lesson plan. Be sure the content of the chart relates to the scope and instructional objectives.
4. Review previous experience charts. Avoid redundant wording. Vary the beginning of each chart; for example, if a previous lesson begins, "Today we . . .," the following charts should be different.
5. Keep sentences short and avoid complicated punctuation. Sentence length should average about seven or eight words at the ten-to-twelve age level, and twelve words at the twelve-to-fourteen level. Pictures combined with words should be used on charts at the primary level.

6. Plan brief, explicit experience charts. If possible, keep them to one page, gearing the vocabulary to the reading level of the group. In planning the experience chart, keep in mind that their verbal responses during discussion will probably be beyond their reading ability.

If the teacher has planned the experience chart in advance, the task of stimulating appropriate discussion and obtaining the desired responses from the student will not be difficult. The strong emphasis on planning experience charts is due to their role in teaching unit subject matter. If experience charts were being used only in relation to teaching skills, less planning would be necessary, but this is not the case with the expanded use of experience charts.

Here are some suggested techniques in using experience charts developed on chart paper.

1. Use an easel large enough to hold 24-by-36-inch newsprint or other lined paper. The easel should be sturdy, and tall enough so that you can write on it comfortably, and the children can see it clearly from their desks. At the secondary level, many teachers find the use of the overhead projector as a more acceptable means of developing experience charts. (See Appendix for plans for constructing an easel.)

2. Experience chart paper can be purchased in a variety of sizes. However, 24-by-36-inch paper provides enough space for lengthy stories and is large enough to use for illustration purposes. Although experience chart tablets can be purchased, they are rather expensive. They are also restrictive in that they contain a standard number of pages. Lined newsprint can be purchased inexpensively by individual sheets. Teachers can bind in tablet form the number of sheets they anticipate using during the unit. Heavy tagboard can be used as a cover to protect the pages.

3. Use a black wax pencil. The type used to mark groceries works quite well. If you are using newsprint, marking pens will soak through. Crayons do not mark black enough to be easily read from a distance.

4. Use cursive or manuscript depending on the ability of your group. In a transitional group, manuscript printing may be used on the chart, but the advanced students may be required to copy in cursive.

5. When possible, record the chart in paragraph form. Occasionally, listing will be necessary; however, avoid frequent use of lists.

6. Prepare two or three leading questions in advance. The questions should be formulated to evoke responses relevant to the content you wish to develop on the experience chart.

7. While writing on the experience chart, you can hold the attention of the students by directing questions to specific students. For example, you might ask about the spelling of a particular word, ask about needed punctuation, or merely ask a student to relate the comment being recorded. Such questions help to keep the discussion going while you are involved in the writing process. It also helps to prevent management problems.

8. Have students read the experience chart aloud after it has been developed. Individual students may be called on to read the entire chart or a portion of it.

9. If it is necessary to copy a chart over after class, avoid changing the content. Sometimes the legibility can be improved if the chart is recopied under more favorable conditions. If grammar or misspellings are corrected, they should be brought to the attention of the class during succeeding lessons.

The teaching of life experience units places considerable responsibility on the teacher in the development and use of experience charts. Many teachers will initially encounter difficulty in developing experience charts that present the content of the unit sequentially. The only shortcut is through good planning and practice. Students soon become acclimated to the technique and assume a major share of the responsibility for constructing the chart during the lesson.

The use of experience charts is not restricted to the recording of unit content. Charts can be designed to meet a number of uses. Once completed, they can also serve a number of purposes, such as (1) to record subject matter of a unit, (2) to develop academic skills, (3) to present seatwork activities, and (4) to administer short tests. They can also be put to a number of instructional uses, such as (1) reviewing a particular lesson or a completed unit, (2) reading, (3) writing experiences, and (4) source of discussion.

Experience charts serve as a means of developing skills and teaching unit subject matter. They also add continuity to the unit and provide a permanent review source. It should be kept in mind that the experience chart plan that the teacher includes in the lesson plan format is merely a guide. The wording of the experience chart developed during the lesson must come from the pupils. (See Figure 10.).

Figure 9 illustrates the relationship of the various steps in preparing lesson plans. After a teacher gains experience in following the procedures, the task becomes less time-consuming. It is important to keep in mind that although a teacher will focus on a sample lesson when writing a lesson plan, the total unit must be kept in mind. A frequent check on the sub-units and general objectives will be helpful.

Numbering Lesson Plans

If a number of units are to be prepared and if it is likely that they will be used again, there are advantages to incorporating a numbering system into the lesson plan format. The system should be kept simple to avoid interfering with the lesson plan writing process. The value of a numbering system is primarily that specific lessons and/or activities can be located quickly. For example, as each unit is taught, an index of scope of lesson statements could be compiled. With a numbering system, it would be a comparatively easy task to locate a given lesson. Some teachers prefer to incorporate a numbering system into lesson preparation. Others find that, because of the many revisions made as a result of teaching a unit, it is less time-consuming to add the numbering system after the unit has been taught and revised. The basic use of a numbering system in a lesson plan is for later reference, not necessarily for teaching the unit.

Sample numbering system:

1. Identifies the scope of lesson statement. Number the statements consecutively in the sequence in which the lessons are taught.
1.1. The second digit identifies the objectives. There may be more than one objective. For example, if there are three objectives for the first lesson, the third objective would be 1.3.
1.1.1. The third digit identifies the activity. Since several activities may be included, be careful to identify each activity with the appropriate objective. See Figure 12 for an example.

The three main parts of the lesson plan requiring identification are the scope of lesson statements, objectives, and activities. The only reason for retrieving resources or experience charts at a later time would be to relate to activities. Consequently, the numbering system need not be extended beyond the activity level. The identification number of the activity can be used to identify the resources and experience chart on the lesson plans. See Figure 12 for an example.

1. Scope of lesson statement (first lesson)
1.1. Behavioral objectives for first lesson
1.1.1. Activity one for objective 1 in lesson 1

Requirements of a Good Unit

Teachers who have taught units know that many changes are made in the unit plans during the process of teaching. Consequently, after you have taught a unit, your end product will differ from the unit plan you began with.

Always Consider the Grouping of Lessons Around Sub-Units Prior to Preparing a Lesson.

Figure 11. Lesson Format Schemata

SCOPE OF LESSON: 5. Acquaint students with different types of handsaws and techniques for using them efficiently.

INSTRUCTIONAL OBJECTIVES	ACTIVITIES	RESOURCE MATERIALS	EXPERIENCE CHART
5.1. To be able to measure and mark a line for sawing accurately to 1/8".	5.1.1. Explain and demonstrate the uses of the various saws. Review measurement skills and give any remedial help needed in the use of a square in marking a straight line for cutting.	5.1.1. Handsaws (cross-cut, rip, coping, keyhole, hacksaw)	5.1.1. Almost every home maintenance project requires some use of basic tools. One of the most useful tools is the saw. There are many kinds of saws. The most common ones are the cross-cut saw, ripsaw, coping saw, hacksaw, and keyhole saw. Each of these is used for different jobs. Can you name these jobs? Before sawing, one must first measure and mark the lumber to be cut. To do neat work, the measurements must be accurate.
	5.1.2. Have students work in pairs. Measure a scrap piece of lumber and mark off a predetermined length to be removed (each pair of students measures and cuts their own board).	5.1.1. Measuring rules 5.1.1. Combination squares 5.1.2. Workbenches or sawhorses 5.1.2. Scrap lumber	
5.2. To be able to use handsaws properly as judged by the teacher.	5.2.1. Before students begin sawing, point out some useful clues and aids: a. Start by using the thumb knuckle to guide blade. Begin by drawing saw toward chest several times.		

134

b. Hold crosscut saw at 45° angle and the ripsaw at 60° angle.

c. To maintain square cuts, check blade often with square.

d. To prevent cutting the table or bench, allow plenty of clearance. Give individual help where needed. Once students have demonstrated mastery, encourage them to help others. Cooperation is a valuable asset.

5.2.2. Cover as many kinds of saws and techniques as time permits. However, the majority of students should master each saw before the class goes on to a different tool.

5.2.3. Point out the opportunities available for the skilled carpenter and encourage the students to think about possible employment in this field.

Vocabulary: measurement, ripsaw, crosscut saw, coping saw, keyhole saw, accurate, 45° angle, 60° angle.

Figure 12. Example of Numbering System

135

The major changes that occur as a result of teaching a unit tend to pertain to the information aspect rather than to basic skills. This happens as a result of teachers' responding to current events and observed student interests that relate to the unit theme. Teachers should not resist making changes, but they should be certain that the changes are warranted. It may be that some of the cues the teacher interprets as reason to alter the unit are really suggesting the need for an additional unit(s) rather than modification of the one being taught.

This chapter has addressed an obvious requirement of a good unit—systematic development to assure good organization, appropriate content, and a sequential structure. Additional requirements have been implied and deserve mentioning.

A good unit should:

. . . stand alone, that is, it should be sufficiently complete that it represents a complete teaching package in terms of teacher direction. To the degree possible, it should be designed so that a teacher other than the developer could implement the unit with the results approximating the intended outcome.

. . . be cumulative, in that the skills, concepts, and information are clearly integrated. The unit should also contribute to the cumulative nature of the overall curriculum of which it is part.

. . . provide instruction in academic skills and concepts, information, and social development. If only one content element is stressed, the potential of the unit is underutilized.

. . . allow for continuous evaluation of pupil progress. Inherent in the evaluation process should be an emphasis on feedback to participating students.

. . . represent an attainable goal for the students who will participate in the unit and for the teacher. In developing units, a frequent error is the construction of one that is too comprehensive for the time allotted to unit teaching. Teachers need to keep in mind the timeframe in which they will be teaching.

Summary

The procedures for developing experience units discussed in this chapter have been used extensively by experienced teachers and teachers in training. Although use of the suggested steps is time-consuming at first, teachers soon become skilled in their use. The preliminary steps fall into a routine that the teacher follows with minimal effort while preparing for the actual writing of lesson plans.

The intent of these guidelines for developing units is to help teachers maximize the benefits of unit teaching. Particular attention has been given to building into units the opportunities for teaching specific academic and social skills. Attention has also been given to helping teachers avoid the pitfall of using units only for informational purposes. Reflected throughout has been a concern for planning units in terms of their relationship to the total curriculum. Units taught in isolation often fall short of their potential as a contribution to instructional programs.

Exercise 4. Develop a lesson representing selected content from Exercise 1 by completing each aspect of the lesson plan format.

SCOPE OF LESSON STATEMENT: _____

(See page 120)_____

OBJECTIVE	ACTIVITIES	RESOURCE MATERIALS	EXPERIENCE CHART
(See page 121)	(See page 125)	(See page 127)	(See page 127)

Exercise 5. Using the lesson plan format suggested in this chapter, have students prepare a unit. On the first three lessons, have them apply the suggested numbering system.

Exercise 6. Design a format different from that presented in Chapter 6. Include the same features. Provide an explanation of the advantage your design has over the one in the text.

ADDITIONAL SELECTED REFERENCES RELATED TO THE PROCESS OF
DEVELOPMENT OF UNITS

BLAKE, KATHRYN A. *Teaching the Retarded.* Englewood Cliffs, N.J.: Prentice-Hall,
1974.
KOLSTOE, OLIVER. *Teaching Educable Mentally Retarded Children.* New York:
Holt, Rinehart and Winston, 1970.

7

Instructional Objectives

The writing of behaviorally stated objectives has become an accepted instructional practice that generalizes across most teaching strategies, and has been demonstrated to be a useful tool for developers of instructional materials. It is probably one of the most useful and generalizable instruction skills.

The skill of writing instructional objectives in behavioral terms is basic to the unit development approach suggested in this book. The developmental steps for writing units require the teacher to prepare instructional objectives for each lesson; the use of objectives is recommended in preparing a year's plan of unit work; the evaluation techniques suggested in Chapter 10 rely on instructional objectives as a frame of reference. Although the reader is referred to this chapter from various sections, specific information on instructional objectives has also been incorporated into other chapters when appropriate.

The intent of this chapter is to orient the reader to the use of instructional objectives in the process of individualizing instruction through unit teaching and to provide experience in writing objectives. Exercises are included at the end of the chapter. The terms *instructional* and *behavioral* will be used interchangeably in describing objectives.

The use of behaviorally stated objectives in instructional planning has received increased attention during the past fifteen years. During the early days of competency based teacher education, emphasis was placed on training teachers to apply task analysis and to write behaviorally stated instructional objectives. This orientation is clearly compatible with the approach to writing units described in Chapters 3 and 4 of this book. However, teachers vary in their proficiency in writing objectives and their attitudes toward the value of the process. It is the author's contention that these variations occur because too frequently teachers are taught to write objectives in isolation and without a direct reference to their use. Taught in the context of developing units, the teacher is able to immediately apply the skill. With the introduction of the individualized educational program (IEP), all teachers, regular and special, who teach handicapped students need to be able to write and interpret short-term objectives. For the most part, short-term objectives take the form of behaviorally stated instructional objectives. The IEP has resulted in making the writing of objectives a required teaching skill. (See Chapter 3 for a discussion on the use of instructional objectives in writing IEPs.)

The development of objectives has a long history in education. Terms such as *aims, goals,* and *outcomes* have frequently been used along with *objectives* to indicate a desired level of achievement or the direction for a particular curriculum area. For the most part, these terms have been used to reflect different levels of specificity. Although they have been used to establish expectancy levels for pupil performance, the more typical application has been to use them within the context of general statements that are somewhat philosophical in nature. Used in this context, they offer little direction to teachers responsible for structuring learning experiences specific to the needs of individual pupils. Nor do they provide much guidance for persons responsible for the selection, modification, and/or development of instructional materials. Consequently, teachers have tended not to perceive objectives or the process of writing them as contributing to their teaching effectiveness in the classroom.

The requirement of preparing IEPs for students receiving special education services was intended to facilitate the delivery of appropriate programs to all students. The component of the IPE related to writing short-term behavioral objectives can serve as an effective tool in the process of individualizing instruction and in the assessment of pupil performance. Objectives written as vague statements cannot accomplish this goal. Since individualization of instruction and pupil assessment are the major responsibilities of the classroom teacher, the teacher must be able to analyze and organize teaching strategies commensurate with pupil ability. At the same time, it is essential that the teacher assess pupil performance to determine the level of competency attained on prescribed tasks. Teachers willing to invest the effort required to become skillful in writing behaviorally stated instructional objectives will find that the skill as well as the objectives will contribute significantly to their efforts at individualizing instruction.

While the short-term objectives are a required element in an IEP, no definition of an objective is provided. Thus, it is necessary to rely on various definitions of objectives and schemes for specifying them that have appeared in the literature. Many such definitions have been written as a result of increased attention given to the use and development of objectives. A review of selected definitions and schemes should be of help to teachers as they develop their own style.

In describing the characteristics of a short-term behavioral or instructional objective as called for in an IEP, Turnbull, Strickland, and Brantley site four essential components. They indicate that each objective (1) must be stated in observable terms; (2) must specify exactly what is expected of the student; (3) must specify acceptable criterion for the student's mastery of the objective; and (4) must specify conditions under which the specific behavior should occur.[1]

Mager defines objectives as follows:

. . . an objective is an intent communicated by a statement describing a proposed change in a learner—a statement of what the learner is to be like when he has successfully completed a learning experience. It is a description of a pattern of behavior (performance) we want the learner to be able to demonstrate.[2]

According to Mager, you have been successful in stating an objective if your statement communicates to the reader your instructional intent. For example, if you have written an instructional objective for a unit lesson, the degree to which your objective communicates your intent can be tested by having another teacher teach the lesson. If students are taught to perform according to the expectations you had in mind when structuring your instructional objective, then it communicates your intent. The scheme that Mager suggests for the specification of instructional objectives includes the following features:

1. Identify a terminal behavior by name; you can specify the kind of behavior that will be accepted as evidence that the learner has achieved the objective.
2. Try to define the desired behavior further by describing the important conditions under which the behavior will be expected to occur.
3. Specify the criteria of acceptable performance by describing how well the performer must perform to be considered acceptable.[3]

General Programmed Teaching defines behavioral objectives in this way: Description of the form of the behavior that instruction is to produce, stated in terms of what the student is to be able to do, the conditions requiring the action, and where appropriate, a standard of accuracy or speed.[4]

1. Ann P. Turnbull, et al., *Developing and Implementing IEPs* (Columbus, Ohio: Charles Merrill, 1978), p. 55.
2. Robert F. Mager, *Preparing Instructional Objectives* (Belmont, Calif.: Fearon Publishers, 1962), p. 3. Reprinted with permission of the publisher.
3. Ibid., p. 12.
4. General Programmed Teaching, *Designing Effective Instruction* (Palo Alto, 1971). printed with permission of the publisher.

They distinguish affective objectives from behavioral objectives by defining affective objectives as "an objective dealing with emotions or feelings indicated by words such as interest, appreciation, enthusiasm, motivation, and attitudes." For purposes of clarification and consistency, their scheme also includes three classifications of objectives, namely:

1. Discrimination Objectives—involves the ability to describe or select two or more similar alternates.
2. Verbal Objectives—involves the ability to write or describe orally.
3. Motor Performance—involves the ability to demonstrate a motor skill.[5]

McAshan presents a comprehensive performance objective approach that differs somewhat from those previously mentioned. He proposes a construct of performance objectives, broken down into specific noninstructional objectives and behavioral objectives. He uses the term behavioral objectives

> . . . to identify a particular type of performance objective. It is interpreted as meaning a performance objective having an identifiable goal which identifies the learner, the program variable, and implies some type of learner behavioral change that can be evaluated as a direct outcome of the goal. This type of objective is a two component statement written in exact terms which includes the first component, the goal, and the second component, the outcome or evaluation of the goal. Its key characteristic is that it not only states the goal but also identifies the instrumentation, performance, activity, or behavior the learner will become involved with as a means of evaluating the success he has achieved as an outcome of the intended goal of the particular objective.[6]

Esbensen, in describing the individualized instruction program developed by the Duluth (Minnesota) public schools, places considerable emphasis on the role of performance objectives. He indicates that

> Objectives are precise descriptions of the behavior that instruction is to produce stated in terms of what the student is to be able to do, the conditions requiring the action, and where appropriate, the standards of accuracy or speed.[7]

The model proposed by Armstrong, Cornell, Kraner, and Roberson for writing objectives classifies them according to the three behavioral domains of cognitive, affective, and psychomotor.[8] These authors also introduce a

5. *Ibid.*
6. H. H. McAshan, *Writing Behavioral Objectives* (New York: Harper and Row, Publishers, 1970), p. 17. Reprinted with permission of the publisher.
7. Thorwald Esbensen, *Working With Individualized Instruction: the Duluth Experience* (Belmont, Calif.: Fearon Publishers, 1968), p. 3. Reprinted with permission of the publisher.
8. Robert J. Armstrong, et al., *The Development and Evaluation of Behavioral Objectives* (Worthington, Ohio: Charles A. Jones Publishing Company, 1970).

new procedure centered on descriptive variables, behavioral variables, and instructional variables. For example, a well-stated objective might focus on a student's demonstrating the use of a ruler in measuring the dimensions of a desk within an accuracy of one-fourth of an inch. In this example, the student is the instructional variable, and the behavior variable is in the cognitive domain. These authors' comprehensive approach to specifying behavioral objectives also extends the use of objectives to program evaluation techniques.

Criticisms of Using Behaviorally Stated Objectives

The practice of developing behaviorally stated objectives has been criticized for two major reasons. First, there is the feeling by some that strict adherence to precisely stated objectives makes learning somewhat of a mechanical process. Implied in this is the concern that the use of narrowly defined objectives prevents the development of cognitive abilities by the students. The second criticism centers on the time-consuming job of stating objectives in behavioral terms. Both criticisms are legitimate under certain circumstances and serve to remind teachers of their responsibility to their pupils and themselves. Task analysis does not have to be so detailed that the teaching strategy does not challenge the child's thought processes.

In reality the teacher who is effectively using instructional objectives as a basis in teaching is using them as a means of individualizing instruction. This approach includes the teaching of cognitive as well as social and motor skills. The formulation of an instructional objective by the teacher may well be aimed at requiring the child to use higher cognitive processes. A major advantage of specifying instructional objectives and the ordering of them by assumed difficulty through the process of task analysis that the teacher is able to determine what level of cognitive processes the pupil is capable of using and can then maintain instruction for the pupil at that level. Unless a teacher employs a system similar to specifying instructional objectives, the teaching of skills and concepts is likely to be less than sequential.

The second criticism pertaining to the time involved in writing instructional objectives must be viewed in terms of the results derived by the teacher. Most teachers become proficient at writing behavioral objectives after a minimum of training. The determining factor regarding the amount of time required to become skilled in writing behaviorally stated objectives is closely related to the complexness of the model followed. If the teacher is primarily concerned with writing objectives for his or her own teaching strategies, the model need not be complicated. The model suggested later in this chapter is very basic but sufficient for the type of objectives required in writing units and short-term objectives included in the IEP. However, it should be noted that many districts provide models to the teachers indicating the degree of specificity preferred. These same persons may also find that the process makes them more effective teachers. The question of time is most applicable in situations where teachers are required to write detailed objectives for everything they teach. Regardless of how efficient they are at the process, it can become very time-consuming if they proceed to write objectives for every skill or concept taught to each child. For purposes of unit teaching, such objectives should be specific; however, they need not cover everything taught through a lesson. Rather, they should focus on the major skills and concepts the lesson has been designed to teach, which in turn should reflect the goals and short term objectives for the individual students. Once teachers have become skilled at writing objectives in behavioral terms, they can determine for themselves how specific they must be in order to present the skill or concept sequentially and obtain evaluation feedback on the child's performance.

Some writers suggest that a teacher should strive for as much specificity as possible. The approach taken in this book supports the point of view that teachers vary in their skill at stating objectives; content varies in the degree of specificity required; and teachers vary in their knowledge of curriculum content, pupil behavior, and teaching techniques. Consequently, it is suggested that teachers strive for specificity through the preparation of behavioral objectives but that the number of objectives developed per lesson be decided upon after they have gained some experience in writing them for unit lessons. For example, if the teacher finds that representative objectives for selected skills rather than a detailed number of objectives are sufficient for planning and evaluating lessons, then little is gained by developing additional and more precise objectives for the same skill or concept. In general, the more difficult a task is for a specific student, the more precise and detailed the objective must be to enable the selection of appropriate learning activities and evaluative procedures.

If teachers find, after writing several unit lessons using behavioral objectives, that they are devoting a disproportionate amount of time to writing behavioral objectives, then they are well advised to develop a model of their own that can be used efficiently and enhances their efforts at individualizing instruction.

The schema or format that you choose to use should be the one that works best for you. *Above all, don't let the task of writing objectives become your end product. The goal is to change the behavior of kids.* Don't invest all of your effort in writing your objectives.

**Advantages of Using Behaviorally Stated
Objectives in Writing Units**

The advantages for teachers and students resulting from the use of behaviorally stated instructional objectives in unit teaching do not differ significantly from those derived in other instructional approaches. However, the advantages become particularly important in unit teaching because of the teachers'
responsibility for determining what is to be taught. In unit teaching, teachers
not only design their teaching activities but also make major decisions on the
curriculum content and when it is taught. Under these circumstances, the use
of behavioral objectives forces them into more precision in planning than
they might otherwise attain. The following advantages are oriented toward
unit teaching, but they are also applicable to other approaches.

1. The process of stating objectives in behavioral terms places teachers in
   a situation where they are called on to examine what they intend to teach
   as well as their motivation for teaching the content.
   a. Objectives designed for unit lessons can be matched with those spe-
      cified on the IEP to determine appropriateness of the unit objectives
      selected.
   b. Objectives representing different levels of competency in a general
      skill area can be developed. This allows the teacher an opportunity to
      check for sequence.
   c. Having developed a series of behavioral objectives for unit lessons and
      subsequently carried out the objectives, the teacher now has a ready-
      made checklist for assessing the content covered through the lessons.
2. Behaviorally stated objectives serve as criteria for teachers to determine
   whether they have actually taught what they intended to teach.
   a. Objectives include criteria for successful performance.
   b. Teachers need only to evaluate the child's performance against the
      specified criteria to ascertain if they have accomplished their intent.
3. The use of behaviorally stated objectives contributes to an evaluative set
   on the part of the teacher. If a teacher consistently evaluates a child's performance, he or she is in a better position to individualize instruction.
   a. Evaluation is a built-in feature of behaviorally stated objectives.
   b. As a result of routinely using behaviorally stated objectives, teachers
      increase their knowledge of each pupil's capabilities and consequently
      should less frequently ask pupils to perform tasks above or below their
      competency level.
   c. They facilitate feedback to students, who can be informed of the per-
      formance level expected of them. They now know when they are suc-
      cessful.

4. Having specified objectives for a specific task, teachers are free to select the activity for teaching the task they feel will work best with the class. The objective merely specifies what the child is expected to attain; it does not indicate the methodology. However, having narrowly defined the task, a teacher is in a good position to consider alternate approaches.
5. Instructional objectives are helpful in translating test findings into teaching strategies. Given the results of formal or informal tests, objectives can be used as a means of planning an instructional program.
6. The use of behavioral objectives increases the opportunity for decision making on the part of students. They can participate in establishing objectives for themselves.
7. A major advantage of building units based on behaviorally stated objectives is that the cumulative effect produces a descriptive definition of what is to be covered through units. They serve the same purpose in terms of providing a frame of reference for explaining your curriculum.
   a. Objectives in sequential form can be used in explaining the curriculum to teachers at other levels and to the administration.
   b. They can serve the same purpose in communicating the curriculum to parents.
8. Having developed the skill of writing behavioral objectives, teachers should be able to critically review commercial materials to determine which material is most applicable to their pupils and the content they intend to teach.

Prerequisites to Writing Objectives

If a teacher plans to use behaviorally stated objectives as a means of improving classroom instruction, the goal must be more than merely learning the task of writing a well-stated objective. The teacher must be concerned with how to analyze a task so that the objectives help to identify prerequisite skills and to delineate the specific skill that will be taught. The teacher's thinking also must be oriented toward pupil behavior. Too often, as teachers, we think in terms of what *we* are going to teach or what *we* want to accomplish with our pupils. This type of thinking is in reference to teacher behavior rather than pupil behavior. A thorough discussion of what is meant by pupil behavior and task analysis is not possible within the scope of this book, but some clarification relative to behavioral objectives is required.

Pupil Behavior

The two major characteristics of behaviorally stated instructional objectives involve (1) emphasizing pupil rather than teacher behavior and (2) specifying precisely what the child is expected to be able to do following instruction. Some teachers encounter as much difficulty with the emphasis on pupil behavior as they do with the precision. This is partially due to procedures often followed in writing lesson plans where teachers write a reminder to themselves to use certain materials, help specific children, and assign certain tasks. Teachers often have a set that focuses on their association with the learner rather than on the behavior of the learner which they are attempting to change.

An understanding of what is meant by the term *behavior* is important if a teacher is to state instructional objectives in behavioral terms. The learning of an arithmetic skill, the development of an attitude, the understanding of a concept, as well as a reduction in the occurrence of disruptive behaviors are examples of changes in behavior. A child is now able to do something he or she previously could not do. For example, a child who has been taught the meaning of the term *reverse* is now able to define it. As the child gains experience with the concept of *reverse*, he or she will be able to apply the term appropriately and respond to directions involving the concept. In essence, the child has learned a concept that is reflected in behavior.

Obviously some behaviors are more easily observed than others. Children who have learned to write their names can easily demonstrate this newly learned behavior. On the other hand, children who have improved in their respect for others are dependent on a situation to arise where they can demonstrate that they respect the rights of peers. Under the latter circumstances, teachers can create a situation that will allow them to observe the child interacting with classmates. In both behaviors, the child is called on to do something that is observable. The child writes his or her name in one case and in the other, shares, takes turns, and is cooperative in a group activity.

Much of what is taught in school involves the acquisition of knowledge that may not necessarily be routinely reflected in the child's overt behavior. For example, we cannot observe thinking, just as we cannot observe the process of learning. We can, however, engage children in activities that require them to perform selected tasks. As they perform, their behaviors expose what they do or do not understand. Thus, as teachers we must plan our teaching strategies so that our pupils are allowed to demonstrate what they have learned. Rather than approaching a lesson with the perspective that you are going to teach Janie the use of the ruler, it is more helpful to approach the situation from the perspective of her being able to use the ruler accurately in measurement tasks. The latter stresses the pupil's behavior as well as the skill.

Task Analysis

A major requirement of making efficient use of behaviorally stated objectives is the capability to break down a general skill or concept into specific tasks. In unit teaching particularly, we find that the skill or concept around which a lesson is planned includes a hierarchy of skills or understandings. For example, in teaching making change, the child must first understand the concept of money, be able to recognize coins, and know their value. In analyzing the global skill, we can determine the prerequisite skills the child must possess as readiness for the specific skill we want to teach. Having done this, we can ascertain the present level of competence and direct our attention to building on this competence in the process of teaching toward the higher level skill.

The development steps for writing units suggested in Chapter 6 represent a point of departure for task analysis within the construct of unit teaching. If you follow these procedures in writing your unit, you will already have made many content decisions prior to planning a selected lesson. As you approach the specification of objectives for a particular skill, it becomes essential that you examine the skill, concept, or information you plan to teach for indications of how it can be broken down into teachable steps. The specificity of these steps will be dependent on the capabilities of your pupils. As you gain experience in applying this procedure, it becomes less difficult to anticipate pupil needs.

Obviously, the more knowledgeable a teacher is of the sequential development of skills and curriculum content being implemented the easier the job of analyzing tasks will be. The approach to developing units presented in this book is designed to assist teachers in extending their knowledge of the curriculum content to be taught through units. However, a teacher may find a need to review the sequential development of academic skills.

In summary, the teacher's prerequisites for writing behavioral objectives include:

1. An orientation toward pupil behavior.
2. Good observation skills which result in being aware of *what* is happening *when* it is happening.
3. A knowledge of curriculum requirements and content.
4.* The ability to analyze tasks and content.
5. The ability to identify the specific behavior that is to be influenced.

A Suggested Model for Writing Instructional Objectives in Behavioral Terms

The primary value of developing objectives in behavioral terms is the precision it brings to the teaching process. If teachers have considered both the nature of the content to be taught and the characteristics of the learner in the process of stating objectives, they should be able to structure a task that will lead to attainment of the objective. Under these circumstances, the chances that the task will be excessively difficult or easy are greatly reduced.

As noted earlier in the chapter, schemes for writing objectives vary in complexness. Some make use of sub-objectives and some do not. Some consider the dimensions of cognitive, adaptive, and psychomotor. Others recommend that the process incorporate consideration of situational variables. For purposes of developing units, a less involved approach is adequate.

In writing units, many teachers have found that a simple format that requires them to be specific but does not involve having to cope with different kinds of objectives or varying levels of specificity is sufficient. This does not lessen the demand for a consistent format. But it does free the teachers to focus primarily on writing objectives for the pupil behavior they desire to influence rather than on the process of writing objectives. The situation would be different if a school system were attempting to develop a comprehensive curriculum based on behaviorally stated objectives. Under these circumstances, they would be well advised to develop a model that assesses representativeness of kinds of learning as well as sequential coverage of content.

The model recommended in this book for writing behaviorally stated objectives for use in developing units includes three major requirements. The objectives must:

1. *Describe* the behavior you want the student to be able to perform. Use specific terms such as to name, to list, to count, to write, to compare, to complete, and so on.
2. Indicate the *conditions* under which the student will be expected to perform.
3. Specify the level of performance you will accept as *successful attainment* of the objective.

If teachers are able to write objectives in behavioral terms that include the three major functions of a good objective—namely, descriptive, condition, and evaluative—then they should be able to write statements that clearly reflect what they intend to teach. For example, if a teacher at the primary level is planning to teach a lesson on color identification, he or she might write an objective as follows:

The student will be able to name red, blue, yellow, and green colors given four appropriately colored objects and verbally instructed to name the color of each one.

Descriptive—to identify colors
Descriptive—to name colors
Evaluative—name color of each object

Some teachers find it helpful to think in terms of questions when they consider the three basic requirements of an objective:

Descriptive: What do I want the student to do?
Condition: What will be given as a means of demonstrating his or her performance?
Evaluative: What will I accept as evidence of successful performance?

In the case of our objectives for identifying colors, the answers to the above questions would be:

1. I want the student to be able to name red, blue, yellow, and green.
2. I will give him or her four objects colored red, blue, yellow and green.
3. I will expect him or her to correctly tell me the color of each object.

In addition to meeting the descriptive, condition, and evaluative requirements, you must be concerned with clarity of wording and the appropriateness of the objective to your students. Figure 13 illustrates a simple model that can be used to evaluate the basic qualities of objectives as you write them. The model is used merely as a check on whether or not the objective meets the basic requirements. It also helps the teacher to determine which aspects of the objective need to be revised. As one becomes accustomed to writing objectives in behavioral terms, there is less need to use the model as an evaluative device.

	CLEARLY STATED	APPROPRIATE TO AGE LEVEL	RELEVANT TO STUDENT	APPROPRIATE TO UNIT
DESCRIPTIVE				
CONDITION				
EVALUATIVE				

Figure 13.   Model for Evaluating Objectives

Clearly stated. The major emphasis is on being certain the objective clearly conveys your intent. Some people suggest that each objective begin with statements such as "will be able to . . ." or "Given . . . student will be able to . . . ." Although for purposes of convenience a teacher may wish to adapt a uniform pattern, it is not essential. The concern should be for clarity, not necessarily uniformity or grammatical structure.

Appropriate to Age Level. The age or ability level of your class should be your frame of reference. You may find that you have developed a well-stated objective, but it is not appropriate for the age level of your group.

Relevant to Student. This feature is somewhat related to age level but it incorporates your knowledge of the interests of your students. In some cases, the objective is important in spite of little perceived interest on the part of students if it is important to their academic or social development. Thus, relevance must also include the importance you place on the objectives for the students. Thus, the objectives stated should correspond to identified IEP objectives.

Appropriate to Unit. This factor is an additional check to be sure you are teaching the skill or concept in relationship to the most appropriate unit. It may be more logically taught as part of another unit.

Summary

Behaviorally stated instructional objectives can be used to assist the teacher in the delivery of individualized instruction. Used in the IEP, as set forth in the requirements, and in unit teaching, the objective facilitates the identification of individual students' current level of performance and in stating the desired outcomes of instruction.

While there exists no universally accepted model for the writing of behavioral objectives, several examples are included in the chapter. One particular model is recommended for the writer of instructional units. The model includes the components of (1) a description of the behavior desired as a result of the instruction; (2) a specification of the conditions under which the student should perform the behavior; and (3) a specification of the level of performance considered for accomplishment of the objective.

An emphasis is placed in the chapter on the importance of keeping in mind the intent of the development of instructional objectives: changing behavior of children, not the writing of objectives as an end product in itself.

Work Exercises

The following exercises are designed to provide practice in writing behavioral objectives as previously described in this chapter. Most teachers will find that additional practice is necessary. Once you feel reasonably comfortable in writing objectives, you are encouraged to proceed with writing objectives as part of lesson plans for actual units you plan to teach. Your skill will improve as you write objectives for lessons, teach activities, and assess pupil performance.

Exercise 7. Global and Instructional Objectives. Differentiating between global and behaviorally stated instructional objectives. Check the appropriate column. Disregard the style in which the statement is written. Focus on the implications of the statement. Some statements, while not meeting all the requirements of a good objective, are definitely more instructional than global.

GLOBAL   INSTRUCTIONAL

_____   _____   1. Understands the basic principles of budgeting.

_____   _____   2. Is able to locate a phone number in a phone book, given a person's first and last names.

_____   _____   3. Given information on quantity and price, is able to determine the best buy.

_____   _____   4. To develop respect for the property rights of others.

_____   _____   5. Is knowledgeable of job opportunities.

_____   _____   6. Provided a local street map, the student is able to locate home, school, and a specified business.

_____   _____   7. Knows the reasoning behind traffic laws.

_____   _____   8. To develop the concept of credit.

_____   _____   9. Is able to tie shoe when provided with verbal instructions.

_____   _____   10. Can pour milk into a glass from a half gallon container.

Exercise 8. Basic Requirements. Analyze the following objectives by identifying the three basic requirements of a good objective. Underline the words reflecting the three functions, using *d* to indicate *descriptive*, *c* for *conditional*, and *e* for *evaluative*. In some cases, two requirements may be in the same phrase.

d   e

1. The student will be able to (write his or her name)(legibly in the appropriate space)(given a job application form.)

c

2. Given a newspaper, the student will be able to locate the section reporting weather conditions.

3. Will be able to tell time verbally within an accuracy of five minutes using a clock that includes only the numerals of 12, 3, and 9.

4. Given five objects of varying sizes, the student is able to place them in order from small to large.

5. Given a list of fruits and vegetables, the student will distinguish between them with 100 percent accuracy.

6. Given a basket of laundry, the student will correctly sort clothes into categories (shirt, socks, etc.).

7. Given a list of various foods, the students will select items representing a balanced meal (one food from each basic food group).

8. While engaged in free time activities, the student will initiate conversation with his peers at least two times per day.

9. When presented with pictures of objects, the students will point to object named.

10. Each day the students will punch their time card prior to going to their work stations after being reminded upon entering the office.

Exercise 9. Use of Evaluative Model. Using your own class or a hypothetical class you can define and rate the following objectives using the Evaluative Model. Revise objectives as necessary. Select your unit topic before rating the objectives.

a. Will be able to demonstrate making change, given a 23¢ purchase and a dollar bill for payment. Four quarters, three nickels, four dimes, and five pennies will be provided.

b. Given a yardstick with quarter-inch markings, will be able to measure a desk top.

c. Student will be able to find a number in a phone book, given a person's name in written form.

d. During family-style meals, the students will serve him/herself proper sized portions of food.

EVALUATIVE MODEL

DESCRIPTIVE				
CONDITION				
EVALUATIVE				
	CLEARLY STATED	APPROPRIATE TO AGE LEVEL	RELEVANT TO STUDENT	APPROPRIATE TO UNIT

Revise objective if necessary:

_____

_____

_____

Exercise 10.   Writing Behavioral Objectives.

1. Unit **Topic:** Measurement
2. Behavior: Correct use of the ruler
3. Write each aspect separately.

Descriptive _____

_____

_____

Condition _____

_____

_____

Evaluative _____

_____

_____

4. Write your final objective in one statement.
    Final Objective: _____

_____

_____

5. Rate your objective against the Evaluative Model in Figure 13.

Exercise 11.   Writing Behavioral Objectives. (Practice Sheet)

1. **Unit Topic:**   Traffic Safety
2. **Behavior:**   Reading crucial safety signs
3. **Write each aspect separately.**

Descriptive _____

_____

_____

Condition _____

_____

_____

Evaluative _____

_____

_____

4. **Write your final objective in one statement.**
   Final Objective: _____

_____

_____

5. Rate your objective against the Evaluative Model in Figure 13.

Exercise 12.   Writing Behavioral Objectives. (Practice Sheet)

1. Unit Topic:
2. Behavior:
3. Write each aspect separately.

Descriptive   _____

_____

_____

Condition   _____

_____

_____

Evaluative   _____

_____

_____

4. Write your final objective in one statement.
   Final Objective: _____

_____

_____

5. Rate your objective against the Evaluative Model in Figure 13.

Exercise 13.   Writing Behavioral Objectives.

1. Read the activities and write one or more instructional objective for your own class.
2. Rate your objective(s) against the Evaluative Model in Figure 11.

SCOPE OF THE LESSON: Involve the pupils in activities and situations which will result in an awareness of their home address as an identifying number.

INSTRUCTIONAL OBJECTIVES	ACTIVITIES	RESOURCE MATERIALS	EXPERIENCE CHART
	1. Introduce the lesson by involving the class in a general discussion of homes and where we live. a. City or country b. Farm, house, apartment, duplex c. One- or two-story house d. On a corner or in the middle of a block e. Color of house f. Big or small house g. Home near other children in the class h. Walk to school or take bus 2. Direct each child to bring to class his or her correct home address (house number, street, town, apartment number if applicable). Note: This should be checked against school records as there may be changes or errors that would need verification. 3. Initiate a project in which each child will make a drawing of his or her dwelling place. Encourage the children to add the family members, pets, etc., to the drawing.	Drawing paper Pencils	We live in a building called home. Our home is our own. It is in a special place called an address. We should know our address.

Sample lesson reprinted by permission from material developed by the Special Education Curriculum Development Center, University of Iowa.

Exercise 14. Writing Behavioral Objectives.

1. Read the activities and write one or more instructional objective for your own class.
2. Rate your objective(s) against the Evaluative Model in Figure 11.

SCOPE OF THE LESSON: Establish an awareness of weight differences and how they are used.

INSTRUCTIONAL OBJECTIVES	ACTIVITIES	RESOURCE MATERIALS	EXPERIENCE CHART
	1. Offer an assortment of objects for examination that have obvious weight differences such as a brick, an empty milk carton, a sheet of paper, etc. Encourage the children to handle them and describe them as being heavy and light.	Block of balsa Block of lignum vitae (or lead)	We know things can be long or short. They can also be big or small. Now we know about heavy and light.
	2. Use the projector to show pictures of paired objects and have the pupils determine the relative weight differences.	Empty milk carton Empty coffee can	Sometimes big things are heavier than little things. Sometimes little things are heavier.
	3. Demonstrate that small objects may be heavy and large ones light by using a large block of balsa and small block of lignum vitae (or lead) and a small sack of lead shot and a feather pillow.	Quantity of dry corn kernels (or wood beads) Overhead projector or opaque projector.	A scale helps us to know what is heavy and what is light.
	4. Put a weight equal to the average weight of pupils in the class on one end of a seesaw. This weight can be adjusted by using small sandbags often available from the P.E. Dept. Let children in turn sit on the other end of the seesaw to see if they are lighter, equal to, or less than the weight.		

Sample lesson reprinted by permission from material developed by the Special Education Curriculum Development Center, University of Iowa.

Exercise 15. Writing Behavioral Objectives.

1. Select a Unit Topic _____

2. Write a scope of lesson statement _____

_____

3. Write a lesson including behavioral objectives.

4. Check your objective against the Evaluative Model in Figure 11.

Instructional Objectives	Activities	Resource Materials	Experience Chart

REFERENCES

ARMSTRONG, ROBERT J. et al. *The Development and Evaluation of Behavioral Objectives.* Worthington, Ohio: Charles A. Jones Publishing Company, 1970.

Designing Effective Instruction. Palo Alto: General Programmed Teaching, A Division of Commerce Clearing House, 1971.

EBENSEN, THORWALD. *Working with Individualized Instruction: The Duluth Experience.* Belmont, Calif.: Fearon Publishers, 1968.

MAGER, ROBERT F. *Preparing Instructional Objectives.* Belmont, Calif.: Fearon Publishers, 1968.

McASHAN, H. H. *Writing Behavioral Objectives: A New Approach.* New York: Harper and Row, 1970.

TURNBULL, A. P.; STRICKLAND, B. B.; and BRANTLEY, J. C. *Developing and Implementing Individualized Education Programs.* Columbus, Ohio: Charles Merrill Publishing Co., 1978.

ADDITIONAL SELECTED REFERENCES

BLOCK, JAMES H., ed. *Mastery Learning Theory and Practice.* With selected papers by Peter W. Airasian, Benjamin S. Bloom, John B. Carroll. New York: Holt, Rinehart and Winston, 1971.

BLOOM, BENJAMIN E., ed. *Taxonomy of Educational Objectives, Handbook I.* New York: David McKay Company, 1969.

BOSTON, ROBERT E. *How to Write and Use Performance Objectives to Individualize Instruction,* Vol. 2. How to Write Performance Objectives. Englewood Cliffs, N.J.: Educational Technology Publications, 1972.

Instructional Objectives: Developing Teaching Strategies for the Mentally Retarded. Iowa City: Special Education Curriculum Development Center, University of Iowa, 1970.

KAPFER, MIRIAM B. *Behavioral Objectives in Curriculum Development.* Englewood Cliffs, N.J.: Educational Technology Publications, 1971.

LYNCH, WILLIAM W. "Instructional Objectives and the Mentally Retarded Child." *Bulletin of Indiana University School of Education* 43 (March 1967):2.

MAGER, ROBERT F. *Analyzing Performing Problems or "Your Really Oughta Wanna."* Belmont, Calif.: Fearon Publishers, 1970.

MEYEN, E. L. *Instructional Based Appraisal System.* Bellevue, Wash.: Edmark Associates, 1976.

NOAR, GERTRUDE. *Individualized Instruction for the Mentally Retarded: They, too, Can Be Winners.* Glen Ridge, N.J.: Exceptional Press, 1974.

PADZENSKY, HERBERT R., and GIBSON, JANE. *Goalguide: A Minicourse in Writing Goal and Behavioral Objectives for Special Education.* Participant Manual, Participant Workbook. Belmont, Calif.: Fearon Publishers, 1975.

PETER, L. J. *Individual Instruction.* New York: McGraw-Hill, 1972.

PLOWMAN, PAUL D. *Behavioral Objectives.* Chicago: Science Research Associates, 1971.

WHEELER, ALAN, and FOX, WAYNE. *A Teacher's Guide to Writing Instructional Objectives.* Lawrence, Kans.: H and H Enterprises, 1972.

8

Unit-Based
Curriculum Planning

Teachers who only teach an occasional unit should place their emphasis on designing the best learning experience possible within each unit and not be overly concerned with the relationship among units. For the most part they will likely select unit topics related to special events, seasons, or holidays. Their use of units will be more to add variety in their teaching than as an instructional methodology. The situation changes, however, as the emphasis on unit teaching increases. If unit teaching comprises more than 10 percent of the teacher's instructional program, then detailed attention should be given to the cumulative contribution of units to the curriculum and the relationship among units. It is not only important to have a well-defined plan of what is to be taught through units, but it is also essential to be able to illustrate the relationship of instruction offered through units to the skills and concepts taught through other instructional modes.

Except for sparsely populated areas, most attendance centers include three or more classes per grade level. Even in special education programs, most attendance centers have several teachers with some assigned responsibility for teaching exceptional children. These circumstances are highly conducive to involving several teachers in the process of preparing unit plans. The trend in some districts to individualize instruction without regard to grade placement is also compatible with a team approach to structuring curriculum plans in terms of instructional units. This chapter will provide practical suggestions on how a district might engage groups of teachers in the process of systematically planning instructional programs that make extensive use of units. The following assumptions are made relative to the suggested procedures:

1. That units represent at least 10 percent of the instructional program.
2. That two or more teachers have responsibility for teaching similar con-

---

This chapter is intended for teachers who allocate a substantial amount of instructional time to unit teaching and who are in a position where they can work cooperatively with other teachers in developing curriculum specifications for unit plans.

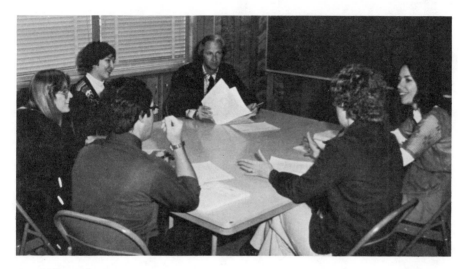

Curriculum planning is a group process.

tent through units to groups of students with comparable learning characteristics.

3. That the district will provide participating teachers with resources for the planning process in the form of consultation, release time, and/or clerical support.

4. That the participating teachers recognize the importance of being able to account for pupil outcome resulting from unit teaching as well as from other dimensions of the curriculum.

Implications of Unit-Based Curriculum Planning

Several implications emerge as the emphasis on unit teaching increases. This is particularly true as the instructional time allocated to unit teaching approaches one-third to one-half of the curriculum. The obvious implication is that students will receive more of their education through unit teaching. Unless the total unit program is systematically planned, there is considerable risk that units taught to individual students will not only lack sequence but may very well be characterized by omissions and redundancies. It is important that some form of curriculum planning process be employed that clearly details the curriculum outcome to be achieved and identifies what will be incorporated into units and what will be covered through other instructional modes.

The primary implications of an expanded emphasis on unit teaching are couched in the context of how effective a teacher is in the process of teaching units. There are, however, some implications that pertain to the teacher's role in curriculum development and to program management.

Development Skills   Unit teaching obviously involves a product: the instructional unit. If the experiences inherent in a unit are to be maximally appropriate to the students involved, it is advantageous if the teacher assumes major responsibility for constructing the unit. The net result is that the greater the emphasis given to units, the greater the need for development skills on the part of teachers. In programs where units will be extensively used, it is reasonable to take for granted that they can be shared among teachers. To implement an exchange of units assumes that the units follow a similar format and are well designed. If extensive use is to be made of units by several teachers, the district should employ a consultant or supervisor who is sufficiently skilled in unit construction to assist teachers in building units and coordinating the development process.

Preparation Time   As has been previously mentioned, it requires time to prepare good units. Although systematic procedures and experience in constructing units will reduce the required time, the more units one has to prepare, the more time one has to allow for development. However, the time demands are not in direct proportion to the number of units produced. What typically occurs in a program emphasizing unit teaching is that series of units are developed that can be adapted to various settings. The consequence is a better return on the teacher's time spent in developing units. Teachers can also cooperate in developing units. Cooperatively developed units often include more varied activities as a result of creativity evolving from teacher interaction in the development of an instructional product. Once a district or program has identified the sequence of skills, concepts, and information to be included and prepared a number of units, the time demands change. The emphasis shifts from preparing complete units to the planning of daily activities and the modification of preplanned activities.

Curriculum Revision   Because of the comprehensiveness of instructional units developed in accordance with the guidelines provided in this book, the unit format results in a more complete picture of what is included in the curriculum than do most other curriculum formats. It is possible to focus revision efforts on objectives, activities, resources, and general content. It is also possible to alter the internal activity sequence within a unit in order to accomplish revision. The latter, of course, would represent a simplified approach to curriculum revision.

Content Control   By design, instructional units specify content as well as teaching techniques. In many ways they are analogous to a text in that the experiences in which the students are to be involved are specified in advance. Thus, once the unit is prepared, there is a certain amount of control placed on the curriculum content. This is not to suggest that teachers will not alter activities during the process of teaching. But it is apparent that the intent of systematically planning a unit is to control content, that is, to be certain that relevant skills, concepts, and information are taught.

Problem Detection Teachers experience a variety of problems in implementing instructional programs. Some of these relate to the behavioral characteristics of students, to student response to teaching style, and to the general features of the classroom climate. The typical approach to resolving an instructionally related problem is to focus on the teacher-pupil interaction. Granted, most such problems are process-related, but the content of what is being taught can also be the source of the problem. Because units describe content as well as technique, the unit represents an additional reference in seeking to resolve instructional problems. It is feasible to examine not only an activity but a complete unit or series of units to identify the factors contributing to instructional problems.

Although not necessarily implications of the approach, there are at least two other concerns that teachers need to be sensitive to when allocating a substantial portion of their instructional time to unit teaching. These concerns pertain to the relationship of *information* to *skills* in unit teaching. One of the major advantages of unit teaching is placing skill instruction in a relevant context. This is particularly significant in working with children who require a highly experiential approach. In many units there is a bona fide body of information that should be taught. In most cases this information provides the context or frame of reference in which skills and concepts are developed. However, there is frequently a tendency to overstress a unit's informational dimension. This occurs because it is much easier to identify information and to design activities for teaching units than to specify skills or concepts. This is more likely to become a problem when teachers develop a year's plan of work by themselves, as described in Chapter 9.

"Givens" in Unit-Based Curriculum Planning

Although few instructional programs are totally unit-based, some teachers organize a substantial portion of their instructional time around unit teaching. Such teachers and those considering broadening their use of units should recognize that there is a set of features associated with unit teaching that must be considered as the instructional emphasis on unit teaching is expanded. The author has chosen to call these "givens." They have been derived from the author's observations of attempts to develop unit-based curriculum by classroom teachers. They should not be interpreted as criticisms of the unit method, but rather as concerns directed toward totally unit-based curriculum for any target student population. They should serve as cues for teachers in developing units.

Although few instructional programs are totally unit-based, some Special Education programs, particularly for mildly mentally retarded students, do implement what could be considered a unit-based curriculum. School districts considering establishing a unit-based curriculum should recognize that there is a set of features associated with unit-based curriculum that must be dealt with. The author has chosen to call these "givens." They have been derived from the author's observations of attempts to develop unit-based curriculum for special classes for the mildly mentally retarded. They should not be interpreted as criticism of the unit method but rather as concerns directed toward totally unit-based curriculum for any target student population. They should serve as cues for teachers in developing units generally.

1. *It is not feasible to develop a totally unit-based curriculum.* A unit-based curriculum is developmental in its orientation, and content must be identified, sequenced, and transformed into instructional units. As long as the teacher is effective in developing and teaching units, the approach works. However, students do have remediation needs. It is in the realm of correction or remediation that a unit-based curriculum falls short. It frequently becomes necessary to use prepared instructional programs in order to correct students' deficits. It would also be unreasonable to assume that sufficient experience could be built into units to accommodate teaching all reading and math skills. This is not to suggest that math and reading are not major goals of unit teaching. However, unless a district is in a position to invest heavily in curriculum development, it would be unwise to assume that teachers will be able to provide quality instruction in reading and math solely through unit teaching.

2. *Unless units can be meaningfully taught in sub-units, they are not sufficiently flexible as a curriculum design.*
   Too often in programs where the curriculum is based primarily on units, those instructional units are the smallest elements in the curriculum. In other words, the only option for altering the curriculum by restructuring what has been developed is to reorder the sequence in which units are taught. The development steps described in Chapter 6 illustrate the concept of using sub-units. If this approach to constructing units is followed, units can be reconstructed using lesson plans, that is, objectives, activities, and resources, as the smallest curriculum element. Regardless of the development procedure followed, the format should allow for breaking units down into elements. The smallest element, however, must remain as a complete teaching activity. For example, it must indicate behavior(s) to be taught, the teaching strategy, and required resources. Typically, a unit comparable to a sub-unit, that is, a collection of planned lessons around a common theme, works best. New units can be developed as a result of

rearranging sub-units. Also, sub-units can be selected from several units to supplement one another.

3. *Evaluating student progress through unit teaching requires constant monitoring.*

    In contrast to teaching with a basic series where the emphasis is on specific skills (for example, math or reading), units of instruction are typically concerned with a broader range of behaviors. Skills are stressed in unit teaching, but considerable emphasis is also given to social development and information acquisition. Consequently, the teacher must sample a wider range of behaviors in determining the unit's successfulness. Techniques such as maintaining *Skills Inventories* (as illustrated in Chapter 10) are effective in assessing student achievement in individual units. A more difficult aspect of evaluating student progress as a result of unit participation relates to cumulative progress—that is, gains as a result of several units and outcomes resulting from incidental experience created by unit activities. When units constitute a major portion of the curriculum, considerable attention should be given to maintaining criterion-referenced skill inventories, anecdotal records, and observation systems in addition to the use of standardized achievement tests.

4. *Unit formats tend to become sacred the longer they are used.*

    A major thesis of this book is that teachers should adhere to a systematic format in preparing units. A particular format has been suggested. Whenever units are to be used in a situation where several teachers are involved, the importance of a systematic and uniform format increases. Since the goal is to encourage all teachers to use a uniform format, all teachers should contribute to format decisions. However, in spite of the advantages of adhering to a common format within a district or program when units are to be shared, there is a tendency for an adopted format to become institutionalized and never changed. Situations do occur that call for format changes. Thus, the format should be reviewed periodically to determine its appropriateness for participating teachers. This does not mean that minor changes are encouraged to satisfy the unique desires of individual teachers. However, it is important to avoid negative teacher reaction to the format or procedures employed in developing units.

5. *Not every teacher can or wants to "teach units."*

    Unit teaching places numerous demands on teachers. First, they must develop the units. Second, emphasis on group teaching techniques requires a wider array of teaching skills than do highly individualized remediation techniques. Basically, unit teaching involves the application of most good teaching techniques. Programs making extensive use of unit teaching should provide inservice training to participating teachers and appropriate teacher techniques. The hesitancy of some teachers to use units is generally related to a lack of experience with units and insufficient information on how to develop and/or teach them.

Developing Specifications for a Unit-Based Curriculum Planning

The same logic that supports the application of systematic procedures for developing units applies to the organization of units into a curriculum. Attention must be given to the identification and sequencing of skills and concepts to be included in units as well as to the determination of what units are to be taught and when. In essence, when the decision is made to allocate a substantial portion of instructional time to unit teaching, two types of planning tasks emerge. The first pertains to planning well-designed units for direct classroom application. The second planning task relates to developing an overall blueprint of unit instruction to which each individual unit contributes. Although individual teachers typically assume responsibility for developing units, the process of structuring an overall unit plan requires broader input and some centralized coordination. In circumstances where the teacher is not part of a larger group engaged in unit planning, a more restricted approach such as that suggested in Chapter 9 is appropriate. The restrictions for individual teachers developing unit plans are primarily a manpower problem. The suggestions included in the following discussion are appropriate regardless of the number of teachers involved. However, it is more feasible to carry them out with a broader talent and manpower base.

If your goal is to develop a long-term plan for unit teaching, that is, a year or more, you must develop a set of specifications that will serve as a frame of reference for the development of actual teaching units. It does not make much difference whether your goal involves unit development to teach language arts to elementary students in regular classes, mentally retarded students in special classes, or students assigned to resource rooms. You still have the same obligation for assuring the student a quality program. Unless a master plan is designed, there is considerable risk that there will be little sequence in the units taught and no assurance that the appropriate skills and concepts have been included. Detailed planning does not guarantee the student a quality education, but it does create a set of conditions conducive to providing quality instruction.

In any instructional program where teachers assume a major responsibility for developing instructional packages, planning increases in importance. Unless specific guidelines are provided, each unit, and ultimately the student's curriculum, becomes unique to the teacher. The net result is that the number of curricula implemented is equal to the number of teachers employed in a program.

Specification Principles

There are no set rules for developing specifications for a unit-based curriculum, but there are principles that warrant consideration. These principles can be used as evaluative criteria in determining the effectiveness of specifications for a unit-based curriculum. It should be kept in mind that the specifications are comparable to a set of blueprints that an architect might develop for a contractor. Just as the contractor builds the structure according to the specifications of the blueprint, so must the teacher construct units according to a set of specifications.

The Unit Plan Specifications Should . . .

. . . Be inclusive of the skills, concepts, and information considered essential to the target student population.

- Consider the total curriculum, not just the content to be covered by units.
- Apply various approaches to task, concept, and content analysis.

. . . Be in balance with the resources available for constructing units. The scope of the curriculum to be covered through unit teaching should represent an attainable development task.

- Every skill or concept included in the specifications must be incorporated in an instructional unit.
- The major resource required in operationalizing a curriculum unit is human talent. The major restriction placed on utilizing human talent is time.
- The specifications for a unit-based curriculum need not be transformed into units the first year. A time schedule should be established.

. . . Be in an organizational format that facilitates unit development by individual teachers and/or groups of teachers.

- Avoid using complex organizational formats and coding systems.
- The structure should allow for easy entry. The teacher should be able to locate specific content without conducting a time-consuming search of specifications.
- The format should provide for a cross-index between the specifications and the units developed for implementing them.

. . . Be in sufficient detail to minimize misinterpretation.

- The purpose of the specifications is to provide direction to teachers in preparing units. Unless the specifications are detailed, units may be developed that do not carry them out.
- The easiest approach to determining whether or not the specifications are sufficient detailed is to check their relattionship to the units developed by teachers in the program.

. . . Be applied as a curriculum-monitoring system in addition to being guidelines for unit development.

- The specifications represent what you feel should be included in the program. Thus, they serve as criteria for determining whether or not the curriculum has been implemented.
- Because the specifications are detailed and organized sequentially, they provide an excellent basis for revision.
- Specifications should be monitored constantly to determine the need for revision.

. . . Be applicable to alternative modes of instruction.

- Although the specifications are being prepared for unit teaching, they should not be unique to unit teaching. In other words, the teacher should be able to use the specifications as guidelines for other instructional techniques.
- This principle can be applied if the specifications are sufficiently detailed and systematically organized.

The Specification Process

The various steps in preparing an instructional unit described in Chapter 6 represent a specification process at the unit level. The six steps represent guidelines for developing specifications to be followed in designing units of instruction. Given the identification of a unit topic, a teacher should be able to produce a quality unit if the steps are followed. In this chapter the emphasis is on developing specifications for a total curriculum or for that portion of the curriculum to be taught through units. The specifications become guidelines for a broad area of curriculum, not for a particular unit. Once the curriculum specifications are available, a teacher has a frame of reference for determining what skills and concepts should be included in unit instruction. In an ideal situation, curriculum specifications are available as a resource prior to preparing instructional units. In reality, few teachers participate in developing curriculum specifications. Consequently, units are designed without the guidance provided by a broader set of specifications. In terms of unit teaching, it is advantageous for teachers to be skilled in unit design prior to participating in the development of curriculum specifications. For this reason, the chapters related to unit development, which receives major attention, have appeared earlier.

Although it is highly desirable that curriculum specifications be developed in advance for all curriculum areas to be included in unit teaching, there is frequently not sufficient time for this activity. The specification process also can occur while the units are being implemented. In other words, as teachers prepare units, they are developing segments of the specifications for the broader curriculum area. The cumulative effect of teaching several units results in a form of specifications for the units taught. Under such circumstances, these specifications are not available for advanced planning. However, they can serve as the basis for specifications relative to subsequent groups of children. The problem is that the skills identified in the unit are organized around the unit topic. For maximum use as specifications, it will be necessary to sort out the skills and organize them according to the skill classifications rather than by unit topics.

Skill Specification Process

One approach to developing curriculum specifications is to identify skills and concepts that are to be included in the curriculum, particularly those to be stressed in unit teaching, and develop what approximate scope and sequence charts. These can be designed using a behavioral-objective format or a skills-listing format. This approach works particularly well in the basic skill areas such as math and reading. However, in areas such as social studies, where content is less sequential, the process is effective, but it is more difficult to reach agreement on the skill placement and concepts sequence. Where units are used to teach or to supplement instruction in specific curriculum areas, the specification process may be restricted to that instructional area. In this circumstance, that specific instructional area would represent the skill classification shown as Step I in Figure 14.

However, special education teachers working with the mentally retarded assigned to special classes might elect to follow the core areas—arithmetic, social competence, communication skills, safety, health, and vocational skills—to represent the skill classification in Step I of Figure 14. Since the specifications constitute scope and sequence charts oriented around skill areas and not unit topics, the selection of skill classifications does not have a substantial influence on the units which will be developed later. The important concern is that the skill classifications be detailed and sequentially organized. At a minimum, they should include the skills and concepts to be covered through unit teaching. Remember that these specifications will be for a curriculum area and not a particular unit. In using the unit development steps described in Chapter 6, the teacher will refer to the specifications in selecting skills and concepts to be incorporated into units. As previously pointed out, the availability of curriculum specifications is a major resource to teachers during the unit development process. In programs where units will be used extensively, the development of curriculum specifications represents a staff development activity. The development of specifications will

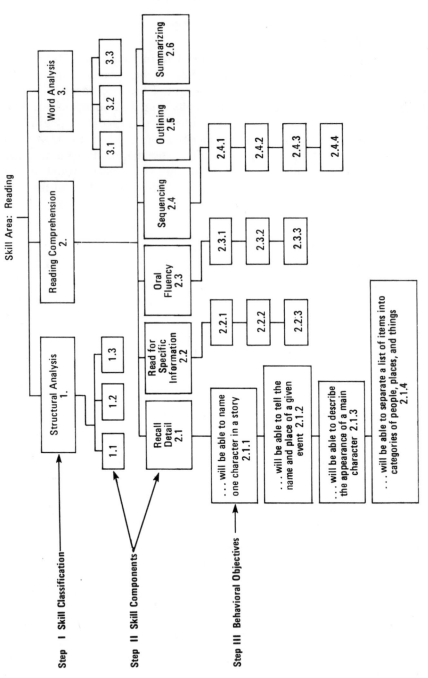

Figure 14. Skill Specification Process
Example: Reading

yield benefits in terms of teachers having a better concept of the content to be included in the curriculum and will also provide a quality control resource in terms of developing instructional units. Without curriculum specifications, teachers lack much-needed direction in terms of the decisions they must make regarding what to include in instructional units.

Step I—Skill Classification Level   This is the most general level in the specification process. There is no set group of skill classification headings. Keep in mind that this is the first of three steps in detailing specifications. If your skill classifications are too specific, for example, "addition facts," it is apparent that you will end up with a large number of skill classifications within the area of math alone. A more appropriate skill classification in math would be "basic operations" or "number concepts."

Examples of Skill Classification

Math	*Reading*
Numbers and numerals	Structural analysis
Operations	Word analysis
Number concepts	Reading comprehension
Problem solving	Punctuation
Measurement	Sentence structure

Step II—Skill Components   This step involves breaking the skill classification identified in Step I into more specific elements. Generally four to five skill elements will be sufficient. If you can only reduce the skill to two elements, then the skill classification is too specific. The skill component level provides a clear definition of what constitutes the skill classifications by breaking the classifications down into clearly described elements. Each component should represent a collection of skills or concepts. The cumulative effect of teaching the skills and concepts reflected in the skill components should comprise those skills and concepts implied by the skill classification.

Examples of Skill Components

Math	*Reading*
1. Operations	1. Structural analysis
1.1 Properties	1.1 Plural
1.2 Symbols	1.2 Singular
1.3 Whole numbers	1.3 Compound words
1.4 Fractions	1.4 Prefixes
1.5 Rational numbers	1.5 Suffixes

Math	*Reading*
2. Measurement	2. Oral language skills
2.1 Weight	2.1. Comprehension of spoken word
2.2 Linear	2.2 Picture interpretation
2.3 Volume	2.3 Auditory memory
	2.4 Discrimination of sounds
3. Numbers	2.5 Rhyming
3.1 Cardinal numbers	2.6 Following directions
3.2 Ordinal numbers	
	3. Reading comprehension
	3.1 Recall detail
	3.2 Reading for specific information
	3.3 Developing oral fluency
	3.4 Sequencing events
	3.5 Outlining
	3.6 Summarizing
	3.7 Classifying

Step III—Behavioral Objectives   This is the most specific level in the specification process. Although behaviorally stated objectives (see Chapter 7) are most effective since they can be directly applied in developing units, some teachers find an outline approach to be more commensurate with their planning style. The intent of this step is to develop a sequential list of behaviorally stated objectives for each skill component. This does not mean that every possible objective need be stated. However, the number of objectives should be sufficient to make clear the skills and concepts to be covered under the skill component. This can become an extremely time-consuming task if assigned to one person; a team approach should be used.

Examples of Behavioral Objectives in Math

Note: The components are not in sequence; they were selected to illustrate the stating of objectives.

1. Number
  1.1 Ordinal numbers
    1.1.1 The student will be able to identify the first object in a set of five objects in response to directions from the teacher.

2. Operations
  2.1 Fractions
    2.1.1 The student will be able to distinguish a half of an object from a whole object.

1.1.2 The student will be able to designate the first and second desks in a row of five desks when asked to do so.

1.1.3 . . . will be able to follow directions correctly when asked to take the last place in line.

1.1.4 . . . will be able to point to the first, second, and third objects when shown a work sheet containing a series of objects.

1.1.5 . . . will be able to identify the first, second, and last objects given a series of objects.

2.1.2 . . . will be able to divide a half circle into four quarter circles.

2.1.3 . . . will be able to separate a set into four subsets each containing a set of 8, 2, or 16 objects.

2.1.4 . . . will be able to identify that each subset is one-fourth of the whole set.

2.1.5 . . . will be able to manipulate the parts of each geometric figure to form a whole when given several plane geometric figures divided into thirds.

Examples of Behavioral Objectives in Reading

1. Reading Comprehension

1.1 Recalling details

1.1.1 The student will be able to report the name of one character in a story.

1.1.2 . . . will be able to tell the time and place a given story took place.

1.1.3 . . . will be able to describe the appearance of the main character in a given story.

1.1.4 . . . will be able to tell what the character did, when asked to describe the main character.

2. Oral Language Skills

2.1 Rhyming

2.1.1 The student will be able to state two words that rhyme.

2.1.2 . . . will be able to identify the words that rhyme given two lines of poetry.

2.1.3 . . . will be able to state which words rhyme, given three stimulus words.

2.1.4 . . . will be able to tell if the words rhyme, given a group of ten words.

1.2 Summary
    1.2.1 The student will be able to separate a list of items into categories of people, places, or things.
    1.2.2 . . . will be able to organize a set of statements into outline form, given direct statements from a story.
    1.2.3 . . . will be able to summarize a given story in five sentences or less.
    1.2.4 . . . will be able to synthesize the ideas, given two stories.

Once the specification process has been completed, teachers have a resource to refer to when teaching skills through units. The skills are organized and presented in three levels of specificity. The specifications also provide a basis for monitoring the curriculum in determining which skills have been taught, when, and in what sequence.

A numbering system is not essential, but it does help in organizing skills by levels. A numbering system has particular advantages when several teachers representing different grade levels are involved in developing or utilizing specifications. As has already been observed, a simple numbering system was used in the examples: 1. = classification level; 1.1 = component level; 1.1.1 = behavioral objective level.

Application Specification Process

While skill specifications are helpful in preparing units, most units place considerable emphasis on information and social experiences. Specifications oriented toward skills do not provide teachers much direction in developing units relative to these dimensions of unit instruction. The same specification process employed for skills and concepts can be followed in detailing specifications that focus on applied content, that is, information, social skills, and the general application of skills. The only difference is that instead of task-analyzing skills, information or the application of skills is emphasized. There are some similarities in this process to the identifying of sub-units as described in Chapter 6 and in the strategies to preparing a year's plan of work in Chapter 9. The difference is in the organizational pattern in which the specifications are detailed. See Figure 15.

Step I—Application Classification This level is equivalent to a unit topic. However, the inclusion of a unit topic at this level does not necessarily mean that the same topic will be developed into a complete unit and taught as detailed in the subsequent specifications. The application components described in the following steps may be combined with application components from other units in the specifications to create the unit that is actually taught. For example, budgeting may be an application component under the classification of "money," and check writing may be an application component under the classification "home management." A teacher may select these two application components and organize them along with other components into a unit. This is the advantage of applying the specification process to the information dimension of curriculum in reference to units. It allows the teacher to examine unit topics that have been subjected to a modified form of task analysis.

Example of Application Classification

Note: Topics will vary depending on age level. They are grouped for illustration purposes by core area.

Arithmetic
Measurement
Time
Budget
Money
Taxes
Salaries

Communication
Telephone
Correspondence
Post Office
Current events
Newspaper

Social Competence
Home
Family
Travel
Vacation
Community

Health
Food
Meal planning
Health habits
Clothing
Weather

Safety
Traffic
Automobile safety
Safety on the job
Electricity

Applying for a job
Planning your future
Occupation
Work responsibilities
Social Security

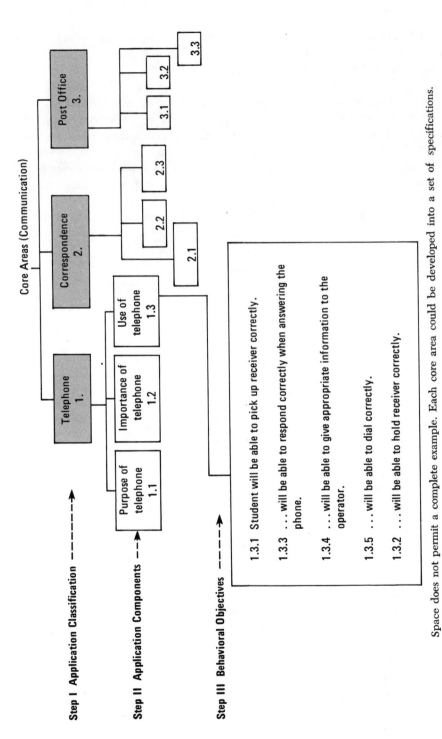

Core Areas (Communication)

Step I Application Classification — — — →

Step II Application Components — — →

Step III Behavioral Objectives — — →

1.3.1 Student will be able to pick up receiver correctly.

1.3.3 . . . will be able to respond correctly when answering the phone.

1.3.4 . . . will be able to give appropriate information to the operator.

1.3.5 . . . will be able to dial correctly.

1.3.2 . . . will be able to hold receiver correctly.

Space does not permit a complete example. Each core area could be developed into a set of specifications.

Figure 15. Application Specification Process

Step II—Application Components   The same process emphasized in the skill component step applies in breaking a unit down into components or sub-units. The goal is to identify major elements of the unit. There is one difference at this step between skills specifications and applications specifications—the number of application components versus skill components. While there may be only five or six skill components, a unit topic may break down into eight or ten application components.

Examples of Application Components

Application Classification	1. Citizenship (primary level)
Application Components	1.1 Respect for authority
	1.2 Respect for police
	1.3 Respect for fire department
	1.4 Respect of size
	1.5 Respect for property rights
	1.6 Care of public property
Application Classification	2. Telephone (primary level)
Application Components	2.1 Purposes of telephone
	2.2 Importance of telephone
	2.3 Use of telephone
	2.4 Parts of telephone
	2.5 Telephone behavior
	2.6 Making personal calls
	2.7 Making emergency calls
Application Classification	1. Applying for a job
Application Components	1.1 Source of job announcement
	1.2 Contact people
	1.3 Procedure to follow
	1.4 Interview behavior
	1.5 Completing form
	1.6 Follow-up

Step III—Behavioral Objectives   The only difference between the behaviorally stated objectives listed in the application specifications and in the skills specifications is in their sequence. In most skill areas, a sequence is built in to the skill acquisition; that is, skill A must be learned as prerequisite to learning skill B. However, in most units there is no set sequence for objectives related to information or social skills. In most cases it is a matter of building a logical sequence. This is not to suggest that the sequence is arbitrarily determined. But it should be noted that if different groups of teachers developed skill specifications, the final sequences of objectives could be very similar. For information or applied specifications, however, the sequence of objectives for a particular unit quite likely would not be similar. However, the sequences could easily be appropriate in both cases. When the emphasis is on information, the factors that tend to influence the sequence depend more on the teacher's preference for organization of content for purpose of instruction than on an inherent sequence from the perspective of the learner. This is highly defensible in the area of information and skill application.

The application specification process can be carried out for each core area. That is, a set unit topic can be selected in each core area. The process can be applied by age level. Topics should vary depending on the age or grade level of the target students.

Examples of Behavioral Objectives

Application Classification	1.	Applying for a job
Application Component	1.1	Source of job announcements
Behavioral Objectives	1.1.1	Student will be able to select most appropriate newspaper for announcing current job openings.
	1.1.2	. . . will be able to locate want ad section.
	1.1.3	. . . will be able to locate employment agency section in classified section of phone directory.
	1.1.4	. . . will be able to contact known employers about possible job vacancies.
Application Classification	2.	Telephone
Application Component	2.1	Use of telephone
Behavioral Objectives	2.1.1	Student will be able to pick up receiver correctly.
	2.1.2	. . . able to respond correctly when answering the phone.
	2.1.3	. . . able to give appropriate information to the operator.
	2.1.4	. . . will be able to dial correctly.
	2.1.5.	. . . will be able to hold receiver correctly.

Summary

The specification processes presented in this chapter approximate the development of scope and sequence charts. Teachers devoting considerable portions of their instructional program to unit teaching are encouraged to develop specifications for at least that segment of the curriculum to be taught through units. Two approaches were presented. The first focuses on skills and the second on unit-related information or applied context. Once completed, the specifications represent a resource for teachers in planning units. They also serve as a reference for principals and/or supervisors concerned with monitoring curriculum. Because of the time required in developing specifications, a team approach is suggested. In situations where only one or two teachers are involved in unit teaching, a modified approach is described in Chapter 9 on developing a year's plan for work.

Exercise 16. (1) Using the guidelines presented in this chapter, prepare a Skills Specifications Chart in the areas of math and reading. Prepare the chart for a single grade level. If it is possible to complete the exercises in cooperation with other teachers, extend the scope to include three grade levels.

(2) Using the guidelines presented in this chapter, prepare an Application Specification Process. Select one core area. If it is possible to complete the exercises in cooperation with other teachers, extend the scope to include all six core areas for at least one age group. Specify the age or grade level. Also, if exceptional children are included in the target population, describe their primary characteristics.

9

Developing a Year's Plan of Work for Unit Teaching

Teachers who occasionally teach units do not necessarily have to be concerned with the relationship among the units they teach. On the other hand, those who devote a major portion of their instructional programs to unit teaching must plan for unit teaching just as they plan for teaching through a prepared curriculum. They must consider the relationship among unit topics and the relative emphasis given to teaching skills within units. One of the most difficult tasks encountered by teachers in organizing their instructional programs is determining which aspects of the curriculum will be taught through units and which will be covered through other methods. While it may not be feasible to anticipate all of the experiences that will be provided through unit teaching during the year, a plan can be developed to represent the general content the teacher intends to cover using this method.

This chapter is designed for teachers who must do their own curriculum planning. If the teacher does not have access to resource people or if he or she teaches in a small attendance center with no other teachers teaching at the same level, it is still necessary to do long-term planning regarding unit instruction. At the same time, it is not reasonable to expect individual teachers to be as comprehensive in their planning as a team of teachers with access to many more resources. This chapter represents a modification of the more comprehensive approach discussed in Chapter 8. Whereas Chapter 8 applies to a team approach to curriculum planning, this chapter is oriented to planning by individual teachers.

A well-designed and effectively taught unit can independently make a significant contribution to a teacher's instructional program. However, few teachers limit their unit teaching to one or two units per year. Most will teach a number of units covering a variety of topics during the year. Collectively, these units may represent a major proportion of the learning experiences engaged in by the students. The topics selected for unit teaching as well as the pattern in which they are taught require careful consideration in developing a year's plan of unit work. An organizational plan facilitates communication with students, parents, fellow teachers, and administrators regarding the curriculum content to be covered through units. The process of preparing a plan requires the teacher to make decisions about both what is to be taught through units during the year and the general pattern in which units are to be taught.

Teachers working in a situation where no structured curriculum is available have fewer resources to rely on when making these decisions. On the other hand, teachers working from a well-designed curriculum must still make decisions about the sequence in which their units will be taught and the content to be covered through unit teaching. It is not practical to suggest the specific content that should be covered through units at any particular age level. The selection of unit topics and the determination of what will be included in selected units must take into consideration the established curriculum or what the teacher perceives as the curriculum. As pointed out in Chapter 3, academic skills as well as informational content can be effectively taught through units. Any restrictions on what can or cannot be taught through units are imposed by teachers themselves. This generally occurs when teachers feel other methods work better for them for certain curriculum facets. The most frequent restriction is to circumscribe unit teaching to encompass areas such as socialization, occupations, information on events, language development, and topics that allow for the application of basic skills taught through more formal approaches such as basal series.

Assuming that the teacher is skilled in writing units, the task of developing a year's plan of unit work becomes one of making decisions about which units will be taught during the year and how they can be organized to maximize their contribution to the instructional program. Teachers who elect to devote a major portion of their instructional program to unit teaching will find it helpful to make a basic plan for the units they anticipate teaching during the year. This does not mean that each unit will need to be written out in detail in advance. However, a blueprint for the year can be developed. Such a plan requires the teacher to make global decisions as to what will be taught through units. Having this type of information available, the teacher is then in a better position to proceed with developing individual units.

The year's plan of work should be viewed as a plan and not as a rigid schedule of units to be taught. They may be altered for a number of reasons. The teacher may decide to consolidate two or three areas of the plan into a single unit, or an event may occur that makes a topic planned for the future more relevant at the present.

A prerequisite to developing a year's plan of unit work is the determination of what is to be taught through teacher-made units and what is to be taught through subject-centered activities. If reading, language arts, and math, for example, are to be taught at specified times during the day and units employed for a short period of time to cover the related social content, then this will, of course, having a bearing on what is to be included in the year's plan of unit work. On the other hand, if major emphasis is to be given to unit teaching, the plan will need to reflect such emphasis.

As previously stressed, units can provide the framework in which the teaching of academic and social skills can be couched. The sequential aspects of these skills should not be altered because they are being taught through units. The informational aspects of units should also be presented sequentially. Teachers in ungraded situations who may have the same children for two or three years must avoid teaching the same concepts and information through repeated unit topics. Each teacher needs to have information on what other teachers are teaching relative to each unit topic. If all teachers in the system are working from a structured curriculum, no problems need arise. In the absence of such curriculum, the yearly plan of unit work proposed by each teacher can serve as a vehicle for communicating what each plans to teach through units during the school year. This makes the year's plan of unit work exceedingly important, particularly where heavy emphasis is being given to unit teaching and where no prescribed curriculum is available as a source of direction to the teacher in developing units.

Developing a year's plan of unit work according to the guidelines presented in this chapter is primarily an individual assignment to be carried out by each teacher. But the process should involve interaction with other teachers. When feasible, the plan should be developed prior to the beginning of the school year. Teachers can begin work on their plans as soon as they know the basic composition of their class. This will probably occur in the spring of the preceding year. The advantage of this timing is that the current year's instructional program is just ending and a firm base exists for making decisions on next year's program. Also, by knowing the units they plan to teach, teachers will be able to anticipate needed materials in time to order for the subsequent year.

While the year's plan of unit work should be geared to the teacher's particular class, the process of developing the plan can be broadened from an individual task to one that involves all special class teachers in a building or in the program. For example, teachers at the primary, intermediate, and junior high levels can collaborate in developing their plans. In many cases, the unit topics will be applicable to all or several of the levels represented in the program. The only differences will be in terms of what is taught under the umbrella of the topic. Having teachers from all levels involved facilitates communication and contributes to better decisions regarding what is to be taught about a particular topic at different age levels. This type of cooperative planning results in a generalized understanding, on the part of all teaching staff members, of the aspects of the curriculum being taught through units. It also encourages continuity and reduces redundancy. (See Chapter 8 for a discussion of team procedures.)

The manner in which a teacher organizes the daily program, as well as the number of units to be taught at one time, will also influence the plan of unit work. If teachers tend to teach two or three units in addition to other aspects of their program, they will likely base their plans on a larger number of unit topics than if they routinely teach only one unit at a time. In the latter situation, the unit topics are likely to be more general and fewer in number.

Guidelines for Planning

In developing a yearly plan for unit work, consideration should be given to formulating a plan that combines efficient curriculum coverage with explicitness. Frequently, the attention given to outlining curriculum content overshadows attempts to make the plan meaningful as a base for communicating the program. It is important that the plan be designed so that it reflects the scope of your unit work and does so in a manner easily understood by your principal, fellow teachers, and the parents of your pupils.

The following features are suggested as guidelines for developing a plan.

1. Select units that allow for teaching skills and concepts that represent major needs on the part of your pupils. This means that typically a teacher will find it necessary to teach more units from one core area than others. For example, if the class tends to be weak in arithmetic skills, a larger proportion of units that lend themselves to providing experience in arithmetic should be selected.
2. Select topics that are relevant and interesting to your group.
3. Select topics that are new to them. Avoid units which are repetitious of units studied in previous classes.
4. Select topics that convey meaning. In other words, in seeking more interesting topics, don't be lured into selecting humorous or vague titles merely for appeal. You can alter the title when teaching the unit. However, for purposes of your plan, stick with meaningful titles.
5. Select a plan format that is easily interpreted to your pupils. While pupil understanding is not the only criteria, it is helpful if students are aware of the general scope of the unit work for the year.

Suggested Approaches

A number of approaches can be employed in developing a year's work plan. Two approaches are offered as a point of departure for teachers in formulating their own approach. While teachers may wish to devise their own style, there is much to be said for uniformity within a school system. Agreement on a basic format will enhance communication on the instructional program. Teachers should be encouraged to explore several approaches prior to making a decision on the one to follow. The sample approaches are geared to two different teacher groups. The *continuum approach* is an example of how teachers who teach only one unit at a time might organize their yearly plan. The *core area approach* represents an example for those teachers who devote time to teaching two or three different units daily. The two illustrative approaches satisfy the five previously mentioned guidelines, yet they differ in order to meet the demands of the two teaching situations described.

Both approaches include the identification of unit topics plus a descriptive statement on the intended content. The content description can be in the form of a *brief outline* or in a series of *outcome statements* oriented toward pupil performance. If the teacher is skilled in writing objectives in behavioral terms, then outcome statements are recommended. However, if the teacher has not developed this proficiency, the formulation of outcomes for a large number of units would be a laborious task and would probably hinder the process of developing the unit plan. The outline form is recommended for most because it lends itself more readily to the planning task. It also is more compatible with the preliminary steps suggested for writing units in Chapter 6. The specification of outcomes in the form of behavioral objectives will take place when writing lessons. However, by the time teachers reach that stage, they will have completed the preliminary steps and be at a better state of readiness for writing objectives. At the plan level an outline form is sufficient.

The purpose of the content description is to indicate what is meant by the unit topic. In other words, a description is given of the general content to be covered and its level of complexity. For example, a teacher at the junior high level may describe the content of a unit on money as follows:

MONEY (using outline format)
      a. Services of the bank
      b. Ways of saving
      c. Establishing a checking account
      d. Writing checks
      e. Balancing a checkbook
      f. Responsibilities that accompany a checking account

MONEY   (using outcome format)

    a. Is able to explain the services of a bank.

    b. Can describe the process of establishing a savings account, buying bonds, and purchasing savings certificates.

    c. Is able to complete all steps necessary in establishing a checking account.

    d. Can demonstrate the appropriate procedure for writing personal checks.

    e. Is able to balance a checkbook accurately.

    f. Is able to describe verbally the responsibilities of having a checking account.

At the primary level a teacher might also select the topic of money. The outline would likely reflect a concern for teaching coin and currency recognition plus an understanding of their values.

If teachers have a prescribed curriculum based on available curriculum outcomes, they would be well advised to follow the established pattern. If behavioral objectives are used in presenting curriculum content, then the task of developing the year's plan of work would be greatly facilitated by the use of outcome statements instead of the outline format. The task then becomes one of selecting outcomes from the prescribed curriculum and incorporating them under the appropriate unit topic. In this situation, the teacher is not called upon to construct the outcomes, as they are readily available from the prescribed curriculum. Few teachers will find themselves in this situation.

Continuum Approach

The continuum approach assumes that a teacher will be basically teaching one unit at a time. The unit may last for several weeks, but no new unit will be introduced until the one presently being taught has been culminated. This type of plan is developed mainly by organizing selected units into a logical sequence and indicating the general content of each unit. The suggestions given below are steps to follow in developing a plan based on the continuum approach. Figure 16 illustrates the relationship among steps.

1. *Identification of Topics*   Identify the units you plan to teach during the year. Teachers should ask themselves the same kinds of questions at this point as suggested during Step 1 of the preliminary steps in writing units. (See Chapter 6) In essence, if they develop a yearly work plan and are careful in unit selection, then most of the work for Step 1 in writing the unit has been completed. Basically, they must be guided in their selection by their knowledge of pupil needs and familiarity with units that

have previously been taught. It is important to select unit topics that facilitate teaching the skills and concepts appropriate to the functioning level of the class. At the same time, the unit's informational aspects must also be meaningful to the pupils. Initially, the topics can be listed in random order. The emphasis at this stage is on the topic and content, not the order. The teacher is merely attempting to identify the units that should be taught during the year. During subsequent steps when the content is outlined, it may be that some unit topics can be merged. A logical order will also become apparent once the content has been outlined.

2. *Content Outline*   Briefly outline the content of each unit. The purpose is to include sufficient information to clarify the content coverage and to convey the intent of the unit to other teachers or administrators who may read the plan. In most cases, eight or nine major points will be adequate. It is advisable to have a colleague read two or three of your brief outlines to check on the meaning they convey. To be sure that the outline reliability conveys your intent, you may find that a more extensive outline is required. It is better to be inclusive rather than to end up with a plan comprised of unit outlines that are too vague. The more complete the outlines are, the easier will be the task of developing them into teachable units later. An attempt should be made to organize the points in the outline sequentially.

3. *Core Emphasis*   Once the brief outlines have been completed, the major emphasis in terms of core areas should be apparent. In other words, a review of the outline should indicate whether the unit is strong in social competencies, communication skills, and so forth.

4. *Sequence Units*   Organize the unit topics into a logical order. In reviewing the brief outlines, you can determine which units are most closely related. The intent is to organize the units so that the content of one unit serves as an introduction to the succeeding one. In addition to the relationship between unit topics, consideration must also be given to timing. Some unit topics are better taught in relation to certain seasons or events that regularly occur at specific times during the year. For example, a unit on the farm might be best taught in the spring or fall, while a unit on transportation could be taught at any time.

5. *Transitional Activities*   After the unit outlines have been developed and organized into sequence, the next step is to describe an activity designed to facilitate transition between units. The activity can be briefly described in a few sentences. You may not use the particular activity to make the transition when actually teaching the unit. However, the procedures enhance continuity.

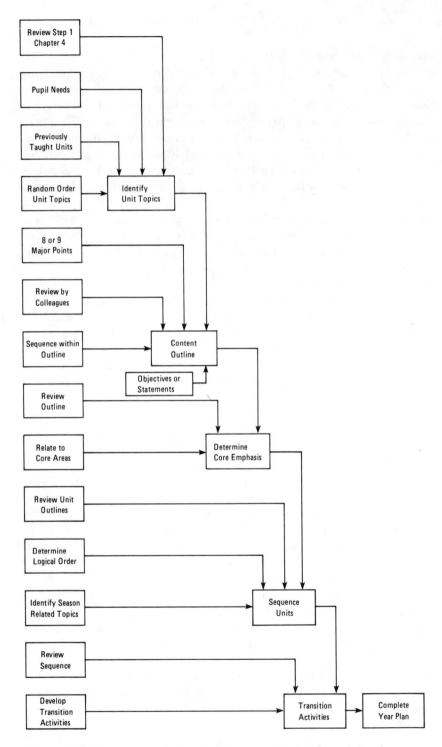

Figure 16. Continuum Approach Schemata—Year's Plan of Work

Examples of Continuum Approach

The following are two sample plans for a year of unit work developed in accordance with the continuum approach. The *first* example utilizes an outline method of describing content. The *second* example is based on the outcome approach to presenting the content.

EXAMPLE 1: CONTINUUM APPROACH USING AN OUTLINE FORMAT

School Orientation (Social Competencies)*

1. The physical layout of the school.
2. Materials and their location in the classroom.
3. Rules in the school and the classroom.
4. Proper behavior in the classroom.
5. Respect for other students' property.
6. Listening and speaking habits in the classroom.

Courtesy (Social Competencies)

1. Respect for teacher and other elders.
2. Proper table manners.
3. Working and playing with others.
4. Use of telephone.
5. Care for toys and other property.
6. Responses to reprimands.
7. Behavior in public places.

Jobs (Vocational Skills)

1. Responsibility for selected jobs in the classroom.
2. Assuming a fair share of work in the classroom.
3. Courtesy in regard to jobs.
4. Completing tasks according to schedule.
5. Importance of safety rules when doing job.
6. Neighborhood jobs the student can do.
7. Jobs the student can do in the home.

*Indicates the core area in which this unit was perceived by the teacher as being strongest.

Home and Family (Social Competencies)

1. Roles of different members of the family.
2. Student's role in helping with the housecleaning.
3. Jobs that can be delegated to the student which must be completed regularly, such as dishes, taking care of pets, and so forth.
4. Jobs the child can do in the yard.
5. Importance of assuming responsibility for a share of the work.
6. Planning family activities.
7. Rooms in the home and their uses.
8. Address and phone number.
9. Direction from home to school.
10. Safety at home.

Citizenship (Social Competencies)

1. The meaning of citizenship in the home, school, community, state, and nation.
2. Need for good citizenship.
3. Respect for others and their property.
4. Respect for flag and other symbols of the nation.
5. Necessity for obeying rules, signs, and signals.
6. Respect for people in authority.

Community Helpers (Vocational Skills)

1. Community helpers and their roles.
2. Role of police officers.
3. Role of firefighters.
4. The medical professions and their services to the community.
5. The librarian and the services the library provides.
6. Services of postal carriers.
7. Recognition of the different types of public transportation.
8. Kinds of help we can obtain from community helpers.

Post Office (Communication Skills)

1. Purpose of the post office.
2. Knowing the location of the post office.
3. How mail is delivered.
4. Writing personal letters to friends.
5. Appropriate procedure for addressing envelopes.
6. Preparing packages for mailing.
7. Knowing where to buy stamps.

Money (Arithmetic Concepts)

1. Recognition of coins and bills up to $10.00.
2. The value of coins to $1.00.
3. Ways of earning money.
4. Basic concept of saving.
5. Uses of money.

Food (Health)

1. Recognition of selected fruits and vegetables.
2. Knowledge of where foods are grown.
3. Function of grocery store.
4. Basic classification of foods.
5. Reasons for needing well-balanced meals.
6. Foods needed daily for a good diet.
7. Ways to cook food.
8. Care for different kinds of food, such as refrigeration.
9. Importance of certain health habits in regard to food, such as brushing teeth after meals, washing hands before eating, and so on.

Health Habits (Health)

1. Importance of getting enough rest.
2. Necessity of seeing a dentist and doctor regularly.
3. Appropriate clothing for different types of weather.
4. Precautions needed to prevent the spread of communicable diseases.
5. Importance of regular exercise.
6. Importance of cleanliness.

Time (Arithmetic Concepts)

1. Purpose of a clock.
2. Telling time.
3. Reading a schedule.
4. Importance of promptness.
5. Days of the week.
6. Basic concept of budgeting time.
7. Reading a calendar.
8. Division of year into seasons.

Seasons (Health)

1. The four seasons of the year and the type of weather associated with each.
2. Safety rules to follow during each of the seasons.
3. Things to do at different times of the year.
4. Health rules to combat colds.
5. Proper clothing for each season.

Clothing (Health)

1. Importance of having clothing that fits, especially shoes.
2. Proper clothing to wear for certain occasions.
3. Selection of clothing that is appropriate for the season.
4. Necessity of changing clothes when they are wet.
5. Importance of changing underclothes regularly.
6. Caring for clothing.
7. Keeping clothes clean.
8. How clothes are made.
9. Responsibility for taking care of one's own clothing.

First Aid (Safety)

1. Necessity for treatment by doctor in severe injuries.
2. People to contact in case of injury.
3. Use of first-aid kit.
4. Treatment for minor injuries.
5. Necessity of cleanliness in the treatment of all injuries.
6. The danger of poisons, sharp objects, and fire.

Safety (Safety)

1. Safe places to play.
2. Necessity of safety habits to prevent accidents.
3. Safety rules necessary at school.
4. Rules of safety needed in the home.
5. Meaning of basic traffic and warning signals.
6. Safety rules needed on the playground.
7. Safety rules needed in traveling.

Transportation (Arithmetic Concepts)

1. Meaning of transportation.
2. Different types of transportation.
3. The concept of distance.
4. Importance of street numbers and how to use them.

5. Safety rules while using public transportation.
6. Safety rules for walking.
7. Purchasing tickets.
8. Behavior while using public transportation.

Telephone (Communication Skills)

1. Identification of different types of telephones.
2. Uses of the telephone.
3. Using the telephone directory.
4. Know good telephone manners.
5. The telephone for emergency calls.
6. Telephone for pleasure.
7. Good habits in using the telephone.

Playtime (Social Competencies)

1. Playing with other children.
2. Sharing and cooperating.
3. Activities appropriate to the particular setting.
4. Games and activities appropriate for different kinds of weather.
5. Good sportsmanship.
6. Following directions.
7. Safety at play.
8. Learning proper care of toys and other property.

Animals (Safety)

1. Animals commonly seen in the community.
2. Animals found on farms or found in the zoos.
3. Types of animals suitable for pets.
4. Handling of animals.
5. Care of animals.
6. Rules of safety applicable to handling animals.
7. Finding homes for lost animals.

Newspaper (Communication Skills)

1. The contents of the newspaper.
2. The newspaper as a source of information.
3. Locating different things in the newspaper.
4. Pictures contained and their messages in the newspaper.
5. The newspaper as a source of entertainment.
6. Importance of reading the newspaper.

EXAMPLE 2: CONTINUUM APPROACH USING AN OUTCOME FORMAT

Family

1. Is able to describe the roles of family members.
2. Knows the names of the family members and is able to write them.
3. Is able to identify jobs in the home that are within his or her capabilities.
4. Understands the concept of "relative" and is able to name grandparents, uncles, and aunts.

School

1. Is able to recognize the school name.
2. Recognizes the teacher, principal, and school secretary and calls them by name.
3. Can locate classroom, restroom, principal's office, and nurse's office.
4. Adheres to school rules.
5. Participates in the fire drill by following directions from teacher.
6. Carries out assigned work tasks in the classroom.
7. Is able to identify classmates by name.

Money

1. Recognizes coins and currency by name and is able to indicate their value.
2. Can demonstrate making change up to combinations totaling five dollars.
3. Is able to compute accurately totals for expenditures up to ten dollars.
4. Can demonstrate an understanding of saving through role-playing exercises.
5. Can explain the services of a bank.
6. Is able to describe the major uses of money in supporting a family.
7. Is able to describe what is meant by earning money.

Time

1. Can tell time accurately to a quarter of an hour.
2. Adheres to the school schedule by being on time.
3. Can identify different kinds of timepieces, such as watches and clocks.
4. Is able to write the days of the week in sequence.
5. Is able to write the months of the year in sequence.
6. Can demonstrate the appropriate method for setting a clock and watch.
7. Is able to estimate with reasonable accuracy the time required to perform a specific task.

Seasons

1. Is able to list the seasons of winter, spring, summer, and fall.
2. Can describe the weather typical of each season.
3. Is able to explain the major activities that occur during each season, for example, planting, hunting, leisure activities, and so forth.
4. Is able to list the months in each season.
5. Recognizes the natural changes that occur in his surroundings during each season.
6. Is able to list the major holidays that occur during each season.
7. Is able to explain the organization and use of the calendar.
8. Can locate the date in the local newspaper.

Grooming and Health Care

1. Practice good health practices related to washing hands before meals, working with food, and so forth.
2. Knows the services of the nurse, doctor, and dentist, and is able to describe what they do.
3. Changes clothing when soiled.
4. Is able to demonstrate appropriate procedures for brushing teeth.
5. Follows good health care practices when ill, such as having a cold.
6. Attempts to take care of clothing by using coatracks.
7. Is able to make simple repairs in clothing.
8. When given a choice of foods, will select food that is healthful.

Community

1. Knows name of community and state.
2. Is able to write name and address.
3. Can locate on a map the major community center such as a school, post office, parks, hospital, and so forth.
4. Obeys traffic signals.
5. Is able to locate designated places in the downtown area independently.
6. Can accurately give directions to a classmate on how to get to designated places.
7. Can describe the roles of community helpers such as police, firefighters, mail carriers, and so forth.
8. Is able to explain simple concepts related to community government.
9. Displays appropriate behavior while visiting places in the community.
10. Is able to list the recreational opportunities in the community.

Telephone

1. Is able to recognize different styles of telephones.
2. Can demonstrate correct use of dial phone.
3. Can recite home phone number.
4. Can demonstrate use of the telephone.
5. Can explain the use of the yellow pages.
6. Is able to obtain a new phone number not listed in the phone book from the operator.
7. Demonstrate good manners when using the telephone.
8. Is able to locate emergency numbers in the phone book.
9. Is able to demonstrate use of coin-operated telephones.
10. Can explain why use of the telephone costs money.

Transportation

1. Able to identify the most frequently used modes of transportation in the community.
2. Can demonstrate appropriate behavior when using public transportation.
3. Is able to explain the costs and can demonstrate payment procedures.
4. Can identify bus stops.
5. Is able to demonstrate good safety practices when using public systems of transportation.
6. Can explain the importance of transportation to the community and to the family.

Measurement

1. Is able to identify measuring instruments, such as scales, yardstick, ruler, tape measure, container, and so forth.
2. Can demonstrate accurate use of measuring instruments typically used at school and in the home.
3. Can calculate differences in measurements.
4. Knows own clothing sizes.
5. Can locate sizes on clothing.
6. Able to estimate basic length and quantity.
7. Can demonstrate computation of cost per measure, for example, cost per yard and per pound.

Foods

1. Is able to recognize common foods and classify them as meats, fruits, vegetables, bread, and so forth.
2. Is able to describe how foods are derived and from what source.
3. Can demonstrate simple preparation of foods for eating, for example, washing fresh fruits, peeling vegetables, and so forth.

4. Can plan a basic menu given a group of foods from which to select.
5. Is able to differentiate foods with high nutrient value from foods with little value.
6. Can list foods normally found together in a supermarket.
7. Is able to explain why some foods must be refrigerated.

The Newspaper

1. Knows the names of local papers.
2. Can identify the main section of the newspaper.
3. Is able to locate features such as the date and the weather.
4. Reads the paper when it is available.
5. Is able to locate information in the want ads section.
6. Can calculate the cost per week, month, and year.

Weather

1. Is able to identify cues that suggest changes in weather.
2. Is able to read a thermometer accurately.
3. Can describe good safety practices under different weather conditions.
4. Dresses appropriately for weather conditions.
5. Is able to relate the need for moisture and sunlight to the growth of plants.
6. Is able to identify on a map the area of the country which has a warmer or colder climate than where student lives.

Leisure Time

1. Plays fairly with classmates.
2. Can locate recreational areas in the community.
3. Knows leisure-type games that can be played indoors.
4. Practices sharing of toys with classmates.
5. Is able to give directions on how to play simple games.
6. Plays as a team member in sports.
7. Returns equipment and games to appropriate places when through using them.

Supermarket

1. Can explain the purpose of the market.
2. Is able to locate the different departments in a supermarket.
3. Can explain the role of the checker.
4. Is able to select assigned items from the shelves.
5. Given the sale price and the regular price is able to calculate the difference.
6. Is able to describe how basic foods are obtained by supermarkets.
7. Can identify foods prepared locally.

Core Area Approach

This approach involves organizing the year's plan of work according to the six core areas. Teachers planning to work on two or three units each day will find this approach most helpful. The process of selecting and describing the units to be included in your plan is similar to that suggested for the continuum approach. However, instead of sequencing the units in a logical order from the first to the last unit you anticipate teaching, categorize the unit topics according to core areas, that is, communication skills, arithmetic, social competencies, health, safety, and vocational skills. The order in which they are taught is determined by the current needs of the pupils and the appropriateness of the unit topic at the time another unit has been culminated. In the continuum approach previously discussed, the teacher established the order as a part of the plan. This is not feasible in this type of plan because it is difficult for a teacher to anticipate the amount of time required to teach each unit. The fact that more than one unit is being taught daily further complicates the task of trying to plan the units sequentially through the core area approach.

Consequently, some units will be taught over a four-week period of time, while others will require five or six weeks to complete. It is possible to accomplish sequence on a tract basis. For example, a teacher who plans to teach three units at different times during the day could develop a plan that groups the units into three general categories. A category might emphasize one or more core areas; the units within each category could be sequenced in a logical order. The teacher would then follow a pattern of introducing subsequent new units from a category, once a unit from that particular category had been completed. Another approach, which is probably more realistic, is to select the units and organize them by core areas. Once the units were grouped by core areas, the teacher would select those to be taught at a particular time by the relevance of the topic and its relationship to the unit being completed.

There is a certain amount of arbitrariness in the organization of units within this plan. Thus, teachers are reminded that the important criteria for teaching a unit are the needs of the student. The plan should not be so rigid that it interferes with this requirement.

The first two steps suggested in the directions for the continuum approach are applicable to the core area approach. To enhance the application of those steps unique to the core area approach, the first two steps are repeated. Figure 17 illustrates the relationship among steps.

1. *Identification of Topics*   Identify the units you plan to teach during the year. Teachers should ask themselves the same kinds of questions at this point as suggested during Step 1 of the preliminary steps in writing units.

(See Chapter 6) In essence, if they develop a yearly work plan and are careful in the unit selection, then most of the work for Step 1 in writing the unit has been completed. Basically, they must be guided in their selection by their knowledge of pupil needs and familiarity with units that have previously been taught. It is important to select unit topics that facilitate teaching the skills and concepts appropriate to the functioning level of the class. At the same time, the informational aspects of the unit must also be meaningful to the pupils. Initially, the topics can be listed in random order. The emphasis at this stage is on the topic and content, not the order. Teachers are merely attempting to identify the units that should be taught during the year. During subsequent steps when the content is outlined, it may be that some unit topics can be merged. A logical order will also become apparent once the content has been outlined.

2. *Content Outline* Briefly outline the content of each unit. The purpose is to include sufficient information to clarify the content coverage and to convey the intent of the unit to other teachers or administrators who may read the plan. In most cases, eight or nine major points will be adequate. It is advisable to have a colleague read two or three of your brief outlines to check on the meaning they convey. To be sure that the outline reliably conveys your intent, you may find that a more inclusive outline is required. It is better to be inclusive rather than to end up with a plan comprised of unit outlines that are too vague. The more complete the outlines are, the easier will be the task of developing them into teachable units later. An attempt should be made to organize the points in the outline sequentially. The organization may change when you develop the unit but to the degree possible the outline of the content should reflect the scope and general manner in which you anticipate organizing the unit.

3. *Core Areas* Having briefly described the unit content, you should organize the topics according to core areas. A review of the unit descriptions should readily reveal the emphasis of the unit. It is likely that more units will be listed under some core areas than others. The pattern of units of core areas should be representative of the needs of the pupils in the class. For example, if your pupil's major weaknesses are in the core area of communication skills, more units should be listed in this core area.

4. *Sequence in Core Areas* The final step is placing the unit topics within each core area in a logical order. Transitional activities are of less value in this approach since teachers will not likely teach the units in a prescribed sequence.

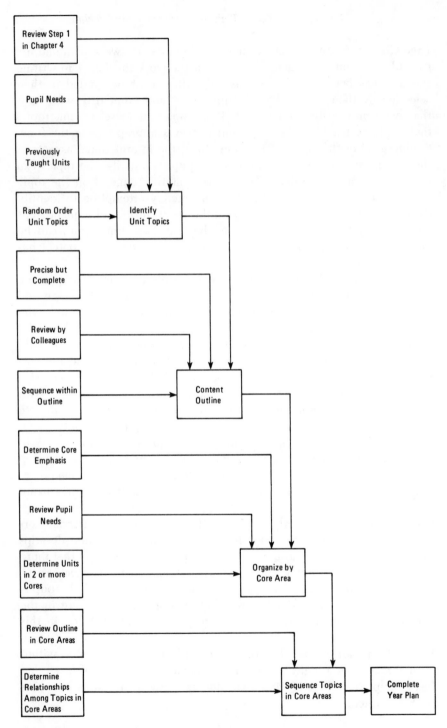

Figure 17. Core Area Approach Schemata—Year's Plan of Work

The following example of a year's plan of work utilizes an outline format. Since the outline format would differ only in the manner in which the content is presented, an example using outcome statements is not included. The reader is referred to the example for the continuum approach.

EXAMPLE: CORE AREA APPROACH USING AN OUTLINE FORMAT

Core Area: Arithmetic

Money

1. Ways to earn money.
2. The use of money.
3. Recognition of coins and bills.
4. Value of coins and bills.
5. Making change for a dollar.
6. Correct use of cent and dollar sign.
7. Saving.

Measurement

1. Basic understanding of inch, foot, and yard.
2. Correct use of the ruler and yardstick.
3. Basic understanding of pint, quart, and gallon.
4. Basic understanding of one-half and full pound.
5. Correct use of the scale.
6. Basic understanding of dozen and one-half dozen.
7. Practical application of measuring tools.

Time

1. Days of the week.
2. Months of the year.
3. Seasonal changes.
4. Introduction of the calendar.
5. Simple daily record-keeping.
6. Concept of half and quarter.
7. Telling time.
8. Setting clock to correct time.

Core Area: Communication Skills

Post Office

1. Purpose of the post office.
2. Location of the post office in the community.
3. Writing simple letters (invitations).
4. Addressing of envelopes.
5. Mailing of letters.
6. Sending of packages.
7. Buying of stamps.
8. Role of the postal carrier.

Telephone

1. Importance of the telephone.
2. Correct use of the telephone.
3. Identification of the parts and their use.
4. Telephone manners.
5. Making personal calls.
6. Making emergency calls.

Current Events

1. Daily use of the newspaper, date, and weather report.
2. Special news items of interest to the class.
3. News items pertaining to holidays.
4. Writing of a class newspaper.

Core Area: Social Competencies

Courtesy

1. Introductions.
2. Saying thank you, please, excuse me, and so forth.
3. Respect for property rights.
4. Table manners.
5. Desirable behavior in public places.
6. Desirable behavior when using transportation facilities.

Home and the Family

1. Members of the family.
2. Responsibility of each member.
3. Sharing.
4. Taking turns.

5. Rooms and their uses.
6. Shelter.
7. Care of the home.
8. Safety and the home.

Community

1. Components of a community.
2. Acceptable social behavior when using community facilities.
3. Responsibility to the community.
4. Community helpers.

Citizenship

1. Respect for authority.
2. Respect for the police department.
3. Respect for the fire department.
4. Recognition of certain signs and signals.
5. Respect of property rights.
6. Care of public property.

Leisure Time

1. Good sportsmanship.
2. Inside games to play individually and in groups.
3. Group games to play outside.
4. Independent games to play outside.
5. Care of equipment.
6. Sharing.

Core Area: Health

Food

1. Identification of fruits and vegetables.
2. Association of name and food.
3. Understanding basic seven foods.
4. Understanding the foods important to specific meals.
5. Source of food.
6. Supermarket.
7. Health habits and food.
8. Manners.

Health Habits

1. Adequate amount of rest.
2. Dental care.
3. Cleanliness.
4. Good grooming.
5. Care of clothing.

Clothing

1. Type of clothing to wear according to the weather.
2. Kinds of clothes for summer, winter, and spring.
3. Change underclothing regularly.
4. Wear proper bed clothing.
5. Prevention of colds.
6. Play clothes, dress clothes, and work clothes.

Water

1. Importance of water.
2. Source of water.
3. Importance of washing hands.
4. Danger of drinking water from ponds, and so forth.
5. Health habits pertaining to public drinking fountains.

Weather

1. Awareness of seasonal changes.
2. The various kinds of weather occurring during each season.
3. The need for rain, snow, wind, sunshine, and so forth.
4. Awareness of safety hazards accompanying the different kinds of weather.
5. Health habits and weather.
6. Wear proper clothing according to the weather.
7. Weather report.
8. Role of the weather forecaster.
9. Months of the year—according to seasons.
10. Days of the week.

Core Area: Safety

Safety and School

1. Classroom safety.
2. Lunchroom safety practices.
3. Playground safety.

4. Use of equipment.
5. Care of equipment.

Safety at Home

1. Electrical hazards.
2. Danger of gas.
3. Care of toys.
4. Stairs and safety.
5. Rugs and slippery floors.
6. Poisons.
7. Refrigerators.
8. Fire safety at home.

Bicycle Safety

1. Traffic rules regarding bicycles.
2. Parking bicycles at school.
3. Care of bicycles.
4. Safe riding habits.

Traffic Safety

1. Importance of traffic laws.
2. Understanding traffic signs, lights, and signals.
3. Correct use of crosswalks.
4. Looking both ways before crossing the street.
5. Playing in the street.
6. Toys in the street.
7. Obeying the police officer.

Core Area: Vocational Skills

Jobs at Home

1. Kinds of jobs which can be done at home.
2. Completing a job.
3. Following directions.
4. Responsibility for doing the same job daily.

Earning Money

1. Allowances and how they are earned.
2. Types of jobs for which youth can earn money.
3. Responsibility for earning pay.
4. Saving principles.

Summary

The development of a year's plan of work requires the teacher to anticipate pupils' needs and to structure a blueprint for unit teaching. While the plan is not rigid, it does serve as a frame of reference in developing the instructional program. It is particularly helpful in communicating with parents, pupils, principals, and fellow teachers regarding the content to be covered. The approach presented in this chapter is oriented toward the teacher who must do curriculum planning without the benefit of resource people. Although the approach is very general compared to the strategies discussed in Chapter 8, the individual teacher using this approach will be able to construct an organizational plan for unit teaching.

Exercise 17. Continuum Approach. Select twenty unit topics applicable to the class you are teaching or to the age level you plan to teach and develop a Year's Plan of Work using the continuum approach. Describe your units in outline form.

Exercise 18. Core Area Approach. Using the units included in Exercise 17, develop a Year's Plan of Work using the core area approach. Describe your units using outcome statements.

10

Evaluation Techniques

How do you know whether or not the unit you just finished teaching on "the community" added to your students' knowledge of the community in which they live? Do you know which students gained the most information? Which concepts were the most difficult for your students? Which were the least difficult? Answers to questions like these are essential if you are to improve your instructional program and ultimately to have a more significant influence on the lives of children for whose education you are responsible. Such answers are not easily derived. While the evaluative data may be obtained in an arbitrary fashion, if evaluation results are to be meaningful to teachers and contribute to better curriculum decisions, the evaluation process must be carefully planned and ongoing. Obviously, there are problems inherent in evaluating the educational progress of children as a result of unit teaching. Most standardized achievement tests are designed to assess pupil progress in the skill area of the regular curriculum and are not entirely applicable for assessing pupil performance based on unit instruction. Many formal assessment instruments are too global and do not provide teachers with the specific information they need relative to planning teaching strategies. These problems dictate the need for designing evaluation procedures as part of each unit.

When teachers commit themselves to individualizing instruction to pupil needs, they become dependent on feedback on the child's performance. To make accurate decisions about the level of difficulty at which a skill should be presented as well as the type of activity that will best engage the student, a teacher must look to the student for the needed information. Students also need feedback; they need to know if they have been successful or if they have failed. If they have failed a particular task, they need to know the nature of the failure so that they can utilize this information in approaching the task from a different perspective. Feedback can also be a source of reinforcement. A teacher's lack of evaluation techniques often results in the postponement of meaningful feedback for the student. The reinforcement that might be forthcoming is delayed and consequently is less meaningful for the learner. Evaluation requires that the teacher closely observe the performance of individual students as well as the group. This practice in itself can have a positive influence on teaching effectiveness.

The benefits to be derived by teachers and pupils from the evaluation process should be sufficient to motivate teachers to apply evaluation techniques in the classroom. The current emphasis on accountability serves to accent this need for evaluation. Barro, in discussing the application of accountability to public schools, states that

> although the term "accountability" is too new in the educational vocabulary to have acquired a standard usage, there is little doubt about its general meaning and import for the schools. The basic idea it conveys is that school systems and schools, or, more precisely, the professional educators who operate them, should be held responsible for educational outcomes—for what children learn. If this can be done, it is maintained, favorable changes in professional performance will occur, and these will be reflected in higher academic achievement, improvement in public attitudes, and generally better education results.[1]

Before procedures for assessing accountability are applied, decisions must be made on what is to be assessed and, in turn, what is to be considered accountability evidence. Once this has been accomplished, a determination must be made relative to teacher contribution to the result of accountability. Barro proposes the following principle:

> Each participant in the educational process should be held responsible only for those educational outcomes that he can affect by his actions or decisions and only to the extent that he can affect them.[2]

He goes on to suggest that teachers should not be held accountable for shortcomings in the curriculum. However, if one examines the role of the teacher in the instructional program, it becomes apparent that he or she serves as a quality control agent and assumes considerable responsibility for the structuring of learning experiences as well as for decisions relative to what is taught and the context in which it is taught. Although there are many constraints placed on teachers who have instructional responsibility for exceptional children in the form of insufficient materials and lack of curriculum direction, the necessity of evaluation is no less than for other teachers.

Guba has indicated that "the primary task in evaluation today is the provision of sensible alternatives to the evaluator."[3] The intent of this chapter is to offer teachers alternatives in the evaluation of their unit instruction.

1. Stephen M. Barro, "An Approach to Developing Accountability Measures for the Public Schools," *Phi Delta Kappan* 52:4 (December 1970), p. 190. Reprinted by permission of Phi Delta Kappan, Inc.
2. Ibid.
3. Egon G. Guba, "An Overview of the Evaluation Problem." A paper read at the symposium on "The World of Evaluation Needs Reshaping," AERA Convention, February 1969.

Although the degree of responsibility varies, the breadth of the teacher's responsibility for evaluation ranges from the assessment of pupil performance on specific learning tasks to the contribution of the instructional program to the total curriculum. The emphasis in this chapter will be restricted to assessing instruction via unit teaching. Three aspects of evaluation will be considered: (1) the collective contribution of unit teaching to the instructional program, (2) the effectiveness of individual units, and (3) pupil performance on specific learning tasks.

Evaluation, assessment, and appraisal are often viewed by teachers as synonymous. The meanings given to these terms usually are oriented to measurement, research, or personal judgments. For purposes of clarification, the definition of assessment by Stephens will be considered as a frame of reference for this chapter.

> Assessment, as used here, is a survey of student functioning. Its purpose is to determine those responses and skills which are adequate and those which need to be taught or improved. The term assessment is used to convey a meaning more specific than "testing." It is distinct from diagnosis which means to identify a disease or abnormality after studying its origin.[4]

Responses will be considered within the context of responding to instruction units as well as to specific learning tasks. This definition places responsibility on the teacher for observing behavioral changes in the students. This means that the teacher must also be concerned with environmental characteristics which produce changes in student behavior as well as with the appraisal of changes themselves. Knowledge of the learning environment necessitates an awareness of pupil-pupil interaction, pupil-material interaction, pupil-classroom interaction, and pupil-teacher interaction. Added to this is a sensitivity to the child's school history and family background. It is not enough to merely assess a child's performance on a particular task without also being cognizant of those variables that contribute to success or failure on the respective tasks. This dimension of evaluation obviously broadens the teacher's responsibility. The learning characteristics of a mentally retarded child combined with a history of poor performance make the evaluation process a complicated but necessary task.

Prerequisites to Evaluation

Prior to engaging pupils in evaluation tasks, teachers must decide what they plan to evaluate and why, as well as how, they anticipate using the results. These decisions will facilitate the selection of appropriate techniques. They

4. Thomas M. Stephens, *Directive Teaching of Children With Learning and Behavioral Handicaps* (Columbus: Charles E. Merrill Publishing Company, 1970), p. 63. Used by permission of Charles E. Merrill Publishing Company.

will also minimize the time commitment of students to the evaluation process. The following are examples of reasons why teachers evaluate instruction. They are presented in an objective format merely for illustrative purposes:

To assess competence in a particular skill that is being taught.

To determine baseline behavior as a basis for planning a unit or a particular lesson.

To obtain information that can be used in revising a unit.

To gain meaningful data for purposes of reporting pupil progress.

To substantiate or refute implications reflected in a pupil's school history.

To appraise the effectiveness of selected activities.

To determine the reaction of pupils to instructional materials.

Each reason requires a different evaluation approach. Certainly you can obtain data during the process of evaluating the performance of a pupil on a selected learning task that may also contribute to the assessment of an instructional unit. However, the evaluation of the pupil's performance should be the major target, and the evaluation process should focus on the child's behavior relative to the selected task.

In addition to circumscribing why an evaluation technique will be applied and specifying the target of evaluation, teachers must allow the behavior to occur. If they are evaluating unit effectiveness, then the unit must be taught and the student allowed to participate in the activities that it includes. If the evaluation target is the performance of an individual child on a task, a situation must be structured that allows the child to perform the task. It may take the form of a test item, a structured situation, or merely observation of the child in a real-life situation that requires performance of the tasks. In order to evaluate the pupil's performance, the teacher must decide on a criterion level for successful performance against which to measure performance. The results then become part of a pool of information on individual pupils and on pupils as a group. The teacher draws on this information when planning the child's program, when making decisions on curriculum content, and when planning units.

In the remainder of this chapter we will discuss evaluation procedures and ways in which the evaluation results can be used in the improvement of classroom instruction through unit teaching.

Evaluating Pupil Performance on Selected Tasks

Individualization of instruction necessitates that teachers be knowledgeable of pupil capabilities and the manner in which they respond to learning tasks. If a teacher approaches teaching with a commitment to enhancing the growth and development of each child, he or she finds that the child is not only the target of teaching, but also the primary resource in determining the best approach. The cues to the learners' needs are reflected in behavior. Their behavior takes many forms. It may be in the realm of performance on structured tasks, in their response to the classroom environment and to others around them, or it may be in the form of nonverbal cues. However, children do express their needs in a variety of forms. The degree to which these expressions communicate is dependent on the awareness of teachers and their capabilities to interpret the implications of observed behavior.

Closely related to the tasks inherent in interpreting behavior is the skill of structuring situations that allow teachers to obtain information on behavior related to specific tasks. This requires an evaluation-type set. Teachers need to be oriented towards assessing student performance. It is not enough to know that Johnny reads at the fourth-grade level or that he has difficulty with the process of division. Teachers must pursue a more analytical approach to evaluation.

The selection of evaluation techniques should be an integral aspect of the planning process teachers engage in when developing their instructional program. Until decisions have been made regarding what is to be taught, there is no basis for evaluation of pupil progress. However, once teachers have decided what is to be taught, they are in a position to develop alternative procedures for assessing pupil performance in the respective area of instruction. Although the evaluation process is dependent on a curricular frame of reference, the curriculum should not be viewed as independent of evaluation. Unless teachers assess pupil performance, they do not know to what extent their instructional program is successful in teaching the curriculum. Without the feedback derived from evaluating pupil performance on specific tasks, they are at a disadvantage in attempting to individualize instruction.

Generally speaking, teachers have two major resources available to them as they integrate evaluation techniques into their instructional program. These include formal and informal procedures. The first is primarily in the form of standardized instruments such as achievement tests, developmental tests, aptitude tests, etc. The latter tests involve evaluation techniques that the teacher can become skilled at devising and administering.

The formal procedures are a resource accessible to most teachers. To use these instruments, the teacher needs to be familiar with their purpose, when they can be effectively used, and what can be gained through their use. For informal techniques to materialize as a resource, the teacher must invest in acquiring assessment skill through informal techniques as well as a knowledge of the various types of informal techniques which can be applied to assessing the behavior he or she is attempting to influence through the instructional program. The advantage of the latter is that once the skill is developed, the teacher has a resource that is always accessible. The informal approach has an added advantage in that the teacher is not bound by predetermined strategies and can be much more specific in assessing pupil performance relative to his or her own instructional program.

Formal evaluation procedures tend to be normative in nature while informal procedures have more of a criterion-reference base. Since normative and criterion measures yield different kinds of information, both will be discussed relative to their application in assessing pupil performance within the context of classroom instruction. Popham and Husek define criterion-referenced and norm-referenced measures as follows:

> Criterion-referenced measures are those which are used to ascertain an individual's status with respect to some criterion, i.e., performance standard. It is because the individual is compared with some established criterion, rather than other individuals, that these measures are described as criterion referenced. The meaningfulness of an individual score is not dependent on comparison to others.
>
> Norm-referenced measures are those which are used to ascertain an individual's performance in relationship to the performance of other individuals on the same measuring device. The meaningfulness of the individual score emerges from the comparison. It is because the individual is compared with some normative group that such measures are described as norm referenced. Most standardized tests of achievement or intellectual ability can be classified as norm-referenced measures.[5]

When a teacher applies a criterion-reference approach in assessing pupil progress, a child's performance is compared only to the level of performance you as a teacher establish as a criterion of success. For example, if your objective is to teach a child to identify coins by indicating their value, you can show him or her a quarter, penny, dime, and nickel and ask the student to label the coins and tell you their value. The criteria for success might be all correct or three out of four correct. The child's performance is being assessed in terms of your criterion. Success or failure is not dependent on how well classmates perform on the item. You obtain information on how well he or she performs the task as well as on how he or she approaches the task and responds to having succeeded or failed. If necessary, you can collect normative-type information by administering the same item to other children. However, normative information in most situations is not necessary if your major goal is to provide experience which allows a child to progress at his or her own rate. What is needed is information on how the student approaches performing a task as a basis for your structuring subsequent tasks. Criterion-ref-

5. W. James Popham and T. R. Husek, "Implications of Criterion-Referenced Measurement," *Journal of Educational Measurement*, Spring 1969, p. 1-9. Used by permission of the publisher.

erence measures in the form of informal techniques provide the needed information.

Normative-type measurement instruments such as achievement tests certainly contribute information which is helpful in planning instructional programs. However, the criterion-reference approach is more appropriate for assessing the results of unit teaching. There are several reasons for this. First of all, the content covered through unit teaching is not uniform to the extent that standardized achievement tests sufficiently sample what is taught through units as differentiated from the total instructional program. Normative measures are generally designed to be global in nature and are not as usable in assessing performance on specific skills. The major advantage of the criterion-reference approach is that it focuses the teacher's attention on the child and the task rather than the child, several tasks, and peers.

Teacher Preparation for Assessing Pupil Performance

Evaluation of pupil performance should be a conscious effort on the part of teachers. It should be carried out in accordance with prescribed purposes. The evaluation tasks in which students are engaged should reflect an awareness of their capabilities and their emotional response to having their skills appraised. To accommodate these conditions requires that teachers examine their own motives for evaluation. Questions such as the following must be answered.

> Are you truly interested in gathering data as a reference for making decisions on the respective pupil's instructional program or are you more interested in obtaining a grade for each student?
>
> Do you plan to make maximum use of the results in terms of improving your overall instructional program? For example, when you find that several students perform unsuccessfully on a variety of tasks are you prepared to re-examine your teaching style and the content of your units?
>
> How do you view feedback to students regarding their performance? Should they receive immediate feedback?
>
> Are you willing to make the investment required to specify instructional objectives to the degree that the performance to be evaluated is explicitly stated?

For the most part these questions fall into the realm of the evaluation set that teachers need as a frame of reference. If teachers feel strongly that they need to measure their own effectiveness, and if they perceive the students as capable of providing information on their own needs as well as demonstrating their competencies, then the teachers have already made considerable progress toward establishing an evaluation program. The remaining requirement is for them to develop evaluation skills.

Basic to the process of evaluation is the specification of what is to be evaluated. The stating of instructional objectives in behavioral terms is discussed in Chapter 7. The reader is encouraged to review this chapter. A well-written instructional objective should include a description of:

1. the desired behavior in terms of the task to be performed
2. the condition under which the behavior will occur
3. what you will accept as successful performance

It should be noted that the above requirements for a good objective are designed to encourage specificity, but they should not be taken literally to the extent that the process of writing objectives becomes an end in itself. Some teachers lose sight of the purpose of writing objectives and become wrapped up in the task of wording them. The more precise you can make the objectives, the easier will be the task of evaluating pupil performance. *However, if a teacher devotes a disproportionate amount of time to writing objectives, the amount of time devoted to evaluation is reduced. The important factor is that teachers attempt to define what they want to measure, formulate an expectancy level for the pupil, and structure a situation that allows the desired performance to occur.*

The expectancy or criterion level may vary with each child. As the teacher gains experience in assessing the behavior of particular children, fewer errors should occur relative to establishing inappropriate criterion levels. While teachers should be able to evaluate most of what they teach, given sufficient time and opportunity, it is not reasonable to expect this to occur. They will find it necessary to evaluate a sample of representative behaviors. It is important, however, that they establish a sequential pattern for the behaviors they select to evaluate. For example, if they are carrying out a plan of pacing pupils through instructional tasks, it is important to evaluate pupil performance at varying points in the sequence of skills so that a determination can be made on whether or not the pupil possesses the necessary prerequisite skills to proceed with subsequent tasks.

As teachers, we need to be reminded that we must share some of the responsibility whenever a child fails at a task we have structured. This is true regardless of the child's intellectual ability. If we have examined the task to determine what skills are required to perform it and if we know the child's capabilities, we can alter the task or the criterion level to increase the child's chances of success. This is not to say that children should be asked only to perform tasks at which they can succeed. The point is that if you are asking children to perform a task far below or above their ability, you learn nothing about them and they gain little in the form of feedback. You also run the risk of discouraging them or, in the case of an exceedingly easy task, you may be misleading them in terms of what they think you expect.

Examples of Informal Evaluation Techniques

When informal evaluation techniques are applied within the context of criterion-reference evaluation, teachers use their judgment in establishing the difficulty of the item. The difficulty level is determined by the criterion set for successful performance. Since this may vary for each child, we find a situation in which a particular evaluation technique can be used in assessing the performance of students with varying abilities merely by raising or lowering the criterion set for success on the task. Consequently, the examples to be presented are not categorized by age or ability levels. Rather, samples of informal evaluation techniques are listed under general topical headings without regard to ability or age levels.

Teachers will find that with minor modifications the techniques are applicable for a wide range of ability levels. Although the examples offered are in the areas of communication skills, arithmetic, and social competencies, the techniques are not mutually exclusive. Some techniques suggested for assessing arithmetic skills can be applied in assessing communication skills. The suggestions are also not exhaustive but are intended to provide assistance to teachers in developing a criterion-reference orientation to evaluation, particularly in assessing the effectiveness of unit teaching.

Communication Skills

LISTENING

Tell or read a story and then ask specific questions regarding the sequence of events and major characters.

Ask a student to summarize a lesson by identifying the main theme of the lesson. You might also ask the student to review previous lessons on the same topic.

Give directions to a child that require two, three, four, or more tasks to be completed. For example, "Pick up the red book on my desk and put it on the shelf where we keep the dictionaries."

Present an audio tape of sounds routinely heard in the home and have the students identify them.

Record a group discussion conducted by students and have pupils identify the speakers. You could also ask them to respond to what was being discussed.

Play a record and have the students respond to the rhythm of the music.

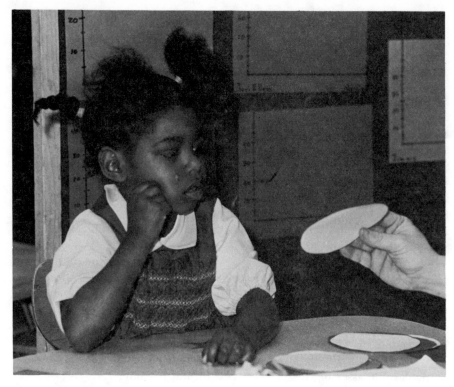

Evaluation may involve individually administered informal tasks.

Read aloud words having similar beginnings and/or endings and have pupils record those that sound alike.

Have students "brainstorm" the sounds they hear on the way to school.

Read aloud sentences and have students identify those that are incorrect. They can also be asked to restate them correctly.

Record radio and TV commercials and ask students to identify the kind of store that would be likely to sell the product—a grocery, drug, or clothing store.

Read the beginning of a story and have the students complete it. The amount of information from the story provided for the students can be varied.

Give the students three categories such as vegetable, fruit, and meat. Then verbally present them with a list that can be sorted into these three categories.

VISUAL

Using a projection device such as an overhead, slide, or opaque projector, project a picture on the screen and have students describe what they see. Specific questions regarding inference can be posed.

Present students with a series of illustrations on cards. Ask them to place the cards in an order that makes a story.

Read a story aloud and ask students to select from a series of pictures those that best illustrate the story.

Present in work sheet form a series of pictures and related words. Have pupils match the words with the appropriate labels.

Use pantomime as a means for presenting nonverbal cues. Ask pupils to indicate what you are attempting to tell them through your gestures and facial expressions.

Project a picture on a screen for a specified period of time and then ask the pupils to reproduce it from memory.

Present a sequential series of pictures illustrating a situation and ask pupils to anticipate what will occur following the last picture.

Give pupils a stack of word cards randomly ordered and have them place the cards in alphabetical order.

Have students locate specific names in the phone book.

Provide the students with a list of familiar words and have them identify those correctly spelled.

VERBAL EXPRESSION

Identify a task and have a student describe verbally how the task should be performed.

Have a child demonstrate proper use of the telephone.

Direct specific questions to students and observe their speech fluency.

Use dramatic play to create situations that require verbal expressions. Be alert for relevance of comments and use of language.

Give children a topic such as "going shopping" and have them state verbally as many things as they can think of that they might shop for during the trip.

Have a child give directions to another on the shortest route to his or her home from school.

Ask a pupil to describe a recent television program.

Use puppets as a means of encouraging verbal expression. Specific instructions can be given to generate the kind of expression you want to assess.

Ask pupils to imitate sounds.

Arithmetic Skills

Have students select a specified number of objects from a large group of objects.

Place several sticks of varying lengths on a desk and have students select the largest, shortest, and so forth.

Present a student with a container and ask him or her to estimate how many cups of water it will hold. Have the child complete the task and determine to what degree the estimate was larger or smaller than what the solution required.

Give a student a story problem that requires him or her to select the appropriate process and derive the answer. This type of problem can be varied to require the student to overlook irrelevant information.

A wide variety of performance tasks can be developed using money. These can include identification and computational tasks as well as tasks requiring the student to anticipate the amount required for a particular expenditure.

Provide pupils with a map and ask them to calculate the distance between two points. The difficulty of the maps can vary from a simplified teacher-made map to a highway map.

Use puzzles as a means of requiring students to discriminate shapes and sizes.

Structure tasks that require pupils to count objects and record the appropriate numerals.

Assign pupils the task of measuring the dimensions of their desks. The proper use of a ruler as well as the accuracy of their measurements can be determined.

Time-telling experiences can be used to assess accuracy. They can also be used to assess time estimation. Students can be asked to estimate how long they think it will take them to perform a particular task, such as going to the office and returning.

Problems using newspaper ads can be developed to assess their understanding of the "best buy." The same exercise can be used to evaluate their understanding of value.

Specific problems involving the reading of a thermometer can be designed to evaluate their ability to read the thermometer, interpret the significance of temperature, and use computational skills.

Computational items involving use of multiplication, addition, subtraction, and/or division skills can be devised and presented individually or collectively in test form. This procedure is more meaningful for the teacher if he or she can observe the pupils' performance and attempt to identify systematic errors.

Create situations that require pupils to utilize arithmetic terms, such as add, larger than, take away, divide, and so forth.

Social Competencies

Develop a brief checklist to assess behavior while on a field trip. For example, did the pupils observe good safety practices or were they courteous to others?

Simulation activities requiring individuals to portray different roles can be used to assess the understanding of behavior appropriate for given situations.

Committee assignments can be used to evaluate the ability of pupils to work together.

Provide verbal description or illustration of appropriate and inappropriate behavior. Pupils can be asked to discriminate between behaviors.

Structure situations that call for specific kinds of behavior and observe the performance of individuals. For example, have a pupil ask for information from another teacher, make an introduction, or lead a group activity.

Assess the frequency with which a child displays a disruptive behavior. Talk with the child about behavior and help the child monitor his or her own efforts in altering the behavior.

Use films involving children at their peer level engaging in social activities. Have the students analyze what is taking place in the film and why.

Have adults purposely engage students in conversation. Obtain feedback from the adult and the student regarding the interaction.

Have students write a script for a play. Ask them questions about the roles they develop for different characters. As the play is cast and presented, observe the interpretation given to the various roles.

OBSERVATION SKILLS

Skill in observation is important to the process of employing informal evaluation techniques. All the evaluation activities previously discussed require the teacher to observe the behavior of pupils and to make inferences from what is observed. If the observation is focused on the child performing a particular task, the job of drawing an inference is enhanced by the circumscribed nature of the task and the anticipated type of response. However, throughout the school day, pupils are performing in less structured situations. They respond to each other in the process of preparing for lunch, they react to assignments, they exhibit a wide array of behaviors that may or may not be observed by the teacher. If a teacher happens to notice a child engaged in an activity, the teacher may or may not make a mental note of what the child is doing. On the other hand, a teacher may watch a child fail at what appears to be a routine activity and infer that the child is unable to perform the task. Whether teachers are observing routine behavior or employing a specific evaluation technique, they must keep in mind that children vary in their behavior. They may be observing the child at a low ebb. For this reason, it is important that teachers not make judgments on a single observation. They should obtain behavior samples over a period of time and under different circumstances. As they observe the child, attention should be given to the surroundings in which the child is performing the activity as well as to preceding events. The child's inability to focus attention on the experience chart might be due to anticipation of the free play activity during recess fifteen minutes hence. Nonresponse to peers during the first hour might be caused by lack of breakfast or the fact that the child encountered a problem on the bus while en route to school.

The variance among and within pupils, coupled with the influence of environmental conditions on the behavior of individuals, complicates the process of evaluation. It also serves to accentuate the necessity of structuring the procedures for gathering evaluation data. Without information on the behavior of individual pupils, the teacher is ill prepared for the task of individualizing instruction.

Although attention has been given to assessing the effectiveness of individual units and their collective influence on the curriculum, the skills required to evaluate pupil performance are applicable regardless of what aspect of the curriculum is being evaluated. The organization of this chapter was designed to illustrate techniques for evaluating pupil performance and to relate these techniques to the process of evaluation within the framework of unit teaching.

Evaluating the Composite Effects of Unit Teaching

The systematic approach for writing units and for developing a year's plan of work suggested in other chapters is evaluation-oriented. Each step requires teachers to make decisions regarding the appropriateness of content as well as the effectiveness of the activities they plan to employ. If they follow these steps, the opportunity for error through the individual units should be greatly reduced. Having completed instruction on the units included in the year's plan of work, the teacher should assess the collective effectiveness of the several individual units taught, in order to determine their contributions to the broader class curriculum goals. Teachers need to determine whether or not they accomplished through unit teaching those curriculum objectives allocated to unit teaching in planning the yearly instructional program. This is not to suggest that teachers ignore opportunities for daily evaluation of pupil performance or avoid evaluating the effects of individual units. Suggestions for evaluating pupil performance are directly applicable to evaluating instruction units. This section is intended to offer guidelines for an end-of-the-year evaluation of the overall effectiveness of the unit teaching program.

Although evaluation of the composite effects of unit teaching cannot be completed until the end of the school year, evaluation should be an ongoing process that requires the teacher to look routinely at pupil performance in reference to the content and skills being taught. A variety of techniques can be structured by teachers for this type of evaluation. Two alternatives will be illustrated. One focuses specifically on unit teaching and does not consider those curriculum aspects covered through other instruction methods. The second is a more comprehensive approach to evaluating the year's instructional program and includes provisions for assessing the total instructional program. The advantages of the former approach is that the teacher can develop an evaluation instrument directly from the work completed during the process of writing behavioral objectives for individual unit lessons. The more comprehensive approach requires that the teacher specify in advance the specific content, concepts, and skills to be included in the overall instructional program throughout the year regardless of the method that may be employed for teaching them. This approach, however, does have the advantage of offering the teacher more detailed information regarding the instructional program and the progress of individual children. It does not separate unit teaching from the other methods employed.

The goal of both approaches is to provide the teacher with objective data regarding the progress of individual children, along with an assessment of the collective class accomplishments during the year. This information can be used as a basis for planning subsequent instructional programs for the same children or for children with similar learning characteristics. The information can also be recorded in a form usable by other teachers who will have the same children in class at other times.

Unit Evaluation Inventory Approach

This approach involves the development of an inventory that includes representative instructional objectives from the units taught during the school year. In other words, it is not necessary to include all instructional objectives. A sample of objectives that reflect the content covered will be sufficient for this type of evaluation. The inventory can be easily constructed by reviewing the lesson plans prepared for each unit during the year and listing the behaviorally stated instructional objectives according to the core areas, namely, arithmetic, social competencies, communication skills, health, safety, and vocational skills. This requires the teacher to make decisions about which core area the task called for in the objective represents. Having done this for each unit, the teacher has a check on the orientation of individual units by core area and can determine the degree of emphasis given to each core area through individual units. The check can also be applied to the total group of units taught during the year. These findings can be compared with the results of the preliminary steps for each unit and the year's plan of work discussed in Chapters 6 and 9.

The major difference, beside the emphasis on unit teaching, between this approach and the more comprehensive approach is that this one cannot be organized into final form until all the units have been developed. As a result, the teacher must develop a record-keeping system which later can be modified into an evaluation form.

If fifteen to twenty units are taught during the school year, the number of instructional objectives that could be recorded and applied to each child will be sizable. For this reason, teachers should select objectives representative of each unit rather than include all the instructional objectives developed through the lesson plans. Since the goal is to evaluate the composite contribution of unit teaching, it is not essential that each objective be included. The following steps are suggested for employing this approach.

1. The performance of each pupil should be evaluated on the individual instructional objectives included in the various lesson plans. As teachers rarely develop all the units they plan to teach during the year in advance, it will be necessary that the performance of each child relative to the respective instructional objectives be recorded on the lesson plans, a note card, or in some other format. This information can later be transferred to the evaluation form.

2. Select those instructional objectives you wish to include in the evaluation inventory. As previously mentioned, all instructional objectives can be included; or if this represents too large a number, then a decision must be made on which instructional objectives are most representative of the units that have been taught.

3. Transfer the instructional objectives to a Unit Evaluation Inventory format (see Figure 18). The objectives can be stated in complete or abbreviated form. The important factor is that the statement of the objectives communicate the task for which the pupil's performance was evaluated.

4. Record the pupil's performance on the evaluation form.

The following two examples are suggested formats for recording the evaluation data. The examples are not inclusive of a year's plan of work in unit teaching. However, sufficient information is provided to illustrate the feasibility of this particular approach. The first example is designed for use with individual pupils, whereas the second applies to a class or a group of students.

Individual Form

This form is self-explanatory. Teachers identify the core areas and list the instructional objectives which have been previously selected. They then record their assessment of the pupil's performance relative to each objective. If they have been careful to record the pupil's performance at the time of the learning experience, they merely transfer the evaluation data. If they have not routinely evaluated each pupil's progress, then it is necessary to structure situations that will allow them to assess performance in those areas specified in the instructional objectives. The column labeled "Unit Source" can be used to identify the unit from which the instructional objective was selected. This necessitates a number being assigned to each unit. The value of this feature is that it helps you gain a perspective on the contribution of individual units to the total unit teaching program.

Comments relevant to the child's performance on specific tasks, for example, interpersonal relations or manner of participation, can be recorded. Care should be taken to record only those comments that will be of assistance to you in revising your units for future students or helpful to teachers who will have the particular student in class the following year. The purpose of the comment section is to add flexibility to the format and to extend its use in the evaluation process.

Figures 18, 19, 20, 21, 22 and 23 illustrate the Individual Form.

Core Area: Arithmetic* Name: Jane		Demonstrates Competence	Does Not Demonstrate Competence	Comment
Unit Source	Instructional Objectives			
3	Given the wage per hour and number of hours to be worked per week is able to estimate income.			
3	Is able to set up a budget that takes into account income and necessary expenditures.			
3	Is able to fill out the necessary forms for establishing a checking account.			
3	Is able to write a check correctly and fill out the check stub accurately.			
1	Given a road map, can determine distance between major cities.			
1	Can identify map symbols and explain their meaning.			
1	Can determine distance between cities on a map and estimate the travel time by car.			
6	Given sales price and regular price on an item, can calculate amount saved.			
6	Is able to compute the sales tax on items costing up to $1,000.00.			
6	Can compute the money to be saved by buying items in quantity.			
8	Is able to accurately change 25%, 50%, and 75% to decimals.			

*Selected from units taught at the junior high level.

Figure 18.   Unit Evaluation Inventory (Individual Form)

Core Area: Communication Skills* Name: Betty		DEMONSTRATES COMPETENCE	DOES NOT DEMONSTRATE COMPETENCE	
UNIT SOURCE	INSTRUCTIONAL OBJECTIVES			COMMENT
2	Is able to write own name from memory in manuscript.			
4	Is able to differentiate between color words and number words; for example, red, two, blue, three, six, white, and black.			
8	Can correctly copy in cursive name and street name from manuscript form.			
9	In listening to words read aloud, can differentiate between rhyming and non-rhyming words.			
8	Is able to correctly demonstrate the use of a dial telephone.			
8	Given a name, can locate the name in the telephone book.			
8	Given a list of ten names, can place them in alphabetical order according to last name.			
10	Given a topic, is able to write complete sentences of at least five words in length.			
11	Given a work sheet with pictures of apples, oranges, bananas, and grapes, is able to write the appropriate name for each in recognizable form.			

*Selected from units for children in the 6-10 age level.

Figure 19. Unit Evaluation Inventory (Individual Form)

Core Area: Social Competencies* Name: Ann		Demonstrates Competence	Does Not Demonstrate Competence	
Unit Source	Instructional Objectives			Comment
1	Is able to stand in line without bothering other children.			
1	Given a description of behavior on the bus, is able to indicate whether it is appropriate or not.			
1	Uses terms such as "please," "thank you," and "excuse me" at appropriate times.			
2	When asked to participate in show and tell, does not share information about the family which is private.			
2	Shares toys with classmates when there are insufficient toys for the group.			
4	Voluntarily contributes to class discussion when the topic is familiar.			
5	When asked to introduce a friend does so in an appropriate manner.			
7	When directed to ask a question of two people engaged in a conversation, waits for an opportunity to say "excuse me" and to pose the question.			
8	When using the telephone, keeps conversation short.			
10	Is able to take correction without complaining or offering an alibi.			
12	Given a set of verbal instructions on a task, is able to communicate them correctly to a small group.			

*Selected from units taught to a group of 6-10 year olds.

Figure 20.   Unit Evaluation Inventory (Individual Form)

Core Area: Safety*		Demonstrates Competence	Does Not Demonstrate Competence	
Name: Joe				
UNIT SOURCE	INSTRUCTIONAL OBJECTIVES			COMMENT
6	Is able to demonstrate the safe use of a saber saw.			
6	When asked to give a knife to another person, hands it to them with the handle first.			
7	Given an illustration of an intersection, can explain the proper way to make a left-hand turn.			
7	Is able to demonstrate the hand signals for stop, left turn			
7	When parking a car on a downhill slope, turns wheels and right turn.			
	toward the curb.			
5	Fastens seat belt prior to starting the engine of a car.			
4	Is able to explain why a person should not turn on a light switch while standing in water.			
4	Given three extension cords with one in need of repair, can identify the one which is unsafe.			
4	Can demonstrate the correct use of a fire extinguisher.			
5	Can explain the correct procedure for putting out an electrical fire in the kitchen.			

*Selected from units taught at the secondary level.

Figure 21. Unit Evaluation Inventory (Individual Form)

Core Area: Health* Name: Johnny		DEMONSTRATES COMPETENCE	DOES NOT DEMONSTRATE COMPETENCE	
UNIT SOURCE	INSTRUCTIONAL OBJECTIVES			COMMENT
1	Can demonstrate the proper procedure for brushing teeth.			
2	Given a menu for breakfast, lunch, and dinner, can identify which one is typically a breakfast menu.			
2	Able to explain why some foods must be refrigerated.			
3	Washes hands after using the rest room.			
4	Wears warm clothing when playing outside during cold weather.			
5	Can explain why he or she should stay home when ill.			
5	Does not put objects such as pencils, crayons, and so on in mouth.			
7	Can explain why meat should be cooked before being eaten.			
7	Given several heads of lettuce, some of which are old, can identify which are fresh.			
7	Is able to distinguish between fresh milk and milk that is sour.			

*Selected from units taught to a class of 6-10 year olds.

Figure 22. Unit Evaluation Inventory (Individual Form)

Core Area: Vocational Skills*		Demonstrates Competence	Does Not Demonstrate Competence	
Name: Betty				
Unit Source	**Instructional Objectives**			**Comment**
1	Is able to identify a source of community help in locating a job, that is, state employment agency, private agencies, and vocational rehabilitation office.			
2	Is able to locate the employment office within a local industry.			
2	Can demonstrate an appropriate procedure for inquiring about job opportunities at a local industry.			
2	Is able to fill out a job application form accurately.			
3	Can explain why it is important to be on time every day at a job.			
3	Has obtained a social security number and keeps it accessible.			
4	Is able to identify jobs that are generally within his or her ability.			
5	Given an example of a job some distance from home, is able to decide a feasible plan for getting to and from work.			
8	Able to demonstrate the use of a time clock.			

*Selected from units taught at the secondary level.

Figure 23. Unit Evaluation Inventory (Individual Form)

Group Form

An alternate format for the Unit Evaluation Inventory can be designed to accommodate the recording of group data, as shown in Figure 24. It has the advantage of reducing the number of forms the teacher must contend with, but it also eliminates the opportunity for recording comments on individual

Core Area: ___Arithmetic___*

Ellen Smith's Class

UNIT SOURCE	INSTRUCTIONAL OBJECTIVES	JOHN 1 2 3	JOE 1 2 3	MARY 1 2 3	SARA 1 2 3	TOM 1 2 3	AUSTIN 1 2 3	DICK 1 2 3	BILL 1 2 3	ANN 1 2 3	JUDY 1 2 3
1	Is able to demonstrate the use of cardinal numbers from one to ten.										
1	Is able to demonstrate an understanding of terms such as up and down, on and under, front and back, etc.										
2	Given a collection of 25 objects, can group them into five equal groups.										
4	Given a group of ten objects and a group of eight objects, is able to identify the larger group.										
6	Is able to rearrange objects on a flannel board into sets and indicate orally the numbers represented.										
7	Given a quarter, dime, and nickel, is able to label them and indicate their value.										

*Selected from units taught to children at 6-10 age level.

1 = Demonstrates competence
2 = Does not demonstrate competence

Figure 24. Unit Evaluation Inventory (Group Form)

students. It has the additional advantage of providing an overview of the group's progress as well as an assessment of an individual's performance.

Because the listing of instructional objectives is the same as for individual forms, only one example is included. However, a teacher who chooses to use the group form rather than the individual form would need to develop an inventory for each core area.

Comprehensive Skill Inventory Approach

In contrast to the Unit Evaluation Inventory, this inventory can be developed prior to the beginning of the school year. The basic feature of this approach is that it requires teachers to specify the skills and concepts they anticipate teaching during the school year. *The specification process discussed in Chapter 8 is compatible with this approach.* Many teachers find that this approach works best in the areas of arithmetic, reading, and language arts. However, it can be modified to accommodate subject matter such as social and vocational skills as well as motor skills. Since the skills are identified before being taught, they can be placed in sequential order within the form. This facilitates assessment and allows the teacher to illustrate graphically the progress of individual pupils as well as of the class as a group. It also enhances teacher evaluation of pupil performances as a routine daily practice.

While the Unit Evaluation Inventory approach focused specifically on unit teaching, this approach is designed to assist the teacher in assessing the overall impact of the instructional program. The emphasis is on the acquisition of skills and knowledge of pupils individually and collectively. Specific attention is given to a broad range of skills and knowledge, whether they were taught through unit teaching or other methods. Teachers electing to use this approach will find that the inventory can evolve from the planning they do prior to the opening of the school year. As decisions are made regarding what is to be taught and the manner in which the instruction will be organized, skills, concepts, and levels of understanding can be selected as the basis for evaluation.

The basic feature of the Comprehensive Skills Inventory approach is that it is representative of the total instructional program. This means that the inventory should accurately reflect what was or, if it is in the planning stage, what will be taught during the year. Obviously, the abilities of children in most classes vary considerably; thus, the inventory should be sufficiently comprehensive to accommodate the more able student as well as those who are less capable.

The development of a Comprehensive Skill Inventory involves many of the same tasks inherent in curriculum development. The process requires a knowledge of pupil needs and an awareness of their performance levels. The selected skills must parallel the curriculum, although the inventory itself need not be organized according to instructional patterns such as unit teaching, academic areas, social activities, or motor skills. The emphasis is on skill and content areas rather than teaching methodologies. Again there is nothing sacred about the format to be discussed, and teachers are encouraged to experiment with formats and procedures that best fit their personal teaching styles.

Many teachers find that even though they are committing a major portion of the school day to unit teaching, the evaluation of pupil progress is best approached from a subject frame of reference. This facilities evaluation of the total program inclusive of unit teaching and acknowledges the integrations of academic skills into the unit teaching aspects of the program.

As is true in any evaluation of pupil progress, the basic skills of arithmetic, reading, and language arts are more easily identified. They also lend themselves more readily to the establishment of evaluation criteria than do areas that are social in nature. If teachers are working from a prescribed curriculum or if they plan the instructional program in reasonable detail, the task of specifying evaluation criteria for the curriculum content is greatly reduced. The aim is to develop an inventory that is representative of the curriculum and includes items of sufficient specificity to yield evaluation information meaningful to the teacher regarding the performance of individual pupils and the class as a group.

For purposes of illustration, sample inventories have been developed for the areas of arithmetic, reading, and language arts. (See Figures 25, 26, and 27.) Inventories could also be developed for other areas, such as social competencies, science, and motor skills. The suggested format is very similar to the format of the Unit Evaluation Inventory. The major difference is the comprehensiveness of the skills, content, and concepts covered. Teachers wishing to make an account of what they feel was learned as a result of unit teaching or other instruction methods can include a column for noting the differentiation. Sample inventories for recording evaluation data on an individual and a group basis are included. Because of the similarities between the two forms, only one sample is included for the group procedure. (See Figure 28.)

Rather than use behaviorally stated instructional objectives to identify the selected curriculum content in the inventory, an abbreviated outline form has been used. This is done because teachers using this approach will most likely be working from a curriculum guide or will not have had an opportunity to develop the content into a lesson format inclusive of instructional objectives.

As with the Unit Evaluation Inventory, information acquired through the use of this procedure can be used to evaluate the contribution of unit teaching to the instructional program, to plan prescriptive teaching programs for individual pupils, as a basis for recording pupil progress, as a means for determining the need for curriculum revision, and as a source of information in providing feedback to students. It has the added advantage of being useful as a reference in determining the appropriate placement of children recommended for assignment to special classes. The child's performance of the skills included in the inventory can be measured and a decision made as to which class approximates his or her ability level. This, of course, would necessitate use of informal evaluation techniques plus a review of the child's previous school performance.

If all special class teachers in the school system utilize this approach, it can have a positive effect on the curriculum. Overlap and omissions become evident when comparisons are made among inventories for different classes. It is also possible to develop a single inventory of the total instructional program with teachers at various levels being concerned only with those skills appropriate to their respective classes. Since the skills and content can be ordered sequentially, the composite inventory can be subdivided according to the level of classes in the program. The difficult task is the initial development of the inventory. This, however, need only be done once and revised annually as the curriculum changes and as ability ranges shift in different classes.

Reporting Pupil Progress

Having obtained evaluation-type data on the performance of individual pupils and on the general effectiveness of units taught, the teacher must make maximum use of the information acquired. Throughout this chapter, reference has been made to the use of evaluation data in the improvement of instruction and in curriculum development. Emphasis has also been given to the importance of providing immediate feedback to students. However, little mention has been made of the contribution of evaluation in reporting pupil progress to parents.

The periodic reporting of pupil progress to parents is a long established practice in our educational system. For the most part, it has taken the form of report cards, home visits, or parent-teacher conferences held within the confines of the school. The nature of the information voluntarily provided to parents by teachers during conferences varies considerably. The report card, however, has served to standardize, within school districts at least, the topics on which progress is reported to parents. In the case of special classes for the mentally retarded, there has been a tendency to devise report cards that differ from the form used in regular classes or to use the same format but omit items deemed inappropriate. Teachers of the mentally retarded, faced with the task of reporting the status of pupils to parents, frequently find they lack sufficient evidence of progress on which to report. Or they find that the data they do have tends to focus on what the child cannot do rather than on capabilities.

	DEMONSTRATES COMPETENCE	DOES NOT DEMONSTRATE COMPETENCE	UNIT INSTRUCTION	OTHER METHODS	

Name:_____

Area: __Language Arts*__

Level: __6-10 C.A.__

	RATING	SOURCE	COMMENT
Verbal expression			
Expresses self clearly			
Uses complete sentences			
Spontaneously participates in discussion			
Expresses ideas in sequence			
Can verbally describe events			
Writing			
Knows purpose for writing			
Reads manuscript writing			
Writes capital and lowercase letters legibly			
Writes a simple sentence			
Writes short stories			
Records in written form words from dictionary			
Shows interest in cursive writing			
Writes labels for pictures and things			
Writes own name and address from memory			
Punctuation			
Uses period and question mark correctly			
Can determine the need for a paragraph			
Capitalizes appropriate words			
Uses common abbreviations, e.g., Mr., Mrs., St., and states			
Listening			
Identifies common sounds			
Identifies rhyming words			
Can differentiate pitch			
Follows directions			
Attends to the speaker			
Spelling			
Spells personal words like name, community, days of week, etc.			
Spells most words needed for writing			
Identifies misspelled words at appropriate reading level			

*This inventory is by no means inclusive.

Figure 25. Comprehensive Skills Inventory (Individual Form)

Name: _____

Area: Reading*

Level: 6-10 C.A.

	DEMONSTRATES COMPETENCE	DOES NOT DEMONSTRATE COMPETENCE	UNIT INSTRUCTION	OTHER METHODS	
	RATING		SOURCE		COMMENT
Pre-reading					
Can sequence ideas					
Shows interest in pictures					
Describes pictures					
Listens attentively					
Imitates actions of teacher					
Shows an interest in reading					
Visual discrimination					
Matches pictures with objects					
Performs puzzles using geometric shapes					
Recognizes letters					
Adequate sight vocabulary					
Auditory discrimination					
Basic phonic skills					
Functional reading					
Reads crucial vocabulary words					
Reads labels					
Reads simple charts					
Contributes to building experience charts					
Has left-to-right orientation					
Knows basic word attack skills					

*This inventory is by no means inclusive.

Figure 26. Comprehensive Skills Inventory (Individual Form)

	Demonstrates Competence	Does Not Demonstrate Competence	Unit Instruction	Other Methods	
Name: _____ Area: Arithmetic* Level: 6-10 C.A.					
	RATING	SOURCE			COMMENT

I. Size and amount (Can differentiate between the following terms when given concrete objects to manipulate)
    A. large–small
    B. big–little
    C. long–short
    D. tall–short
    E. wide–narrow
    F. empty–full
    G. heavy–light

II. Number skills
    A. Numbers one to ten
        1. Counts one to ten by rote
        2. Applies understanding of rote counting–one, two, three . . . ten
        3. Writes numerals one to ten
        4. Recognizes words "one" to "ten"
    B. Can identify plus and minus signs
        1. Identifies and understands meaning of + and — signs
        2. Can read words "plus," "minus," "add," "subtract"

*This inventory is by no means inclusive.

Figure 27. Comprehensive Skills Inventory (Individual Form)

Skill area: __Reading__

		SKILL	ANN 1 2 3	BARB 1 2 3	DICK 1 2 3	JUDY 1 2 3	BARRY 1 2 3	BLAKE 1 2 3	DON 1 2 3	JOE 1 2 3	SAM 1 2 3
UNIT INSTRUCTION	OTHER INSTRUCTION										

1. Demonstrates competence
2. Does not demonstrate competence

Figure 28. Comprehensive Skills Inventory (Group Form)

255

If implemented, the procedures for evaluation discussed in this chapter will provide an ample base for reporting pupil progress. If teachers can put into practice the idea of criterion-reference evaluation, they have a ready-made resource of evaluative data that can be shared with parents. They can illustrate for parents examples of specific tasks and show them how their child fared on the item. If they have developed a Comprehensive Skills Inventory, they have a frame of reference for explaining to parents what has thus far been covered and what will be taught during the remainder of the year.

In other words, the by-product of routinely assessing pupil performance can be the creation of an information resource on individual pupils and class performance which can serve as input for your reporting system. Parents frequently do not understand what is implied by a report which says that Mary reads at the 3.1 reading level and is working at the 2.7 grade level in arithmetic. They seek meaningful information that tells them explicitly what Mary can or cannot do.

Report cards or conference guidelines that employ broad categories such as reading, arithmetic, social studies, science, and so forth, are not very helpful when attempting to communicate with parents. This is particularly true in terms of reporting pupil progress in areas covered through unit teaching.

Summary

The evaluation of pupil performance is essential to the improvement of instruction. Unless teachers assess the effectiveness of their teaching efforts, their educational decisions are subject to considerable error. It is important for teachers to approach their daily instruction with an evaluation set that motivates them to look for evidence that their teaching is changing the behavior of their students.

Although formal evaluation procedures can be applied in assessing the performance of the mentally retarded, standardized tests for the most part are not designed to cover the content typically taught through units. However, this situation should not be used as an excuse for not evaluating the results of unit teaching. Skill inventories can be developed by teachers as a frame of reference for evaluating their instructional program. The type of inventory presented in this chapter builds on the use of criterion-reference evaluation techniques. These techniques are informal in nature. They require that teachers identify the behavior to be changed and establish a criterion level they will accept as evidence that the child has successfully performed the task. They then must allow the student to perform the task incidentally or structure a situation that requires him or her to perform the task under conditions that can be observed.

The results of evaluating pupil performance are necessary for individualizing instruction, helpful in revising curriculum, important as a source of feedback to students, and essential to the provision of needed input for reporting pupil progress to parents. The results of evaluation contribute to improved instruction.

Exercise 19. Develop a Unit Evaluation Inventory. Select three units written by yourself or other teachers. Select specific skills from these units and develop a Unit Evaluation Inventory using the following form.

UNIT EVALUATION INVENTORY
(Individual Form)

Core Area: _____

Name: _____

UNIT SOURCE	INSTRUCTIONAL OBJECTIVES	DEMONSTRATES COMPETENCE	DOES NOT DEMONSTRATE COMPETENCE	COMMENT
		RATING		

Exercise 20.   Develop Comprehensive Skills Inventory. Assume you are teaching
a group of primary level mildly mentally retarded children. Develop a Comprehensive Skills Inventory in the area of language.

COMPREHENSIVE SKILLS INVENTORY
(Individual Form)

	Demonstrates Competence	Does Not Demonstrate Competence	Unit Instruction	Other Methods	
Name:_____					
Area:_____ Level___					
	RATING		SOURCE		COMMENT

Exercise 21. Develop a Comprehensive Skills Inventory. Assume you are teaching a junior high level group of mildly mentally retarded children. Develop a Comprehensive Skills Inventory in the area of arithmetic skills.

COMPREHENSIVE SKILLS INVENTORY
(Individual Form)

Name:_____

Area:_____ Level ___

	DEMONSTRATES COMPETENCE	DOES NOT DEMONSTRATE COMPETENCE	UNIT INSTRUCTION	OTHER METHODS	
	RATING		SOURCE		COMMENT

Exercise 22. Develop a Comprehensive Skills Inventory. Assume you are teaching a senior high level group of mildly mentally retarded pupils. Develop a Comprehensive Skills Inventory based on vocational skills.

COMPREHENSIVE SKILLS INVENTORY
(Individual Form)

	DEMONSTRATES COMPETENCE	DOES NOT DEMONSTRATE COMPETENCE	UNIT INSTRUCTION	OTHER METHODS	
Name:_____					
Area:_____ Level__					
	RATING		SOURCE		COMMENT

Exercise 23.   Criterion for objectives. Describe a criterion measure for each of the following objectives.

1. Given four objects, the student will be able to order them according to size from smallest to largest.

2. Given specific information about a job vacancy, the student will be able to demonstrate correct procedures for applying for a job.

3. Using a real stove, the student will be able to determine accurately if the oven is heating according to the temperature dial.

REFERENCES

BARRO, STEPHEN M. "An Approach to Developing Accountability Measures for the Public Schools." *Phi Delta Kappan* 52, no. 4 (December 1970).

GUBA, EGON G. "An Overview of the Evaluation Problem." A paper read at the symposium on "The World of Evaluation Needs Reshaping." AERA Convention, February 1969.

POPHAM, W. JAMES, and HUSEK, T. R. "Implications of Criterion-Referenced Measurement." *Journal of Educational Measurement* (Spring 1969).

STEPHENS, THOMAS M. *Directive Teaching of Children with Learning and Behavioral Handicaps.* Columbus: Charles E. Merrill Publishing Company, 1970.

ADDITIONAL SELECTED REFERENCES

FRANK, A. R.; RETISH, P. M.; and CROOKS, F. C ."Developing a Skills Inventory." *Teaching Exceptional Children* (Winter 1971):81.

GALLAGHER, PATRICIA A. *Positive Classroom Performance Techniques for Changing Behavior.* Denver, Colo.: Love Publishing Company, 1971.

HALL, R. VANCE. "Responsive Teaching: Focus on Measurement and Research in the Classroom and the Home." *Focus on Exceptional Children* 3, no. 7 (December 1971).

HIVELY, W., and REYNOLDS, M. C., eds. *Domain-Referenced Testing in Special Education.* University of Minnesota: Leadership Training Institute/Special Education, 1975.

JOBES, N. K., and HAWTHORNE, L. W. "Informal Assessment for the Classroom." *Focus on Exceptional Children* 9, (2) (April 1977):1-13.

LOVITT, TOM; SCHAFF, MARY; and SAYRE, ELIZABETH. "The Use of Direct and Continuous Measurement to Evaluate Reading Materials and Pupil Performance." *Focus on Exceptional Children* 2, no. 6 (November 1970).

MEYEN, EDWARD L., and HIERONYMUS, ALBERT N. "The Age Placement of Academic Skills in Curriculum for the EMR." *Exceptional Children* 36 (January 1970).

MEYEN, E. L. "Instructional Based Appraisal System." Bellevue, Wash.: Edmark Associates, 1976.

MINSKOFF, ESTHER H. "Creating and Evaluating Remediation for the Learning Disabled." *Focus on Exceptional Children* 5, no. 5 (October 1973).

SEMMEL, MELVYN I., and THIAGARAJAN, SIVASAILAM. "Observation Systems and the Special Education Teacher." *Focus on Exceptional Children* 5, no. 7 (December 1973).

YOSHIDA, R. K.; FENTON, K. S.; and KAUFMAN, M. J. "Evaluation of Education for the Handicapped." *Phi Delta Kappan* (September 1977).

11

Seatwork Experiences

Unit teaching requires the teacher to use techniques that allow students to extend their knowledge beyond the planned unit lessons. It is also necessary to use independent and small group activities as a means of individualizing instruction. Well-designed seatwork experiences play a major role in the process of unit teaching.

In spite of the wide array of instructional materials available on the commercial market, most teachers find it necessary to develop many of their own supplemental materials. The majority of teacher-made materials are used by students in independent study situations or in small-group activities approximating peer teaching. The development of seatwork experiences is not an easy task. The major problem encountered in designing seatwork relates to the inability of some students to work independently. This characteristic is frequently accompanied by the inability to sustain attention for very long periods of time and difficulty in following directions. These characteristics place the teacher in a position of having to invest additional effort in designing seatwork experiences with attention-holding features and in the structuring of verbal and written directions within the comprehension level of such pupils.

Teachers also face a situation similar to the development of criterion-referenced evaluation techniques. They have to have a specific objective in mind for the seatwork activity, be sensitive to the child's ability level, and structure the activity so that the child understands what is expected. Provisions must also be structured for making feedback on performance available to the pupil. When these conditions are considered along with the learning characteristics of students and the amount of time devoted to seatwork activities, the necessity of teacher planning becomes apparent. Too often teachers do not have sufficient time for planning seatwork activities, or view such activities as noninstructional. Teachers who require pupils to engage in poorly designed seatwork activities run the risk of discouraging children from participating in independent activities or of creating a situation in which the experiences are primarily "busywork," not contributing to the instructional program. These circumstances frequently result in management problems or poor attitudes toward learning on the part of pupils.

The designing of meaningful seatwork experiences requires the teacher to be a skilled and creative developer. In unit teaching the teacher's instructional effectiveness is greatly influenced by his/her ability to construct a quality unit. The same situation is true in designing seatwork experiences. The teacher must be able to determine the student's needs, specify an objective or at least an intended outcome, be able to structure an activity related to the objective, communicate directions to students, and assess performance. Because students are expected to do the seatwork experience without direct supervision, the teacher must be able to help the student see the intrinsic value of completing the exercise or be able to construct the experience in a manner appealing to the student. It takes a skilled teacher to consistantly develop seatwork exercises that extend instruction and that enhance the independent performance of students.

For the purposes of unit teaching, seatwork will be defined as *activities in which students can engage independently or in small groups with a minimum of teacher supervision.* They may take the form of committee assignment on projects, individualized work sheets, or various media such as film strips, Language Masters, audio tapes, single loop films, or peer-conducted exercises. While the term "independent activities" is probably more appropriate than "seatwork," the latter term is used to differentiate classroom activities from field trips or other activities engaged in by students informally or formally outside the classroom.

Viewed within this context, seatwork activities can serve several purposes. They can be used as a vehicle for extending the teaching of skills and concepts initiated through unit lessons. Used in this manner, the seatwork activities can be incorporated within the lesson presentation or employed at the conclusion of the lesson. They can be designed as behavior reinforcers. If the tasks are geared to the ability level of the pupil and relevant to the content of the unit currently being worked on, the experience can provide the learner with meaningful feedback. This in turn becomes a means of reinforcement. They can also be organized to make use of novelty features that hold attention but do not interfere with the learning experiences built into the activity. In this case, the form of the activity serves as a diversion for the learner even though the content of what is to be learned through the activity is compatible with what is being taught through units or other aspects of the curriculum.

The application of previously learned skills and concepts is an important use of seatwork. Used in this fashion, the activities are not intended to teach a skill or concept, but rather are utilized as a means of providing practice in applying skills or concepts in which the learner has some competency but is not as proficient in the particular skill as the teacher would like. This is differentiated from practice for the sake of practice. There may be occasions when the teacher will ask pupils to engage in drill exercises. When making such a decision, teachers should give serious consideration to the effect that this request might have on the motivation of the pupils. If they can demonstrate to the pupils the necessity for completing the task or if it can be presented to them within a context that holds their attention, then it can probably be carried out without negative effects.

An important but indirect contribution of well-designed seatwork is in the area of behavior management. While some teachers use seatwork activities as a means of keeping students busy and diverting their attention from disruptive activities, seatwork can be used in a positive manner in behavior management. If the seatwork activity is designed as a learning experience geared to the ability level of the pupils, and perceived by them as relevant, then the chances are increased that they will pursue the activity with a minimum of teacher supervision. This allows the teacher time to give individual attention to other pupils and/or to prepare for a subsequent learning experience.

Tips on Planning Seatwork Activities

1. Identify the particular skill or concept you are attempting to reinforce or teach through the activity. If the activity relates to a specific unit or lesson, be sure the relationship of the activity to the lesson is obvious to the student.

2. Analyze the task from the perspective of determining what type of activity would be most appropriate for the task. Avoid extensive reliance on paper-and-pencil activities that take the form of drill exercises. Vary the type of activities used during the day as well as within particular units.

3. Estimate the amount of time required for your pupils to complete the activity. You may find it necessary to vary the nature of the activity or its scope in order to accommodate the different ability levels represented in your class.

4. In formulating the directions to be given students, use vocabulary words you know they understand. In some cases, verbal directions will be sufficient; however, when feasible, both verbal and written directions should be provided. Use questions or illustrations to check their understanding of directions.

5. If the activity is a group project, be sure that all participants understand their roles.

6. Review the activity to make certain that all needed materials and equipment are available. If media equipment is to be used, check the students' ability to operate them.

7. Although seatwork is intended as an independent activity, remain accessible so that you can provide help when needed.

8. Decide in advance how and when you will provide feedback to the students. If they are to receive a grade, inform them when the assignment is made.

Use of Commercially Prepared Work Sheets

A number of commercial firms are marketing prepared work sheets in the form of ditto masters. For the most part, these are developed around unit themes such as weather, measurement, and time, or they are designed as review exercises for the development of basic skills. While teachers should not rely on them entirely, there are advantages in using commercially prepared work sheets. For example:

1. They can be purchased in advance and thus are accessible when needed.

2. They are generally legible and reflect a professional appearance.

3. They are relatively inexpensive considering the time required on the part of teachers to develop their own work sheets.

4. They generally employ varied styles of type and use better illustrations than most teachers can develop within the time available to design seatwork activities.

While there are times when the influence of these advantages will cause teachers to employ commercially prepared work sheets, there are certain cautions to be considered. Teachers must be selective in the work sheets they choose to use. Not much is gained if the work sheet does not offer the experiences they want to provide the students. Many teachers find it helpful, when developing a unit, to review available commercially prepared work sheets on the unit topic and decide in advance which ones would probably be appropriate in supplementing specific lessons to be included in the unit. They are then in a position to anticipate the number and kinds of seatwork activities they must develop through their own efforts.

In using commercially prepared work sheets, you may find that some are too comprehensive and/or attempt to include too many different concepts within the same activity. Teachers should be alert for these problems and either modify the work sheet or develop their own. It is difficult to anticipate the effectiveness of a particular work sheet with individual students. Consequently, if a work sheet containing several concepts is to be used, teachers may find it necessary to conduct the activity as a group exercise rather than as an independent activity.

If teachers find a set of commercially prepared work sheets for a unit they will be teaching, in addition to reviewing the individual work sheets in terms of the number of concepts presented and the organization of the exercises, they should also check the series to see whether work sheets on the same concept are presented at different levels of difficulty. They may find, for example, that work sheets are available regarding the use of the ruler for measuring to an accuracy of one inch; however, no exercises are available for more precise uses of the ruler. In this case, they might choose to use the one that is available and develop additional work sheets on the same concept but at a more difficult level. When reviewing a series of prepared work sheets on a topic, teachers should not assume that the sequence in which the work sheets are ordered is necessarily sequential in terms of prerequisite skills required to perform the tasks. They will need to make their own decisions regarding the sequence in which they will use the work sheets if they adopt the entire series.

Commercially prepared work sheets can be effectively employed in unit teaching if the teacher is selective and does not depend upon them as the only source. Because of the convenience of commercially prepared work sheets, teachers must guard against their overuse in the classroom. Many teachers have tended to use such work sheets to the extent that they become the dominant type of independent activities engaged in by their students. This contributes to circumstances in which students are easily distracted and may cause students to develop negative attitudes toward similar learning tasks. It is important to keep in mind that experience presented as seatwork appear to be and in fact are teaching exercises. If a student perceives the teacher as placing little value on the assigned seatwork or merely using the assignment to occupy the student, problems related to motivation are likely to occur.

Evaluation of Seatwork Activities

Just as it is important for the teacher to know whether or not the child has learned a particular concept, it is important to know if the child has failed or succeeded at an assigned seatwork activity. The child's need for feedback also is as important in seatwork activities as it is in testing situations. Evaluation of seatwork activities extends beyond the assessment of pupil performance on a particular task. If teachers are to make maximum use of seatwork activities in structuring learning experiences for children, it is important for them to obtain information about the effectiveness of particular activities as well as information regarding their own efficiency in designing seatwork experiences.

Evaluating Pupil Performance

1. Be sure pupils understand how their participation will be evaluated; in other words, what you are expecting from them in the way of performance. In the case of work sheets, the type of response desired is relatively obvious. However, in terms of group activities your objectives may be less obvious. Give them some indication of how their participation will be evaluated.
2. Monitor the participation of pupils in the activity while it is in process. Some students may not understand the directions and consequently will be unable to pursue the task unless additional directions are offered.
3. If work sheets are being used, correct the papers and provide feedback as soon as possible. When grading papers, look for recurring errors that reflect a skill deficiency.
4. If the child's paper is below your expectations, check to make sure he or she understood.
5. Frequently, teachers find that there is insufficient time available to grade papers and provide immediate feedback to students. When this occurs, there are alternatives which can be employed by teachers to facilitate the correcting of papers and the subsequent provision of feedback to students relative to their performance. For example:
   a. In group activities, individual pupils can be given the correct responses and serve as a group leader or teacher substitute.
   b. Work sheets can be designed to include the key so that students can grade their own papers.
   c. Papers can be exchanged with peers for purposes of grading.
   d. Correct responses can be recorded on the chalkboard or on experience charts and grading done as a group exercise.

When keys are provided or when peers grade each other's papers, checks should be made at the time of grading to identify systematic errors. If a student is allowed to continue making systematic errors, the teacher has set the stage for unnecessary failure. For example, in grading a spelling assignment, should he discover that the student consistently places the "i" before the "e" in words where the correct sequence is "ei," the student is not misspelling independent words, rather he is making the same error repeatedly. Attention to this type of mistake is particularly important.

To avoid embarassment resulting from grades or examples of corrections, spend time early in the year working on attitudes. Try to establish the idea that between correcting someone else's paper, we are helping them and that the paper is theirs. Thus, a grade is their private property. Granted, this attitude may not be easy to achieve. There will be situations in which it will be in the best interest of some children if peers are not used in evaluating work sheets. On the other hand, if the teacher is doing a good job in planning seatwork activities, the evidence of children failing them routinely should be greatly reduced.

Evaluating Teacher-Designed Seatwork Activities

Criteria for assessing the effectiveness of seatwork activities include the degree to which the activity carries out the instructional objectives and the benefit derived by pupils through participation. There are questions which the teacher can pose as an informal technique for assessing the seatwork activities employed in the instructional program.

1. Is the activity meaningful and functional; is the skill used in a situation as close as possible to the way it would be utilized in real life?
2. Does the activity really require the use of the skill or reinforce the important concept? Make sure the activity reinforces the skill you intend and not just the skills of cutting, pasting, copying, and so on.
3. Does the activity require too many other skills in addition to the one being emphasized? Are any of these secondary skills too difficult?
4. Can the students do the activity independently; is it within their ability range and experiential background?
5. Are materials, supplies or equipment needed for the activity available in sufficient quantities for the particular classroom situation?
6. Will the activity require the students to think; is it challenging enough?
7. Does the activity allow students to use problem-solving techniques in a meaningful way?
8. Is the activity reasonably interesting, attractive, and varied?
9. Is the amount of teacher preparation time required to develop and produce the activity within reason?
10. Will the activity engage the students in independent work for a sufficient period of time, or will it take too long to complete?
11. Can the activity be done quietly if other instruction is taking place in the classroom?[1]

1. Reprinted by permission from *Developing Appropriate Seatwork for the Mentally Retarded,* Special Education Curriculum Development Center, University of Iowa (Iowa City, April 1969). Supported in part by grant from U. S. Office of Education Project No. 6-2883.

Developing and Sharing Seatwork Ideas

As you accumulate evaluation information on seatwork activities over a period of time, it will become apparent that your class responds better to some types of activities than to others. The response pattern is likely to vary from group to group. In some cases, students prefer certain activities because of specific inherent features. If you can identify these features, it may be possible to capitalize on them by incorporating them into other activity forms. You may also find that your students' preference is influenced by your enthusiasm for particular activities. Be alert for this situation, because you may unconsciously be causing some activities to fail due to your personal preference for others. While you may not be able to alter your behavior, you should at least attempt to identify why some activities work and others do not.

The ease of designing work sheets containing exercises has resulted in a few standard formats being used by most teachers and commercial producers of seatwork material. This is in part due to the appeal of paper pencil exercises combined with the assumed limitations and use of the mode. Teachers who are sensitive to how students respond to seatwork assignments attempt to vary the design of seatwork exercises. The simplest form of variance is to vary the mode, that is, paper pencil exercises, small-group assignments, production tasks, or preparations for forms of participation. Another strategy is to develop options within each mode. For example, develop several alternative ways of designing paper and pencil exercises to teach the same skill.

Teachers must keep in mind that in instructional situations where the teacher is interacting with the student, changes are made in an almost extemporaneous manner when it is sensed that the student is not responding. Activities may be abruptly altered or halted if the teacher perceives such a need. Or the teacher may reinforce or ignore particular behavior to influence pupil performance. When the student is engaged in seatwork exercises, the teacher must depend on the exercise, directions given, and the student's involvement. Creative designs greatly help.

Some teachers find it helpful to keep a file on seatwork assignments that tend to be appealing to students and effective in teaching particular skills. They will often attach a note to the work sheet describing the exercise, indicating the objectives of the assignment, identifying the type of student completing the task, and recording the amount of time required. Recorded in this manner, teachers can exchange ideas and examples of effective seatwork. Over time the pooling of seatwork ideas among even 3 or 4 teachers will result in extensive inventory of examples. In some cases, a teacher will be able to use examples obtained from other teachers, however, in most cases the ideas and formats will be of help in redesigning experiences.

Seatwork and Unit Teaching

Unit teaching is frequently presented as a group instructional method. While this is true in the context that group participation is essential to unit teaching, individualization is also an important component of effective unit teaching. Certainly the goal is not to teach the same skills and concepts to all students at the same time. The primary manner through which individualization occurs centers on the instructional skills of the teacher. A secondary but important vehicle for differentiating instruction through units is seatwork experiences. Teachers can vary the level of difficulty, scope, format, and type of seatwork depending on the observed needs of students. In some situations seatwork might be assigned to a group of students while the teacher continues to work with another group. The use of seatwork for purposes of individualizing instruction is important to unit teaching.

The discussion in Chapter 6 on core activities applies to seatwork. It is helpful after completing the core activities step to review the core areas and develop a list of possible seatwork experiences that might be used to teach skills or concepts related to each core area. This can be used as a resource in planning unit lessons.

Care should be exercised when using seatwork with units to avoid the use of drill practice. Such exercises related to number facts, spelling, etc. are useful, but should be presented as practice exercises on specific skills and not as experiences directly related to unit topics. The reason is that drill exercises are frequently perceived by students as "less than exciting." There is no reason to risk relating negative experiences to units if avoidable.

In using seatwork, make certain that the students see the relationship between the seatwork assignment and the unit group work. It may be necessary at times to involve students in designing experiences that will help them in their unit work. Because units are organized around a theme familiar to students, they tend to have a vested interest in the content and are willing to participate in decisions pertaining to what is expected of them. Teachers should capitalize on this interest and allow students to contribute ideas regarding activities that can be carried out individually and in small groups to further their understanding. The development skills required of teachers to construct units are generic development skills and can be easily taught to students. As developers, they can ease the teacher's job and add to the unit teaching climate.

Summary

Student participation is essential to effective unit teaching. The alert teacher will find no shortage of opportunities for engaging students in unit work. However, the nature of their involvement must not be restricted to group discussion or completing work sheets comprised of drill exercises. Teachers must be creative in varying the type of seatwork activities used. They must also approach the development of seatwork with the perspective that such activities are instructional in nature and are an inherent part of unit lessons. Just as the teacher needs feedback from students on their reaction to seatwork assignments, they need information from the teacher on their performance.

Exercise 24. Creating and Categorizing Seatwork Activities. Write a behavioral objective for a unit lesson. In a "brainstorming" fashion generate as many seatwork activities as you can that would be applicable to teaching the objective. Having done this, categorize your activities according to the following types.

a. Work sheet
b. Group project work
c. Use of media
d. Individual projects

Now select one activity from each category and develop the activity at two levels of difficulty.

Exercise 25.   Writing Directions. Assume you are teaching a unit on foods to a group of fifteen children at the primary level. Further assume that you plan to use the following work sheet as a means of providing the pupils with experience in associating the names of fruits and vegetables with illustrations. Write directions for the exercise that convey to the students what they are to do.

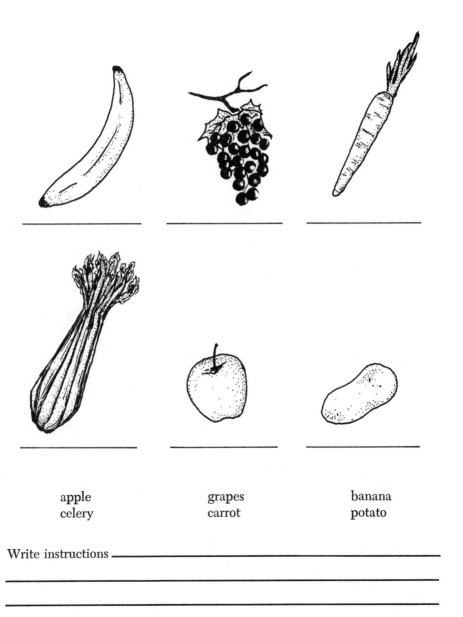

apple   grapes   banana
celery   carrot   potato

Write instructions _____

_____

_____

Exercise 26.   Correcting Work Sheets. Using the following example of a work sheet, design and/or describe three ways in which the work sheet could be corrected by students independently or as a group.

Coins

Write the name of each coin in the space provided.

How many nickels make a quarter? ....

How many pennies make a dime? ....

How many pennies make a quarter? ....

How many quarters make a half dollar? ....

Write the following values using numbers.

Three dollars ....

Four dollars and thirty cents ....

Ten cents ....

Eight dollars and forty-six cents ....

Fifteen dollars ....

Exercise 27.   Identifying Concepts. List the different concepts included in the following example of a work sheet.

**U.S.D.A. Grade 'A' Pearl Brand
Young 6 to 8Lb. Sizes**

HEN
TURKEYS.............$2.79
Each

TURKEYS
U.S.D.A. Grade 'A' Pearl Brand

**7Lb. Average
Each............$2.79**

---

1. How big are the turkeys that are advertised? ....
   (Is this saying the same thing in two different ways?)
2. How much do the turkeys cost per pound? ....
3. Is there any difference in the brand in the two ads? ....
4. Could some turkeys weigh more than 7 pounds? ....
5. Could some turkeys weigh less than 7 pounds? ....
6. Is it important to check the weight of each turkey that you buy? ....

BIBLIOGRAPHY

Special Education Curriculum Development Center. *Developing Appropriate Seatwork for the Mentally Retarded.* Iowa City: University of Iowa, 1969.

ADDITIONAL SELECTED REFERENCES RELATED TO THE
DEVELOPMENT OF SEATWORK

CHEYNEY, JEANNE S. "It Worked for Me." *Grade Teacher* 85 (January 1968):33.
CHRISTOPLOS, F. "Programing for Children With Learning Disabilities." *Journal of Learning Disabilities* 2 (1969):45-48.
DARROW, HELEN FISHER, and VAN ALLAN, R. *Independent Activities for Creative Learning.* New York: Bureau of Publications, Teacher's College, Columbia University, 1961.
FRANK, ALAN R. "A Study of Selected Variables in the Preparation of Seatwork for the Mentally Retarded." Unpublished doctoral dissertation, University of Iowa, 1970.
FUCHIGAMI, ROBERT Y., and SMITH, ROLAND F. "Guidelines for Developing and Evaluating Seatwork Materials for Handicapped Children." *Education and Training of the Mentally Retarded* 3, no. 3 (October 1968).
GREENMAN, GLADYS. *Independent Work Period.* Washington, D.C.: Association for Childhood Education, 1941.
JORDAN, LAURA J. "Effective Seatwork for the Educable." *Education and Training of the Mentally Retarded* 3, no. 2 (April 1968).
OTTO, CAROL C. "The Tape Recorder as an Aid in Teaching Slow Learners." *Wisconsin Journal of Education,* January 1967.
RASMUSSEN, MARGARET, editor. *Homework.* Washington, D.C.: Association for Childhood Education International, 1963.

12

Sample Units

The major problem in providing sample units is that some readers may view them as a standard. That is not the intent. Rather, they provide an illustration of units that have been written by classroom teachers in accordance with the procedures described in the previous chapters. The sample units do not represent highly sophisticated units which have been revised several times. The sample units are not complete units, in that only selected lessons have been included. However, the lessons are representative of the content projected for each unit.

The first unit, on *Time*, is intended for the intermediate level class. The second unit, on *Home Safety and Maintenance*, was also developed for the intermediate grades. Both units include complete preliminary steps and selected lesson plans.

In reading the units, keep in mind that they represent the perspective of the teachers who wrote them. You might have selected different content and/or employed other instructional techniques.

Unit Topic: Time[1]

This unit on time was selected for illustrative purposes primarily because of the extensive use made of sequential seatwork. The sample lessons represent only the portion of the unit pertaining to telling time. Lessons regarding the social and vocational implications of time would also be included if the unit were developed in detail. The reader will note that the lessons in this unit differ considerably from those in the unit on *Home Safety and Maintenance*. One reason is the skill orientation of the time unit; the other is that it is designed for an older group of children. This unit was written for use with mildly mentally retarded children in intermediate grades.

1. Modified and reprinted by permission of Corydon Crooks, who developed this unit while a graduate student at the University of Iowa.

I. RATIONALE

The ability to handle the concept of time is crucial to the adjustment of all children. The affairs of the individual and of all members of a community are organized and to some degree controlled by various aspects of time. Most of us are awakened by the clamor of an alarm clock, and the activities of the ensuing day are governed by whether it is a workday, a Saturday, or a Sunday. The changes of the seasons and the ticking away of seconds are extremes that are separated by many aspects and applications of time-related concepts.

Because some children lack the ability to grasp spontaneously the abstract aspect of time, they often meet with difficulties at home, at school, and in the community. Therefore, a unit of instruction designed to teach time in a concrete and meaningful manner should be indispensable in contributing to the overall adjustment of these children.

The following pages will provide some guidelines and ideas for presenting a portion of the subject of time over a fifteen-day period.

II. SUB-UNITS

A. Recreation
B. Seasons
C. Science
D. Measurement
E. Jobs
F. Money
G. Holidays
H. Newspaper

III. OBJECTIVES

The following concepts and skills should be accomplished as a result of the teacher's work in this area.

1. To develop the different concepts of time through knowledge of the seasons, the calendar, and daily time (clock usage).

2. To develop the ability to tell time in hour, half-hour, quarter-hour, and five-minute units and to be able to relate this ability to everyday usage. Note: It is reasonable to expect that some pupils will be able to work in smaller time units. When this is the case, these pupils should be encouraged and reinforced. The exercises should be altered to make use of and to give practice in their refined ability to use the clock.

3. To develop time concepts in general terms, that is, early, late, now, then, morning, afternoon, day, night, yesterday, tomorrow, A.M., P.M., and so forth.

4. To identify various consequences related to time. For example:
   a. What might happen if you are late for school?
   b. Will going to bed early give me more energy for working and playing? Why?

    c. Would a two-hour walk make me tired?

    d. Would a half-hour run make me tired?

    e. What happens if we are late for the school bus?

    f. Why do you need to turn on the TV at a certain time for your favorite program?

IV. ACTIVITIES

The following list of activities has been arranged according to various competencies. This list is not intended to be complete but should be used as a guide and a suggestion for the general level of competency that may be expected. We recognize that individual differences will determine the level of achievement to a considerable degree and that though teacher expectations should be optimistic, not all children will reach the same level. Some will go beyond our expectations, some will fall short of them. Adjustments will have to be made to modify the activities appropriately for various individuals in the class.

A. *Arithmetic Activities*

1. Make a calendar for this month. This can be both a group project and an individual one.

2. Construct a demonstration clock for the bulletin board.

3. Make a season wheel.

4. Tell the time given various locations of the hands on a demonstration clock using whole-hour, half-hour, fifteen-minute, and five-minute intervals.

5. Count the number of days, weeks, months before or after an important date such as a birthday, Christmas, or Thanksgiving.

B. *Social Competency Activities*[2]

1. List some problems resulting from being late for school, work, and so forth.

2. Role-play a situation that might occur when tardy for a class, work, or a date.

3. Work as a group to construct bulletin boards to illustrate holidays.

4. Clap hands to keep time with a metronome.

5. Do simple rhythm steps in time with a metronome.

6. Participate in elementary group dances that require some sense of rhythm to execute.

2. These particular activities were selected from sample lessons included in *Planning on Arithmetic Curriculum*, Special Education Curriculum Development Center, University of Iowa (Iowa City, 1968). Reprinted with permission.

C. *Communication Skills Activities*[3]

1. Read the day, month, and year on newspapers, magazines, books, and so forth.
2. Obtain schedules of the departure and arrival of postal pickups at the post office.
3. Obtain timetables from the bus depots.
4. Make out time schedules for daily activities.
5. Write invitations to another class to attend a class function at a certain time and date.
6. Write friendly letters indicating the date and time of the letter as well as the date and time of certain events that have occurred.
7. Role-play making arrangements with a friend to go to a movie— time, date, place, and so forth.

D. *Safety Activities*[4]

1. Call the local hospital to determine the times that doctors are on duty.
2. Demonstrate safety precautions to be taken related to seasonal sports.
3. Figure starting times for trips so that destinations may be reached without careless hurrying.
4. Role-play possible accidents that might occur as the result of hurrying because of tardiness.
5. Call hospital to determine the regular hours as well as emergency hours that are followed.

E. *Health Activities*

1. Plan different menus to correspond to the various holidays and seasons.
2. Read to determine the amount of sleep needed each night.
3. List the detrimental effects of eating too rapidly.
4. Construct and discuss a bulletin board showing pictures of appropriate clothing for various occasions, time of day, and season of the year.
5. Demonstrate the length of time to leave thermometer in the mouth.
6. Take the pulse and respiration of a classmate using a stopwatch.
7. Watch a film related to the timing of artificial respiration.

3. Ibid.
4. Ibid.

F. *Vocational Competency Activities*

1. Interview personnel from local businesses and factories to determine the working hours.
2. Visit a larger business that utilizes a time clock—have the manager demonstrate and explain its function.
3. Investigate the number of hours various community workers spend on the job (police officers, grocer, teacher, truck driver, doctor, and so forth.)
4. Compute a simple hypothetical wage for a worker who works a set number of hours for a certain rate. Emphasize that time may indeed be equivalent to money.

V. RESOURCES

It is desirable to identify and plan how you will use the resources for your lessons. Be certain that all resource materials for any particular lesson have been assembled beforehand and that you are thoroughly familiar with them. Audiovisual equipment should be set up and ready for only the flick of a switch to become operative. Threading film or tape, focusing, screen placement, and so on should be done before the class begins. It is often helpful to have one or more of the class members "certified" as an A-V "technician." This leaves the teacher free to utilize the movie, filmstrip, or whatever to greater advantage. This is also reinforcing to the pupils who have been qualified to assume this responsibility.

A list of resources that may assist in teaching this unit follows. The teacher should use any available films and books that will serve to enrich the presentations, whether they are listed here or not.

A. *Materials*

Newspapers	TV schedules in newspapers
Books and magazines	*TV Guide*
Calendars	Clock and watches
Demonstration clock	Pictures of sundials and clocks
Hourglass	Projector (slide, movie, overhead)
Films	Bulletin board and materials

B. *Films*

The following films are listed in the *Catalog of Educational Films* published by the Audiovisual Center at The University of Iowa.

Mail orders for films may be sent to:

Audiovisual Center
Division of Extension and University Services
The University of Iowa
Iowa City, Iowa 52240

1. *The Calendar: Story of its Development;* (U-5066)
2. *The Story of Measuring Time: Hours, Minutes, Seconds;* (U-6037)
3. *The Calendar: Days, Weeks, Months;* (U-4024)
4. *Children of Switzerland;* (U-776)
5. *How to Measure Time;* (U-5684)
6. *What Time Is It?;* (U-3346)

C. *Books*

Abisch, Roz. *Do You Know What Time It Is?* Prentice-Hall, Inc., 1968.

Borland, Kathryn K. *Clocks, From Shadow to Atom.* Follet, 1969.

Jupo, Frank. *A Day Around the World.* Abelard Schuman, 1968.

Mendoza, George. *The Scarecrow Clock.* Holt, Rinehart and Winston, 1971.

Piltz, Albert. *Time Without Clocks; How Nature Tells Time.* Grosset and Dunlap, 1970.

Roy, Cal. *Time Is Day.* Astor-Honor, 1968.

Waller, L. *A Book To Begin on Time.* Henry Holt and Co., 1969.

VI. VOCABULARY

A working vocabulary relevant to the subject of time is necessary. The following list should be in the repertoire of intermediate level children. These should be familiar as sight words, although many pupils will be able to write and spell some of these words.

day	: (colon)	late	alarm	May
week	channel	A.M.	set	June
month	program	season	wind	July
year	television	spring	decade	August
calendar	TV	summer	P.M.	September
second	holiday	fall	morning	October
minute	sun	autumn	night	November
today	moon	winter	afternoon	December
tomorrow	stars	Sunday	evening	timetable
tonight	time	Monday	noon	motel
yesterday	hour	Tuesday	now	clock
past	hand	Wednesday	January	leap year
present	face	Thursday	February	century
future	clock	Friday	March	half-hour
o'clock	early	Saturday	April	quarter-hour

Lesson 1

SCOPE OF THE LESSON: To introduce the subject of months and seasons and to relate them to our lives.

INSTRUCTIONAL OBJECTIVES	ACTIVITIES	RESOURCE MATERIALS	EXPERIENCE CHART
1. Each child shall be able to tell his or her birthdate and either write it on paper or point to the proper date on a yearly calendar when asked to do so.	1.1° Have each pupil draw a birthday cake on heavy, white paper. Children should draw on the cake the number of candles that would represent their age. Under the cake each child shall letter name, present age, and birthdate (month, day, year).	White drawing paper Colored drawing paper Pencils Felt pens Crayons Rulers	Our date of birth is important to remember. We need to know the day, month, and year of our birth. List each child's name and birthdate.
	1.2. Let each child cut out a candle from colored paper and then put name and the numerical date of birthday on it. These candles should then be attached to a cake with his or her birth month lettered on it. These birth month cakes will be prepared by the teacher and put on a bulletin board or as decoration in the room.	Cake cut-outs (the teacher should prepare these before class) Stapler, thumbtacks, cellulose tape or paste Large calendar for the year	
	1.3. Use an existing large yearly calendar (or make one) and have each child place a small name disc over the correct day and on the right month for his or her birthday. This can serve as a reminder for parties to the class.		

°1.1 indicates first activity with objective number 1.

296

Lesson 2

SCOPE OF THE LESSON: To continue activities related to the seasons and months.

Instructional Objectives	Activities	Resource Materials	Experience Chart

1. The child shall demonstrate a knowledge of the months and seasons by being able to read and/or write the name of each month (with reasonable spelling), know its numerical place in the yearly sequence, and arrange the months into seasonal groups when asked to do so.	1.1. Construct a season wheel similar to the one on page 133.
	
	1.2. Discuss the seasons by having the children consider:
	a. weather characteristics
	b. tree foliage and plants
	c. animals' seasonal habits
	d. changes in animals' coats
	e. seasonal activities
	  (1) school
	  (2) sports
	  (3) farm
	  (4) recreational
	
	1.3. Relate the seasons to the months using the season wheel and a large calendar. Show the relationship between the succession of the months and the passage of the year through the seasons.
	
	1.4. Each child can make a seasonal scrapbook with the seasons and months lettered at the top of each page. Paste appropriate pictures on the pages.
		Season wheel (see page 314) made of stiff cardboard.
		
		Magazines for pictures
		
		Paste
		
		Scissors
		
		Crayons
		
		Notebook paper
		
		Construction paper for notebook covers
		
		Stapler
			We have four seasons during the year. The weather changes during each season.
			
			Winter (cold)
			December
			January
			February
			
			Spring (cool and rainy)
			March
			April
			May
			
			Summer (hot and sunny)
			June
			July
			August
			
			Fall or Autumn (cool)
			September
			October
			November

Lesson 3

SCOPE OF THE LESSON: To introduce seasonal holidays to further knowledge about seasons and months.

INSTRUCTIONAL OBJECTIVES	ACTIVITIES	RESOURCE MATERIALS	EXPERIENCE CHART
1. Each child shall participate in a discussion of seasonal holidays by making at least one appropriate verbal contribution.	1.1. Introduce the subject of seasonal holidays by talking about each of the four major holidays observed during the winter, spring, fall, and summer (Christmas, Easter, Thanksgiving, Fourth of July).	Ditto copies of the exercise Season Fun for each pupil (page 317) Crayons Transparency of Season Fun for projection on a screen or the chalkboard	We celebrate many holidays during the year. Some holidays are winter holidays and some are summer, spring, and fall holidays. Christmas comes in the winter. Easter comes in the spring. The Fourth of July comes in the summer. Thanksgiving comes in the fall.
2. Each pupil shall complete the Season Fun Exercise (page 317) by coloring the pictures and by writing (or verbalizing) the proper responses to fill in the blanks.	2.1. The children shall be encouraged to color the sketches accompanying Season Fun. 2.2. Finish the exercise by having each pupil complete the sentences by writing the appropriate words in the blanks.	Note: A transparency of the lesson being worked on will help the teacher and pupils during group discussion of a lesson. Overhead projector	

Lesson 4

Scope of the Lesson: To provide for a review of the seasons and the months.

Instructional Objectives	Activities	Resource Materials	Experience Chart
1. Each pupil shall complete the Review of the Seasons exercise on page 316 to the teacher's satisfaction.	1.1. This exercise can be done as a joint project with the whole class participating and answering the questions. Those children who have the ability can do the exercise as seatwork.	Ditto copies of the review exercise on page 316.	Use a copy of the exercise on page 316 as the experience chart. After each child has completed it, the exercise can be done on the chart and the pupils can correct their own papers.
	1.2. Using the exercise as a group review, project the exercise using a transparency of page 316 for group discussion and deciding the correct answers.	Thermal transparency of the exercise Wax pencil for use on the transparency Overhead projector	
	1.3. Either as the result of group discussion, or of individual seatwork, individual children can copy or provide the answers on their own initiative and complete the exercise on dittoed copies of this review.		

Lesson 5

SCOPE OF THE LESSON: To introduce and to provide learning experiences in the use of the calendar.

INSTRUCTIONAL OBJECTIVES	ACTIVITIES	RESOURCE MATERIALS	EXPERIENCE CHART
1. The pupil shall complete Calendar Exercise 1 on page 319 according to the instructions. The pupil may use a current calendar as an aid.	1.1. The teacher shall read the instructions to the first calendar exercise and demonstrate how to do the exercise either on the chalkboard or by using the overhead projector and a transparency of the lesson. A calendar of the current month should be prominently displayed.	Large calendar for the current month Ditto copies of Calendar Exercise 1 for each member of the class—see page 319. Thermal transparency of the exercise Wax pencil Overhead projector	The Calendar The calendar helps us keep track of the days, months, and years. Some calendars sit on the desk and some hang on a wall. We have four calendars in our classroom. This is the month of March. March has 31 days.

Lesson 6

SCOPE OF THE LESSON: To provide for continuing exercises to strengthen knowledge about the calendar.

INSTRUCTIONAL OBJECTIVES	ACTIVITIES	RESOURCE MATERIALS	EXPERIENCE CHART
1. In a class discussion each child shall demonstrate by accurate statements, and to the teacher's satisfaction, that he or she has sufficient knowledge about the calendar to answer the questions on pages 319-320.	1.1. The pupils can take turns reading the questions on pages 319-320, either from their own copies of the exercises or from projected transparencies.	Copies of pages 319-320 Thermal transparency of each page	We can tell what is today by looking at the calendar. March 1976 S M T W Th F S 1 2 3 4 5 6 7 8 9 10 11 12 13 14 15 16 17 18 19 20 21 22 23 24 25 26 27 28 29 30 ㉛
2. Each pupil shall complete the supplements to Calendar Exercise 1 on page 319-320 by writing the correct answer on the dittoed copies of the exercises. The pupils who are unable to meet writing skills needed may supply the answers verbally.	2.1. After a discussion of the question has elicited a correct answer, the teacher should write the answer on the transparency with wax pencil. Pupils can then write the answers on their individual copies. Note: The use of an overhead projector with this exercise can reinforce reading skills and provide a model for writing the answers. The exercises on pages 330-1 have been presented in small groups so that the pupils will not be overwhelmed by a full page of questions. The teacher shall use discretion concerning the number of questions that the class can tolerate during one class session on Time.	Overhead projector Wax pencil	Today is Wednesday, March 31, 1976.

301

Lesson 7

Scope of the Lesson: To strengthen skills in using the calendar.

Instructional Objectives	Activities	Resource Materials	Experience Chart
1. Each child shall complete Calendar Exercise 2 to the teacher's satisfaction and within the time allotted by the teacher.	1.1. Calendar Exercise 2 (page 321) can be done as a class activity using individual copies as well as a projected transparency. The teacher may administer this lesson in a manner similar to the previous one.	Copies of Calendar Exercise 2 for each pupil. See page 332. Thermal transparency of the exercise Overhead projector Wax pencil Calendar for the current year	Record Calendar Exercise 2 from page 321 on the chart and complete as a group activity.

Lesson 8

SCOPE OF THE LESSON: To continue to provide exercises and activities that utilize the calendar.

INSTRUCTIONAL OBJECTIVES	ACTIVITIES	RESOURCE MATERIALS	EXPERIENCE CHART
1. Each child shall make at least three appropriate contributions to a discussion concerning the exercise on page 317. 41.	1.1. With the help of individual copies of Calendar Fun and a projected image of the work sheets, discuss and verbalize the answers to all of the questions on the three sheets.	Individual copies of Calendar Fun Thermal transparency of the exercises Wax pencil	Dates to Remember My birthdate is _____. Today's date is _____. My teacher's birthdate is _____. The last day of school is _____.
2. Each pupil shall complete the three parts of Calendar Fun either by writing the answers in the spaces provided, or by verbalizing the answers to the teacher.	2.1. Each child shall write the correct answers to the seatwork activity in the spaces provided. Those who cannot write sufficiently well may verbalize the answers. 2.2. Utilize the questions on the work sheets to stimulate a time-related discussion that goes beyond the scope of the work sheet. Note: As with the questions following Calendar Exercise 1, the number of questions per page has been kept to a nonthreatening number.	Overhead projector Calendar for the current month	

Lesson 9

SCOPE OF THE LESSON: To introduce and provide a variety of experiences for teaching and strengthening knowledge and skills associated with using a clock or watch.

INSTRUCTIONAL OBJECTIVES	ACTIVITIES	RESOURCE MATERIALS	EXPERIENCE CHART

1. Each child shall demonstrate that he or she can correctly and with little hesitation tell time by full hours, half-hours, quarter-hours, and five-minute intervals by reading aloud the correct time from a demonstration clock, a projection of a clock face, a wall clock, or a watch when asked to do so. Note: The limitations and abilities of individuals must be recognized and the goals set must be individually realistic. Not every child will be capable of reading a clock or watch at five-minute intervals, for example.		Transparency of a clock face
		
		Overhead projector
		
		Assortment of clock faces—enough so each child can have one at his or her desk. Use small demonstration clocks, old watches or alarm clocks with the hands intact and movable.
			Clocks
			Clocks help us in telling time. We have a clock in our classroom.
			Some of us have wristwatches.
			Clocks have *hands*.
			  The long hand tells the minute.
			  The short hand tells the hour.
			  Some clocks have second hands which move fast.

2. Each pupil shall participate in the discussion of clocks and watches and their function by making at least one appropriate contribution during the discussion.	2.1. The teacher will introduce the clock to the class using a projection of a clock face from an overhead projector or by using a *large* demonstration clock. It is recommended that each child have a small clock face with movable hands, a watch, or an alarm clock to use at the desk during these exercises. Old, nonfunctioning clocks with the faces and hands in-		

304

tact would be adequate. These can be procured from parents, friends, Goodwill or Salvation Army stores, etc.

2.2. As a part of the previous activity the teacher should evaluate the ability of the members of the class to use a clock by showing a variety of settings on the demonstration clock using full-hour, half-hour, quarter-hour, and five-minute graduations.

3.1. Involve the class in a discussion of the length of the hands on the clocks and watches. Ask them to discriminate between the long one and the short one on clock faces and watches of different sorts and sizes.

4.1. Provide for practice in reading time by discussing time-related situations and by having pupils take turns in showing their ability to set the hands to a variety of discussed times and/or to read the clock set to different readings.

Examples: "How does the clock look when we watch a TV program at 6 o'clock?" "When the clock is like this (set the hands to 12 o'clock) and it is daytime, it is time for (*lunch*)."

3. Each child shall demonstrate the ability to discriminate between the minute and hour hands by indicating (pointing or touching) the correct one when asked to do so.

4. Each child shall provide at least one correct answer to a time-related situation that requires reading time from a clock or watch.

Lesson 10

SCOPE OF THE LESSON: To provide for more activities in using the clock.

INSTRUCTIONAL OBJECTIVES	ACTIVITIES	RESOURCE MATERIALS	EXPERIENCE CHART
1. Each pupil shall complete Clock-Face Exercises 1 and 2 in a manner commensurate with assessed ability and to the teacher's satisfaction. Note: This exercise calls for writing the correct time in numerals and words. If writing the words is too advanced for any of the pupils, that part of the exercise may be modified. Always keep in mind, however, that we are concerned with gains in learning as well as strengthening what has been previously learned.	1.1. Use the overhead projector to help moderate a discussion of the exercises in the project. The class may decide collectively or individuals may take turns suggesting what times are shown on each of the six faces. With each decision, have each child write first in numerals (on the top line) then in words, on the bottom line) the time represented on each clock face. This shall be done on the individual copies by each pupil. Note: Instructions for Exercises 1 and 2 appear on page 323.	Ditto copies of the exercises on page 142 for each pupil Thermal transparency of the exercise Overhead projector Wax pencil	Record exercises 1 and 2 from page 323 on the experience chart. After the pupils have been given the opportunity to work independently on the exercise, work then as a group exercise. Have the pupils explain how they completed each example.

Lesson 11

SCOPE OF THE LESSON: Continue to provide experiences that will develop clock-reading skills.

INSTRUCTIONAL OBJECTIVES	ACTIVITIES	RESOURCE MATERIALS	EXPERIENCE CHART
1. Each child shall draw the hour and minute hands in the proper relative positions according to the times given under each clock face in Exercises 3 and 4. Attention must be given to the difference in the lengths of the hour and minute hands. The teacher should expect at least 5/6 of each exercise to be correct.	1.1. Distribute copies of Clock-Face Exercise 3 to each pupil and explain the exercise. Use the overhead projector to demonstrate how to draw lines in their relative positions and of the correct lengths. Use a ruler or straightedge and wax pencil on the acetate transparency.	Ditto copies of Clock-Face Exercises 3 and 4 for each child Rulers or straightedges for drawing lines to represent hands Demonstration clock Clock transparency	Record Exercises 3 and 4 from pages 324-325 and repeat the process suggested in Lesson 10.
	1.2. Use the same techniques with Clock-Face Exercise 4. Note: As in other exercises, it may be of advantage to the pupils to instigate the exercise as a group project. However, the individual pupil should be encouraged to strike out independently as quickly as possible.	Assortment of clocks as in Lesson 9 Transparency of the lessons Wax pencil	
	Exercise 3 is on page 324.		
	Exercise 4 is on page 325.		

Lesson 12

SCOPE OF THE LESSON: Provide for further activities to strengthen clock use.

INSTRUCTIONAL OBJECTIVES	ACTIVITIES	RESOURCE MATERIALS	EXPERIENCE CHART
1. Each child shall complete Clock-Face Exercise 5 by numbering the dots correctly on the clock faces and by drawing the hands in the correct positions. The difference between the hour and the minute hand should be easily recognized. Accuracy should be at least five correct out of six. Note: The pupils may write the numbers around the perimeter of the clock faces if this is easier for any of them. They should, however, attempt to keep the numbers small and directly relative to each face.	1.1. Distribute copies of Clock-Face Exercise 5 (page 326) to each pupil. 1.2. Project a transparency of the exercise to help explain it to the pupils and to demonstrate how to do the exercise. 1.3. Discuss and do, as a group, one or two parts of the exercise using the projected copy. The teacher may want to make additional practice examples for group work by using an acetate sheet and a wax pencil to construct similar problems.	Ditto copies of the exercise (page 326) Transparency for use with the overhead projector Plain acetate sheet Wax pencil Rulers or straightedges for drawing hands	In telling time, we must be careful to read the correct time. We must look closely at the hour hand and the minute hand. Some clock faces do not have numbers. We need to know where the numbers are supposed to be. This will help us tell time. The time is the same.

Lesson 13

SCOPE OF THE LESSON: Improve clock skills.

INSTRUCTIONAL OBJECTIVES	ACTIVITIES	RESOURCE MATERIALS	EXPERIENCE CHART
1. Each child shall participate in a discussion of the Clock-Face Exercises 6 and 7 and shall correctly (five out of six accuracy expected) write the numbers on the faces, write the time in numbers on the top line and the time in words on the bottom line under each face.	1.1. By now the children should be fairly competent in reading time correctly and should be able to fill in the numbers on the faces, write the time in numbers and in words as directed. 1.2. As in other exercises, the overhead projector may be an asset. Exercises 6 and 7 are on page 327.	Ditto copies of the exercise for each pupil Transparency of the exercise	Record Exercises 6 and 7 from page 327 on a chart as a means of correcting students' work.

Lesson 14

SCOPE OF THE LESSON: Introduce the use of the clock as a means of timing and scheduling activities.

INSTRUCTIONAL OBJECTIVES	ACTIVITIES	RESOURCE MATERIALS	EXPERIENCE CHART
1. Each child shall be engaged in activities 1.2 and 1.3 and shall supply at least three correct answers to each set of questions.	1.1. Use the demonstration clock or the overhead projector and/or individual clocks, and so forth in the following ways.	Transparency demonstration clock. Large demonstration clock Wax pencil	No experience chart is necessary for this lesson.
	1.2. Set a demonstration clock to a time (example: 3 o'clock) then ask the pupils what time it will be in 5 minutes, 15 minutes, 30 minutes, an hour, and so on. Do this as a group exercise and give each child an opportunity to respond. Use a variety of clock settings.	Individual clocks as in Lesson 9	
	1.3. Do as in 1.2 but ask the pupils what time it was 15 minutes ago, an hour ago, and so on.		

Lesson 15

SCOPE OF THE LESSON: To provide a continuation of clock-related activities.

INSTRUCTIONAL OBJECTIVES	ACTIVITIES	RESOURCE MATERIALS	EXPERIENCE CHART
1. Each pupil shall complete Exercise 8 by writing, in numerals, the correct answers to the questions in the exercise. Expected accuracy should be at least 80%.	1.1. Distribute copies of the exercise and read each of the five questions from a projection of the exercise. Pupils may be asked to do the reading whenever possible. 2.1. The pupils shall determine individually the correct answers and write them in the spaces provided. Exercise 8 is on page 328.	Ditto copies of the exercise (page 328) Transparency of the exercise	Half an hour equals 30 minutes. One hour equals 60 minutes. A quarter of an hour equals 15 minutes. Half past means 30 minutes after the hour. For example, half past ten is the same as 10:30. Before assigning Exercise 8 on page 147 to the class, complete the following as a group activity. Ask volunteers to draw hands on the clock faces indicating the appropriate time. 12:15 1:30 2:40 5:20 7:00

311

Lesson 16

Scope of the Lesson: To further skills in clock-related time situations.

Instructional Objectives	Activities	Resource Materials	Experience Chart
1. Each pupil shall complete Exercise 9 by either writing the numerals (except for part one of the fourth question) in the blank spaces or by giving the correct answer verbally.	1.1. Using the projection of the transparency of the exercise, discuss how to do these clock-related problems. 1.2. Encourage the children to make contributions by asking the whole class similar questions. This could develop into a game similar to a spelldown, with the person who gets the correct answer having the privilege of asking a child on the other "side" a question from a bank of problems or an original problem. Exercise 9 is on page 329.	Ditto copies of the exercise (see page 329) Transparency of the exercise	Have the class participate in developing a daily schedule. The following is an example. School starts at 8:30 We have arithmetic at 9:00 Reading begins at 9:30 Recess 10:00 Units 10:15 Lunch 11:30 School begins 12:15 Language 12:15 P.E. 1:15 Music 1:45 Study time 2:15 We go home at 3:00

Birthday Cake Exercise

Have each child draw a birthday cake on the order of the one shown. Have the children letter their own names, ages, and birth dates including the month, day, and year under the drawing. The correct number of candles should be drawn on the cake to represent the child's present age. The whole drawing can be colored and used as a bulletin board decoration to remind the class to prepare for birthday celebrations.

JACOB PETERS-11 YEARS
MARCH 17, 1965

Season Wheel

This season wheel can be made of stiff paper or tagboard and should be large enough so that the whole class can see it (at least 24″ diameter). If the inner wheel is a separate disc, one exercise could be to turn the discs until the seasons line up with the proper months. The wheel can also be colored, and pictures cut from magazines showing seasonal activities can be grouped in clusters around the appropriate season.

Month Flower

Fill in the missing letters to complete the names of the months. Also, give each month its proper number, starting with January as month number 1.

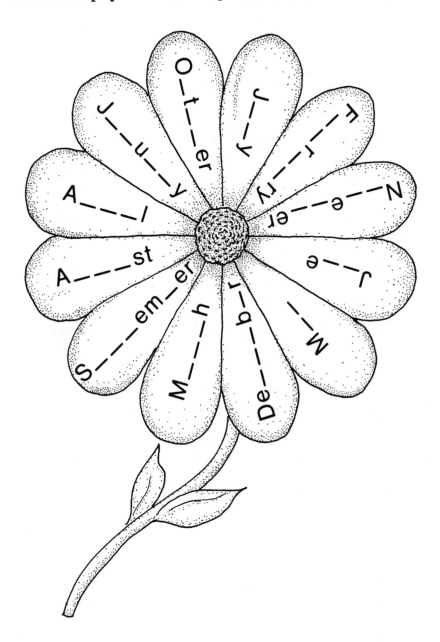

Facts About the Seasons

1. Fill in the missing letters to complete the names of the months.
2. Fill in the blanks from the list of words below so that the sentences make true statements.

1. In J .... y it is usually .... but in J .... u .... y it is the .... season so it is snowy and ....

2. M .... h, A .... l, and M .... are all in the .... of the year. They are the ....rd, ...th, and the ....th months.

3. The Thanksgiving month is N .... m .... r. It is the month that comes in the .... and is the ....th month of the year.

4. The last month of winter is F .... r .... y and the first month of summer is J ....

5. Christmas comes during the month of D .... m .... r. It is in the .... and is the .... month of the year. The next year begins with J .... ry.

6. We start school in S .... t .... b .... r. This month begins the .... season.

7. The 8th month is A .... u ....

8. A summer month that comes after July that is usually a very hot month is A .... u .... t.

9. O .... b .... r is the middle month of the .... season.

10. The winter months are .... but in the .... it is warm.

| spring | fall | cold | warm | 3 | 5 |
| summer | winter | hot | last | 4 | 11 |

Season Fun

We celebrate Thanksgiving in the .... during the month of ....

Our nation's birthday is in the .... on the ....th of ....

Christmas comes in the .... during the month of ....

A religious celebration in the .... is Easter.

Review of the Seasons and Months

Write the correct answer in each blank.

    1. School begins in the ....

    2. Christmas comes in the ....

    3. Easter is in the ....

    4. You play in the snow in the ....

    5. In the .... it is usually very hot.

Draw a line between opposites.

    Example: Fast ———— Far
                Hot ———— Slow
                Near ———— Cold

Winter	First
Past	Tomorrow
Yesterday	Spring
Autumn	Summer
Last	Future

Write in the months in the spaces under the correct season.

Calendar Exercise 1

The Calendar

1. Letter in the name of this month in the top space of the calendar form.
2. Letter in the names of the days of the week in the seven spaces on the second line.
3. Complete this month's calendar by filling in the numbers of the month, being sure to start the first (number 1) on the right day of the week.

Names and Dates

1. What day of the week is the last day of this month? ....

2. Write the numbers (dates) of the days of this month that are all on a Sunday. ...., ..., ..., ..., ...

3. Write the days of the month that are all on a Tuesday.
   ...., ..., ..., ..., ...

4. What day of the week did the first fall on this month?

5. What is today's date (number of the day)? ....

6. What was yesterday's date? ....

Names of Days and Months

1. What was yesterday's day-name? ....

2. What will be tomorrow's date? ....

3. What will be tomorrow's day-name? ....

4. What was the day-name of the first of this month? ....

5. What day is today? ....

6. Write the names of the following:

   This month ....

   Next month ....

   Last month ....

Counting the Days

1. There are .... days in this month.

2. There are .... days in a week.

3. Next month will have .... days. (consult a calendar for the year)

4. Last month had .... days.

5. What day did last month begin on? ....

6. What day will next month begin on? ....

Calendar Exercise 2

Days of the Month

1. Write in the days of the week on the second line in the form above.
2. Make Sunday the first day of this month; write the number 1 under Sunday in the third line.
3. Make Tuesday the last day of this month; number all the days up to and including the space under Tuesday on the last line.
4. How many days are there in this month you have made? ....
5. How many months have the same number of days as your month? ....
   Suggestion: Get a calendar for this year to help you.
6. What is the least number of days there can be in a month? ....
7. In this month you have made what is the date of:
   The second Tuesday? ....   The third Sunday? ....

Birthday Days

Note: You will need to use this year's calendar for help in answering these questions.

1. What is today's date? ....
2. My birthday is the .... of ....
           (date)   (month)

3. This year my birthday falls on the .... day of the week. This is ....

4. I will have to wait .... months, ... weeks, and .... days until my birthday is here.

5. There are .... days in a week.

School Days

Note: You will need to use this year's calendar for help in answering these questions.

1. But, there are only .... days to a school week.
2. This year school began on the .... of ....

3. This year school is over on the .... of ....

4. The days of the week are: (1) ....

   (2) ....   (3) ....

   (4) ....   (5) ....

   (6) ....   (7) ....

5. Christmas is the .... of .... and falls on the .... day of the week which is ....

Vacation Days

Note: You will need to use this year's calendar for help in answering these questions.

1. January 1st this year was on what day of the week? ....

2. This year Christmas vacation begins on the .... of .... and we go back to school on the .... of ....

3. There are .... days to the Christmas vacation.

4. How many days was the Thanksgiving vacation? ....

5. What other vacations are there during the school year and what are they? ....

Clock-Face Exercise

Exercises 1 and 2

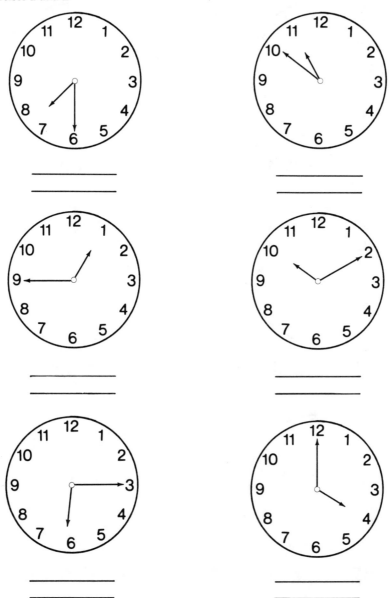

On the top line under each clock face write the correct time in numerals. On the second line under each clock write in words the time shown by the position of the hands.

Exercise 3

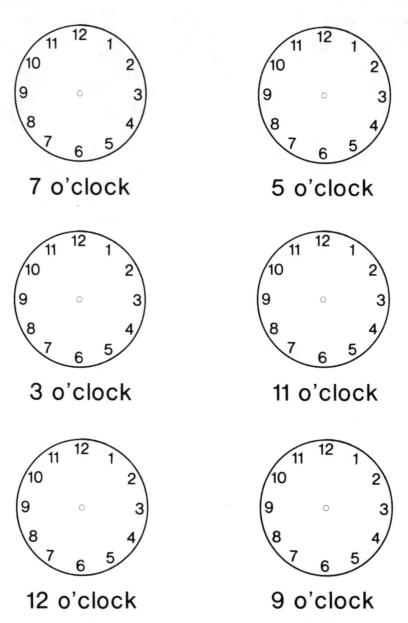

7 o'clock

5 o'clock

3 o'clock

11 o'clock

12 o'clock

9 o'clock

Draw the hands in the proper positions to show the times given under each clock face. Be certain the hands are drawn to show a difference in length between the minute hand and the hour hand.

Exercise 4

Draw the hands in the proper positions to show the times given under each clock face. Be certain the hands are drawn to show a difference in length between the minute hand and the hour hand.

Exercise 5

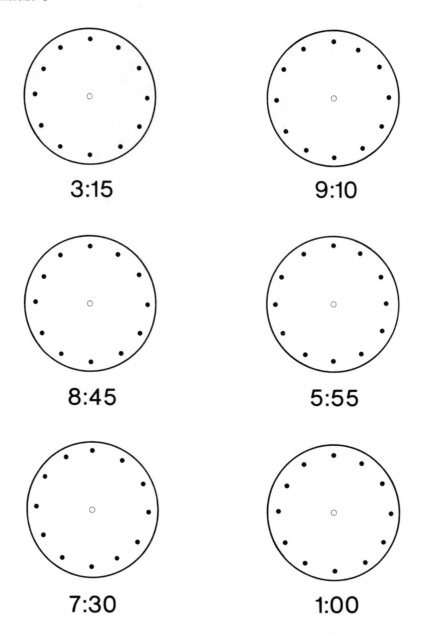

3:15

9:10

8:45

5:55

7:30

1:00

Write the numerals on each clock face, and then draw the hands in the proper position (and lengths) to show the times given under each clock.

Exercises 6 and 7

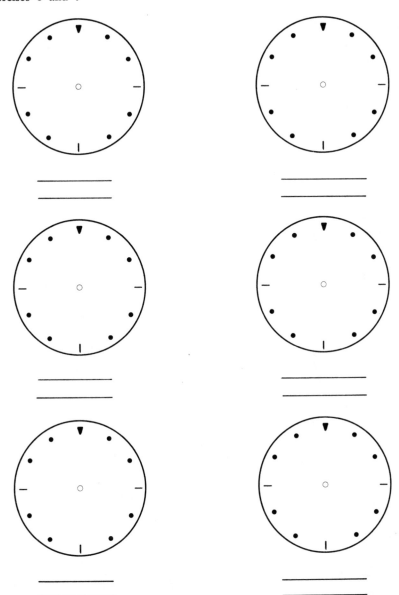

Write the numerals on the clock faces and then:
1. On the top line under each clock face write in numerals the time indicated by the position of the hands.
2. On the second line under each clock face write the time in words.

Exercise 8

In fifteen minutes the time will be ....

Half an hour ago the time was ....

In 90 minutes the time will be ....

In five minutes the time will be ....

Twenty minutes ago the time was ....

Exercise 9

How many minutes is it before 4:30? ....

If the TV program we wanted to watch was at 8:00 o'clock, how late are we? ....

If the bus leaves at 2:45, how much time is left?
....

The football game begins at 1:30. Are we late or not? .... If we are late, how many minutes late? ....

New Year's begins at 12:00 midnight. How long do we have to stay up to see the New Year in?
....

Unit Topic: Home Safety and Maintenance[3]

Instructional Level—Intermediate

I. RATIONALE

Knowledge of efficient home maintenance practices and appropriate safety procedures represent areas of the curriculum that are complementary in nature. A program on safety and accident prevention would not be complete without addressing the sometimes overlooked areas of home maintenance and safety. Of particular concern is the fact that accidents continue to account for the greatest proportion of childhood deaths. There is even some indication that the death tool is increasing for certain groups of youngsters, most notably those between the ages of five and fourteen (Solomon 1977).

It would be unwise to assume that appropriate home maintenance and safety practices are taught or even stressed in every child's home. Further, it should not be assumed that all children are capable of generalizing appropriate maintenance and safety practices between environmental settings. Devoting a unit of the total curriculum specifically to home maintenance and safety would better insure that the child develop adequate knowledge, skills, attitudes, and habits required for decision making in day-to-day home life.

This unit is based upon the notion that a well-maintained and safe home environment is of central importance to every individual. The unit is also based on the belief that every individual must assume a certain amount of responsibility in their own home environment. Lastly, it is recognized that successful and independent living in later life requires at a minimum that the individual be able to manage and maintain a safe home environment.

II. SUB-UNITS

    A. Basic First Aid
    B. Emergencies
    C. Drugs and Poisonous Substances
    D. Indoor Maintenance and Safety
    E. Outdoor Maintenance and Safety
    F. Play and Sports Equipment

3. This sample unit was developed by Judy Mantle while a graduate student at the University of Kansas.

III. GENERAL OBJECTIVES

1. To learn a distinction between safe and unsafe home environments.
2. To develop an understanding of the need for creating and maintaining a safe home environment.
3. To develop an understanding of individual responsibility for maintaining a safe home environment.
4. To develop an understanding of the consequences that might occur if a safe home environment is not maintained.
5. To develop an understanding of the importance of reacting quickly and without panic in emergency situations.
6. To develop communication skills necessary for reporting emergencies.
7. To learn and practice basic first aid skills.
8. To learn the names, purposes, and precautions to be taken with common household drugs and poisonous substances.
9. To learn appropriate ways to care for and handle household pets.
10. To develop an understanding of safety precautions to be exercised when utilizing and storing tools, garden equipment, and household appliances.
11. To create an awareness of safety precautions applicable to play and sports activity in the home.
12. To learn to effectively communicate a variety of precautions and practices that contribute to a well-maintained and safe home environment.

IV. CORE AREA ACTIVITIES

A. *Arithmetic Activities*

1. Develop concepts of time to coincide with taking medication a designated number of times per day.
2. Use telephones to dial the appropriate telephone number for emergency assistance. Use stopwatch to time for efficiency.
3. Count and report the number of articles that appear in a local newspaper resulting from poor home safety practices over a two-week period of time.
4. Make a graph depicting safety hazards that have caused home accidents in the local community based on reports in the local newspaper.

B. *Social Competence Activities*

1. Ask questions of resource person (fireman, pharmacist, nurse).
2. Host a room-sponsored safety fair. Have students explain to students from other classes various home safety practices. Dem-

onstrations and displays of home safety practices would be presented.

3. Assign committees to develop components of a safety checklist, which would be utilized to examine each child's home environment for safety hazards.

4. Field trip to veterinarian.

C. *Communicative Activities*

1. Use telephones to report emergencies to poison control, fire department, police department, and to acquire ambulance service.

2. Plan, prepare, and arrange bulletin board for depicting home safety practices.

3. Design a pamphlet on home safety. Explain features of the pamphlet to the entire class.

4. Distinguish safe and unsafe home safety practices that are presented via a slide-tape presentation. The student must be able to identify and present measures for correction of the condition both verbally and in written form.

5. Show slides of hazardous conditions in the home. The student must determine the dangerous conditions, tell why it is dangerous, and what measures could be taken to alleviate the hazardous condition.

6. Write to local and national organizations requesting pamphlets and brochures on home safety and maintenance.

D. *Health Activities*

1. Identify, describe, and demonstrate and/or explain the function of common household first aid supplies.

2. Develop a list of components for a home first aid kit.

3. Present empty containers of popular over-the-counter drugs.

4. Write a short explanation of what one could do in their home to insure that young children do not have access to medicine, drugs, pills, and other hazardous substances, etc.

5. Invite school nurse to speak to the class on first aid procedures and medicine and drugs in the home.

E. *Safety Activities*

1. Design telephone pads to include emergency numbers of the fire and police department, neighbors, poison control, hospital, parent's work number and ambulance service, etc.

2. Collect pictures of where falls might happen. Show them to the class. Tell how the situation might be prevented.

3. Have each student plan emergency escape routes from all areas of their house.

4. Present empty containers of poisonous substances and have students identify various types of poisonous substances commonly found in the household.
5. Role-play possible accidents that might occur as a result of leaving various items around the home.
6. Divide class into several small groups. Provide each group with a written statement of a hazardous situation in the home. Allow a short time for group collaboration and decision making regarding the situation. Rotate presenters from each group to explain situation and group decision for solving problems.

F. *Vocational Activities*
1. Pass around items from tool kit. Have students say the name and tell the function of each tool.
2. Have students cut out catalogue, magazine, and newspaper advertisements of tools, garden equipment, and household appliances. Make a poster. Discuss how to care for and store tools, garden equipment, and household appliances.

V. RESOURCE MATERIAL

A. *Books*
These books are available through the Lawrence Public Library, Lawrence Kansas.
Bendick, Janne. *Emergency Book*. Chicago, Il.: Rand-McNally, 1967.
Boyer, Richard. *Safety on Wheels*. Fayetteville, Georgia: Oddo Press, 1974.
Greenbank, Anthony. *A Handbook for Emergencies: Coming Out Alive*. Garden City, New York: Doubleday, 1976.
Langman, Harold. *Watch Out*. New York: Parents Magazine Press, 1968.
Shapp, Martha. *Lets Find Out About Safety*. New York: Watts Press, 1975.
Smardge, Norah. *What a Silly Thing To Do*. Nashville: Abingdon Press, 1967.

B. *Workbooks*
Hunter, W. F., and LaFolette, P. L. *Directing Language Skills*. New York: McGraw-Hill Book Company, 1978, p. 108.
Hunter, W. F., and LaFolette, P. L. *Acquiring Language Skills*. New York: McGraw-Hill Book Company, 1978, p. 98.

C. *Films*

Films may be selected from the following list. They are available through:

> Film Services
> 746 Massachusetts
> Lawrence, Kansas 66044

First Aid on the Spot
Are you ready . . . or not?
Poison around the House
In Case of Fire
House of Accidents
I'm No Fool with Fire
Poison Plants
First Aid for Children: I Can Do It Myself
First Aid for Little People
Safe Living at Home
Safety as We Play
Safety with Fire

D. *Miscellaneous*

Slide-tape presentation (teacher-made)
First aid kit
Resource people—nurse, veterinarian, fireman, pharmacist, physical
   education teacher
Newspapers
Projector (slide, movie, overhead)
Catalogues
Tool kit
Flash cards
Cassette player
Pictures of accidents and injuries
Containers of over-the-counter drugs and prescriptions
Containers of other household poisonous substances
Telephone book
Teletrainer telephones
Art supplies
Bulletin board

VI. VOCABULARY

accidents
access
adhesive tape
adult
advantage
alcohol
ambulance
animals
appliances
articles
aspirin
assistance
band-aid
basement
bathroom
bedroom
bicycle
bite
bleeding
broken
bucket
burn
catalogue
caution
checklist
children
chisel
choke
closet
committee
condition
container
cotton
cupboard
curtains
dangerous
demonstration
dial

dining room
direction
disadvantage
display
doctor
driveway
emergency
environment
entranceway
equipment
escape
evacuation
examine
file
fire
fire extinguisher
first aid
gauze
garage
hammer
hand drill
hazard
hedge trimmer
hoe
hose
household
hydrogen peroxide
illness
immunize
indoor
injury
insect
kitchen
lawnmower
living room
maintenance
magazine
medication

neighbors
newspaper
nurse
ointment
outdoor
over-the-counter drug
panic
pliers
police
practice
precautions
prescription drug
putty knife
rake
reporting
responsibility
resource
routes
ruler
safe
scissors
screwdriver
sidewalk
situation
smoke alarm
sparks
stairwell
telephone
tweezers
unsafe
veterinarian
warning
window
wrench
yard

Unit: Home Safety and Maintenance

Lesson 1

SCOPE OF LESSON:
1. Introduce the unit topic on home maintenance and safety.
2. Develop the concepts of safe and unsafe home environments by presenting situations for comparison.
3. Develop an understanding of the need for creating and maintaining a safe home environment.

INSTRUCTIONAL OBJECTIVES	ACTIVITIES	RESOURCE MATERIALS	EXPERIENCE CHART
1. Is able to demonstrate interest in home maintenance and safety practices by participating in class discussion.	1. Present large flash cards of the following words in order to create interest and initiate discussion of key unit concepts. Students should write down each word and their definition of each word. a. Environment b. Maintenance c. Safe d. Unsafe e. Hazard f. Dangerous	Large flash cards	We must all be concerned with home maintenance and safety practices. There are many different areas in a home environment. Some areas of a home may be more dangerous than others. It is important that we know the difference between safe and unsafe conditions in and around a home.
2. Is able to identify various areas that comprise a home environment.	2. Initiate a class discussion of each word. Reach group consensus on a definition of each word and determine how each word relates to home maintenance and safety practices. Write words and definitions on transparencies.	Overhead Projector	
3. Is able to list areas of the home that are likely to be most dangerous and explain why they are dangerous.			
4. Is able to distinguish between safe and unsafe home conditions via a slide-tape presentation.	3. Have the students identify various rooms and areas of a home environment (indoor and outdoor). Prompt if necessary, to create an awareness of a variety of spaces commonly found in home environments such as: a. Indoor 1. Living room 2. Kitchen 3. Dining room	Overhead Projector	

4. Bedroom
5. Bathroom
6. Entranceway
7. Stairwell
8. Closet
9. Cupboard
10. Basement
11. Garage

b. Outdoor
1. Yard
2. Driveway
3. Sidewalk
4. Stairway

4. Have students list areas of the home environment they think are most likely to be dangerous and explain why. Call upon students to share ideas with the rest of the class.

5. Using a slide-tape presentation, show pictures of safe and unsafe conditions in various home environments. Have students write whether each picture depicts a safe or unsafe home environment. Go back through slides and discuss. This activity may serve as a pretest for the unit.

Teacher-made slide-pre-presentation

6. Explain that the culminating activity for the unit will be to host a Safety Day, where other classes will be invited to visit and view displays and demonstrations that depict a variety of home maintenance and safety practices.

Vocabulary: Environment, maintenance, safe, unsafe, hazard, dangerous, indoor, outdoor, living room, kitchen, dining room, bedroom, bathroom, entranceway, stairway, closet, cupboard, basement, garage, yard, driveway, sidewalk, condition, practice.

Lesson 2

SCOPE OF LESSON:
1. Review experience chart and vocabulary from introductory lesson.
2. Create awareness as to what can happen as a result of unsafe home practices.
3. Create awareness of individual responsibility in alleviating hazardous conditions in the home.

INSTRUCTIONAL OBJECTIVES	ACTIVITIES	RESOURCE MATERIALS	EXPERIENCE CHART
1. Is able to read aloud and answer questions pertaining to experience chart from previous lesson.	1. Review experience chart from introductory lesson. Have students read the chart aloud.	Experience Chart—Lesson 1 Sample folder	Unsafe conditions in the home may result in serious accidents or injuries. We must all take responsibility for recognizing and correcting hazardous conditions in our own homes. People of all ages can be injured if home conditions are unsafe.
2. Is able to write definitions of words from previous lessons.	2. Introduce the idea of developing a home safety folder, which will be displayed on Safety Day. The notebook is to include a daily accumulation of vocabulary words with the students' own definitions of the words.		
	3. Ask students to verbally give their definition of selected vocabulary words from introductory lesson.	Flash cards	
3. Is able to read and comprehend a potentially hazardous home situation, write possible consequences and determine the action to take to alleviate the hazard.	4. Students should then write their own definitions of words from previous lesson.		
	5. Hold up flash cards of the words *accident* and *injury.* Discuss the meaning and causes of each word.	Flash cards	
	6. Film—"House of Accidents"	Film	
	7. Show slides of home hazards and have students write the consequence that could result in their own home if the hazard was left unattended. Students should assume that younger children will visit the home if there are no younger brothers or sisters. Descriptions of hazardous conditions could include:	Slide presentation	

a. window curtains near a stove
b. spilled milk on kitchen floor
c. broken toys
d. sharp knife left on kitchen table
e. clothes left on bedroom floor
f. old rags piled in the basement
g. bicycle left in the driveway
h. horseplay in the bathroom
i. sparks from toaster when plugging it in
j. bottle of aspirin left on table by bed.

8. Develop written solutions to each problem. Then discuss what action could be taken to correct the hazardous condition.

9. Design a cover for the Safety Day Folder.

Folders—Art Supplies

10. Students should add vocabulary words and handout to folder:

Vocabulary: accident, injury, window, curtains, kitchen, broken, knife, bedroom, basement, sparks, aspirin, responsibility, condition.

Lesson 3

SCOPE OF LESSON:
1. Review experience chart and vocabulary from previous lesson.
2. Orient student to elementary first aid principles.
3. Create an awareness of the types of first aid supplies that may be useful in the home.

INSTRUCTIONAL OBJECTIVES	ACTIVITIES	RESOURCE MATERIALS	EXPERIENCE CHART
1. Is able to read aloud the experience chart from the previous lesson.	1. Review experience chart from Lesson 3. Briefly quiz students on major concepts and vocabulary words from previous day.	Experience chart	It is important to know when and how to use the appropriate first aid procedure. It is also important to know what to do and what *not* to do in case of serious injury. First aid supplies should be kept in a place in the home where one can get to them quickly.
2. Is able to verbally define vocabulary words from previous lesson.	2. Guest speaker—school nurse. The nurse will demonstrate first aid practices for common minor injuries.	Resource person —School nurse	
3. Is able to verbally name first aid supplies.	3. Show pictures of appropriate ways to store first aid supplies.	First aid supplies Pictures	
4. Is able to role-play basic first aid techniques.	4. Display and pass around basic first aid supplies typically used in the home. Should say aloud the name of the first aid supply.	First aid supplies	
	5. Have students get a partner and practice techniques. First aid procedures should be presented verbally and demonstrated by each student.		
	6. Have students (in pairs) role-play situations where first aid procedures are required. They should be given a written paragraph describing the situation, read it aloud to the rest of the class, and verbally explain the procedures they would follow. Involve entire class in discussion of role-play situation.		
	Vocabulary: same as previous lesson.		

Lesson 4

SCOPE OF LESSON: 1. Review experience chart and vocabulary from previous lesson.
2. Develop an understanding of the usefulness of a well-maintained first aid kit or medicine cabinet.

INSTRUCTIONAL OBJECTIVES	ACTIVITIES	RESOURCE MATERIALS	EXPERIENCE CHART
1. Is able to read aloud the experience chart from previous lesson.	1. Review experience chart from Lesson 3. Have the students read the chart aloud. Briefly quiz them on major concepts.	Overhead projector	All of us should know about basic first aid. There are many types of first aid supplies that may be useful in the home. If injuries are serious, it is important that we get help from an adult. Parents should be told about any first aid that is given.
2. Is able to verbally define vocabulary words from previous lessons.	2. Briefly quiz students on selected vocabulary words from previous lessons.	Overhead projector	
3. Is able to formulate a definition and purpose of first aid from class discussion.	3. Film—First Aid for Children: I Can Do It Myself	Film	
4. Participate in a group to develop a list of first aid supplies and their uses.	4. Have students write the phrase, "First aid is . . . ," and prepare their own definition. Initiate a group discussion of what first aid is and when it should be used.		
5. Is able to role-play basic first-aid treatment for selected emergency situations.	5. Develop entry for Safety Day Folder entitled "First Aid Supplies for the Home." Have students participate in a group to develop a list of first aid supplies. Rearrange groups to enhance the sharing of ideas.		
6. Is able to write a thank you letter to school nurse.	6. Present pictures of minor injuries that commonly occur in home environments. Review the basic first aid procedures for the following:	Pictures of accidents and injuries	
	a. Bleeding from minor cuts and scratches		
	b. Nosebleeds		
	c. Minor puncture wounds		
	d. Burns		

341

Lesson 4 *(Continued)*

Instructional Objectives	Activities	Resource Materials	Experience Chart
	e. Sprains f. Splinters g. Sunburns 7. Discuss what to do and what not to do in case of serious injury. Discuss the importance of informing the parent or adult of all accidents and injuries. 8. Have students write a thank you letter to school nurse. Vocabulary: First aid, bleeding, burn, adult, scratch, sprain, splinter, sunburn, cotton, gauze, band-aid, scissors, adhesive tape, tweezers, hydrogen peroxide, alcohol, first aid cream.		

Lesson 5

SCOPE OF LESSON: 1. Review experience chart and vocabulary from previous lesson.
2. Create awareness of common household drugs and hazardous substances.

INSTRUCTIONAL OBJECTIVES	ACTIVITIES	RESOURCE MATERIALS	EXPERIENCE CHART
1. Is able to read aloud and answer questions pertaining to experience chart from previous lesson.	1. Review experience chart from Lesson 4. Briefly quiz students on major concepts and vocabulary words from previous day.	Resource person—Pharmacist Containers of over-the-counter and prescription drugs Work sheet Abbreviations Containers of other hazardous substances Antidote	There are important differences between over-the-counter and prescription drugs. It is important to know how to use drugs in a safe manner. Many common household cleaners and supplies can be dangerous to the body if they are not used for their intended purpose. Storing drugs and hazardous substances in a safe place away from young children can prevent many accidents and injuries.
2. Is able to distinguish between over-the-counter and prescription drugs.	2. Resource person—Pharmacist Present containers of over-the-counter drugs and prescription drugs. Have children read labels aloud, helping them understand and interpret cautions, warnings, and directions for safe use.		
3. Is able to identify and explain precautions to be taken with drugs in the home.	3. Discuss abbreviations that are found on labels, such as oz., fl. oz., T. tbs., t. or tsp., hr.		
4. Is able to identify and list the precautions to be taken with other hazardous substances in the home.	4. Have students read labels. Determine the dosage for adults and children. Determine time of dosage.		
5. Is able to write a short story on how drugs and hazardous substances should be stored in the home.	5. Present containers of other hazardous substances in the home such as: mothballs insect killers drain cleaners paint thinners gasoline hair spray roll-on-deodorant		
	6. Pass the containers around. Have students read the labels and cautions aloud.		

343

Lesson 5 *(Continued)*

Instructional Objectives	Activities	Resource Materials	Experience Chart
	7. Have students make a list of these and other hazardous substances they can think of which are found in their own homes. 8. Write a short story on how drugs and hazardous substances should be stored in the home. Vocabulary: prescription, over-the-counter, caution, warning, directions, substances, antidote.		

Lesson 6

SCOPE OF LESSON:
1. Review experience charts and vocabulary from previous lessons.
2. Develop an understanding of emergency communication procedures.
3. Develop an understanding of desired behavior in an emergency situation.

INSTRUCTIONAL OBJECTIVES	ACTIVITIES	RESOURCE MATERIALS	EXPERIENCE CHART
1. Is able to read aloud and answer questions pertaining to experience chart from previous lesson.	1. Review experience chart from Lesson 5. Briefly quiz students on major concepts and vocabulary words from previous day.		When there is an emergency, we must be prepared to act quickly. One should know what emergency services are available and what telephone numbers of those services are. Getting help as quickly as possible may save someone's life. Everyone should know emergency escape routes for their own home. Acting calmly and without panic in an emergency is very important.
2. Is able to dial emergency phone numbers.	2. Design a telephone pad that includes emergency phone numbers for: a. Fire Department b. Police Department c. Hospital d. Ambulance Service e. Neighbors f. Poison Control g. Parents' work number	Telephone book	
3. Is able to design emergency escape routes for own home.	3. Using telephones, practice dialing the emergency numbers and asking for assistance. Have students time each other. Record accuracy.	Teletrainer-Telephones Stopwatches Film	
4. Is able to write a paragraph on the behavior to display in emergency situations.	4. Film—*In Case of Fire.*		
	5. Instruct students to draw a floor plan of their home. They should then draw escape routes to be utilized in emergency situations.	Construction paper Crayons	
	6. Have students write a paragraph on why it is important to keep calm and not panic in an emergency situation.		

345

Lesson 7

SCOPE OF LESSON: 1. Review experience chart and vocabulary from previous lesson.
2. Develop an understanding of potential dangers created by the improper use of electrical appliances.
3. Develop understanding of safety, practices for specific areas of the home.
4. Create awareness of routine housekeeping responsibilities and desirable personal habits for home maintenance and safety.

INSTRUCTIONAL OBJECTIVES	ACTIVITIES	RESOURCE MATERIALS	EXPERIENCE CHART
1. Is able to read aloud and answer questions pertaining to experience chart from previous lesson.	1. Review experience chart from previous lesson. Have students read the chart aloud.		If electrical appliances are not utilized and cared for appropriately, fire hazards could develop. Each area of the home invites certain kinds of accidents. Certain precautions should be taken in each area of the home. Keeping things in their appropriate place will help prevent accidents and falls.
2. Is able to make a list of safety precautions to be utilized with electrical appliances.	2. Resource person—Fireman. The fireman should discuss fire prevention measures for each area of the home. Other topics, such as storage of flammable items, smoke alarms, and use and care of electrical appliances should be presented.	Resource person—Fireman	
	3. Have students cut pictures of electrical appliances out of catalogues. The pictures should be posted on a large piece of poster board to make a collage. The students should then make a list of safety precautions to be taken when utilizing electrical appliances. Share ideas in class discussion.	Scissors, catalogues poster board	

Lesson 8

SCOPE OF LESSON: 1. Develop an understanding of safety practices for specific areas of the home.
2. Create awareness of routine housekeeping responsibilities and desirable personal habits for home maintenance and safety.

INSTRUCTIONAL OBJECTIVES	ACTIVITIES	RESOURCE MATERIALS	EXPERIENCE CHART

1. Is able to participate in a group discussion and formulate ideas for safety practices in each area of the home.
 	
2. Is able to identify articles in the local newspaper that discuss accidents in the home.
 	
3. Is able to write to organizations and request pamphlets and brochures on home safety and maintenance.
	1. Divide students into groups. Each group is to formulate a list of safety practices to be applied in each area of the home, such as:
	  a. Kitchen
	  b. Bathroom
	  c. Stairways and Halls
	  d. Bedroom
	  e. Living Room
	  f. Attic, Basement, Garage
	
	2. Have groups present their ideas for each area. Rotate presenters. Compile ideas. Write them on transparencies. Develop a home safety checklist for students to evaluate their home.
	
	3. Have students scan local newspaper and circle the articles depicting accidents or injuries resulting from poor home safety or maintenance practices. Have students add up the number of articles. Divide the types of accidents of injuries into categories. Make a graph of the types of accidents or injuries depicting the causes of the accident or hazard.
	
	4. Have students write to local and national organizations to request pamphlets and brochures on home safety and maintenance.
		Overhead projector
		
		Newspaper
		Construction paper
			Each area of the home invites certain kinds of accidents. Everyone should develop routine habits to help prevent accidents. Keeping things in their appropriate place will help prevent accidents and falls. Local and national organizations have ideas to help us keep our homes safe.

Lesson 9

SCOPE OF LESSON: 1. Develop an understanding of the appropriate procedures for care and handling of household pets.

INSTRUCTIONAL OBJECTIVES	ACTIVITIES	RESOURCE MATERIALS	EXPERIENCE CHART
1. Is able to discuss the proper care and handling of animals.	1. Visit a local animal hospital. Ask the veterinarian to speak to the class about appropriate methods for: a. Holding and handling animals b. Feeding animals c. Importance of not taking food or toys away from animals. d. Playing with animals e. Immunizing animals 2. Discuss various aspects of the field trip. Vocabulary: veterinarian, immunize		No experience chart

Lesson 10

SCOPE OF LESSON: 1. Create an understanding of appropriate function and storage of tools and equipment.
2. Create an awareness of potential hazards in the outdoor home environment.
3. Develop an understanding of first aid and emergency procedures as they relate to common outdoor accidents in the home environment.

INSTRUCTIONAL OBJECTIVES	ACTIVITIES	RESOURCE MATERIALS	EXPERIENCE CHART
1. Is able to label basic household tools and garden equipment. 2. Is able to identify potentially hazardous conditions in the outdoor home environment. 3. Is able to role-play emergency procedures for common outdoor accidents.	1. Hold up pictures of household tools and garden equipment with labels under the picture. Have the students say the name of the item. Then hold up flash cards with pictures and no labels. Have the students write the name of the item. Go through cards again and have them check their work. Items could include: *Tools* a. saw b. pliers c. hand drill d. file e. hammer f. wrench g. chisel h. ruler i. screwdriver j. putty knife k. snippers *Garden Equipment* a. lawn mower b. hand shovel c. shovel d. rake e. hedge trimmer f. hose g. bucket h. hoe	Flash cards	It can be fun to work with tools, and it can be fun to work in the yard. We must remember that tools are necessary for many kinds of work, but they can be dangerous. It is important to utilize and store tools in a safe way. Tools that do not work correctly should be repaired.

Lesson 10 (*Continued*)

Instructional Objectives	Activities	Resource Materials	Experience Chart
	2. Pass around items from tool kit. Call upon students to tell the function of each tool.	Tool kit	
	3. Discuss how to care for and store tools and garden equipment.		
	4. Using a slide presentation, have students identify and write down potentially hazardous conditions in the outdoor home environment. Have them list ways to correct the hazardous situations.	Slide presentation	
	5. Show pictures of common outdoor accidents. Have students role play first aid and emergency procedures they would take in specific situations. Vocabulary: saw, pliers, hand drill, file, hammer, wrench, chisel, ruler, screwdriver, putty knife, snappers, lawn mower, hand shovel, shovel, rake, hedge trimmer, hose, bucket, hoe.	Flash cards	

Lesson 11

SCOPE OF LESSON:
1. Review vocabulary and experience chart from previous lessons.
2. Emphasize importance of inspecting toys and play equipment frequently.
3. Develop an understanding of the importance of storing play and sports equipment in an appropriate fashion.
4. Create awareness of the types of hazards that can develop if play and sports equipment are not utilized appropriately.

INSTRUCTIONAL OBJECTIVES	ACTIVITIES	RESOURCE MATERIALS	EXPERIENCE CHART
1. Is able to read aloud and answer questions pertaining to experience chart from previous lesson.	1. Review experience chart and vocabulary words from previous lesson.		If play and sports equipment are to be safe and if you want them to last a long time, it is necessary to take good care of them. Serious accidents or injuries can result if toys and play equipment are used and stored carelessly.
2. Is able to list reasons why it is important to inspect toys and play equipment frequently.	2. Write the names of different kinds of toys used both inside and outside the house. Have students list reasons why it is important to inspect toys and play equipment frequently.	Overhead projector	
3. Is able to discuss reasons for and ways of storing play and sports equipment in an appropriate manner.	3. Have physical education teacher lead a discussion on the reasons for and the ways of storing play and sports equipment in an appropriate manner.	Resource person—Physical Education teacher	
4. Is able to draw cartoons of what could happen if toys and play equipment are not utilized, cared for, or stored appropriately.	4. Have students draw cartoons (stick figures) of accidents and injuries which could result if play or sports equipment is misused.	Construction paper Crayons	

Lesson 12

Scope of Lesson: 1. Prepare for Safety Day.

Instructional Objectives	Activities	Resource Materials	Experience Chart
	1. Collect materials and prepare displays for Safety Day.		
	2. Role-play and practice demonstration for Safety Day.		

Bibliography

ARMSTRONG, ROBERT J. et al. *The Development and Evaluation of Behavioral Objectives*. Worthington, Ohio: Charles A. Jones Publishing Company, 1970.

BARRO, STEPHEN M. "An Approach to Developing Accountability Measures for the Public Schools." *Phi Delta Kappan* 52, no. 4 (December 1970).

CALDER, C. R. "The Curriculum-Instruction Continuum with Respect to Mainstreaming of Handicapped Children." In *Instructional Technology and the Education of All Handicapped Children*, edited by R. Heinrich and S. C. Ashcroft. Columbus, Ohio: National Center on Media and Materials for the Handicapped, 1977.

CROOKS, CORYDON. "Time." Unpublished doctoral dissertation, University of Iowa.

Designing Effective Instruction. Palo Alto: General Programmed Teaching, A Division of Commerce Clearing House, 1971.

EBENSEN, THORWALD. *Working with Individual Instruction: The Duluth Experience*. Belmont, Calif.: Fearon Publishers, 1968.

Federal Register, 42 (163) August, 1977.

GUBA, EGON G. "An Overview of the Evaluation Problem." A paper read at the symposium on "The World of Evaluation Needs Reshaping." AERA Convention, February 1969.

JOHNSON, MAURITZ, JR. "Definitions and Models in Curriculum Theory." *Educational Therapy* (April 1967).

KELLY, EDWARD J. *Elementary School Social Studies Instruction: A Basic Approach*. Denver, Colo.: Love Publishing Co., 1979.

LEMBO, JOHN M. *The Psychology of Effective Classroom Instruction*. Columbus, Ohio: Charles E. Merrill Publishing Co., 1979.

Life Experience Starter Units Set No. 2. Special Education Curriculum Development Center. Iowa City, Iowa: University of Iowa, 1969.

MAGER, ROBERT F. *Preparing Instructional Objectives*. Belmont, Calif.: Fearon Publishers, 1968.

McASHAN, H. H. *Writing Behavioral Objectives: A New Approach*. New York: Harper and Row, 1970.

McCANDLESS, B. R. *Children Behavior and Development*. New York: Holt, Rinehart and Winston, 1967.

MEYEN, E. L. *Instructional Based Appraisal System (IBAS)*. Bellevue, Wash.: Edmark Associates, 1976.

ODEN, C. W., JR., "Desegregation and Mainstreaming: A Case of Deja Vu." In *Mainstreaming and the Minority Child*, edited by R. L. Jones. Reston, Va.: The Council for Exceptional Children, 1976.

PEPPER, F. C. "Teaching the American Indian Child in Mainstreaming Settings." In *Mainstreaming and the Minority Child*, edited by R. L. Jones. Reston, Va.: The Council for Exceptional Children, 1976.

PHENIX, PHILLIP, H. "Curriculum." *Philosophy of Education*. New York: Holt, Rinehart and Winston, 1958.

Planning an Arithmetic Curriculum. Special Education Curriculum Development Center. Iowa City, Iowa: University of Iowa, 1968.

POPHAM, W. JAMES, and HUSEK, T. R. "Implications of Criterion-Referenced Measurement." *Journal of Educational Measurement*, Spring 1969.

SOLOMON, K. J., M.D. In *A Sigh of Relief, the First-Aid Handbook for Childhood Emergencies*, edited by M. I. Green. New York: Bantam Books, 1977.

Special Education Curriculum Development Center. *Developing Appropriate Seatwork for the Mentally Retarded*. Iowa City, Iowa: University of Iowa, 1969.

STEPHENS, THOMAS M. *Directive Teaching of Children with Learning and Behavioral Handicaps*. Columbus, Ohio: Charles E. Merrill Publishing Company, 1970.

TURNBULL, A. P.; STRICKLAND, B. B.; and BRANTLEY, J. C. *Developing and Implementing Individualized Education Programs*. Columbus, Ohio: Charles Merrill Publishing Co., 1978.

WILLIAMS, W. J., and STITH, M. *Middle Childhood Behavior Development*. New York: Macmillan Publishing Co., 1974.

Lesson 13

SCOPE OF LESSON: 1. Host A Safety Day

INSTRUCTIONAL OBJECTIVES	ACTIVITIES	RESOURCE MATERIALS	EXPERIENCE CHART
	Other classes and parents should be invited to attend and participate in Safety Day. A number of displays and demonstrations depicting activities throughout the unit may be exhibited. Students should actively participate in demonstrations of home safety practices and procedures where possible. At the end of the day present certificates that acknowledge achievement in home safety and maintenance techniques.		

REFERENCES

CROOKS, CORYDON. "Time." Unpublished doctoral dissertation, University of Iowa, 1971.

Life Experience Starter Units Set No. 2. Special Education Curriculum Development Center. Iowa City: University of Iowa, 1969.

Planning An Arithmetic Curriculum. Special Education Curriculum Development Center. Iowa City: University of Iowa, 1968.

SOLOMON, K. J., M.D. In *A Sigh of Relief, the First-Aid Handbook for Childhood Emergencies,* edited by M. I. Green. New York: Bantam Books, 1977.

Appendixes

Sample Individualized Educational Plan

INDIVIDUAL EDUCATION PROGRAM

Student Name or ID # _____ Date of Birth _____ Grade _____

Parent/Guardian _____ Address _____ Phone _____

School District _____ Attendance Center _____

Primary Language of Home _____ Is English spoken or understood _____ Ethnic _____

I.E.P. Date _____ Primary Area of Exceptionality _____ (Code 1-12)

Placement/Planning/Review Team: Signature   *Instructional Team: Signature*

Principal _____   Principal _____

Parent _____   Parent _____

Student (when appropriate) _____   Teacher _____

Teacher _____   Special Teacher _____

Special Teacher _____   Other (specify) _____

Psychologist _____   Other (specify) _____

Social Worker _____

Speech and Language _____

Other (specify) _____

Summary of Present Level of Educational Performance:

Strengths   *Weaknesses*

_____   _____

_____   _____

_____   _____

_____   _____

Reprinted with permission from the Central Kansas Cooperative in Education, Salina, Kansas.

NAME _____

Annual Goal—Priority # ( ) _____

Short-Term Objectives (Written in Measurable Terms)	Name & Position of Person Responsible	Hours Per Week	Implementation Date	Completion Date	Special Methods and/or Materials	Comments

STUDENT'S NAME _____

Program Review (required to be reviewed four (4) times yearly)

Review I

Reviewing date: _____

Reviewed by: _____

Comments: _____

_____

_____

Review II

Reviewing date: _____

Reviewed by: _____

Comments: _____

_____

_____

Review III

Reviewing date: _____

Reviewed by: _____

Comments: _____

_____

_____

Review IV

Reviewing date: _____

Reviewed by: _____

Comments: _____

_____

_____

I.E.P. _____
Name

Educational Services Recommended: (Ideal)

☐ Self-contained
☐ Resource Room
☐ Itinerant   Specify _____,
☐ Home
☐ Institution   Specify _____,

Educational Services Provided:

Services	Date Initiated	Amount of Time Assigned	Anticipated Duration
_____	_____	_____	_____
_____	_____	_____	_____
_____	_____	_____	_____
_____	_____	_____	_____
_____	_____	_____	_____

_____ % Regular

_____ % Special

Justification for Placement Recommendation:

Experience Chart
Easel Directions
for Building*

LIST OF MATERIAL

4 - 1" x 2" x 72" legs

4 - 1¼" x 1" x 36" back base for sides

4 - 1" x 3" x 36" back base and front base

2 - 1" x 8" x 36" top back base

1 - 1" x 4" x 36" top cap

2 - 32¾" x 42½" x ½" cellotex or chalkboard

1 - 14½" x 34" x ¼" plywood or hard board for storage area bottom

4 - 6" heavy duty clipboard clips

8 - ½" x 36" quarter round trim

*Designer unknown.

Glossary

Annual goals. Activities or achievements to be completed or attained within a year. Annual goals are required to be stated for handicapped children when writing individualized education programs (IEPs), as directed in Public Law 94-142.

Assessment. A survey of the skills currently present and absent in learners.

Competency-based instruction. Instruction designed to meet predetermined objectives, with measures of performance used to evaluate obtainment of those objectives.

Comprehensive skill inventory. A listing of all skills taught in the school year.

Continuum approach. The logical sequencing units of instruction throughout the school year.

Core areas. Areas of learning, such as communication, arithmetic, social competence, safety, health, and vocation.

Core area approach. The organization of units of instruction by core areas resulting in instruction occurring simultaneously on several units.

Due process. Used in an educational context, the term refers to procedures and policies established to ensure equal educational opportunities for all children. P. L. 94-142 contains due process procedures specific to handicapped children.

Evaluation. A measure of the changes in pupil performance and the instruction responsible for those changes.

Exceptional children. Children whose performance in school-related behaviors varies from the norm to the extent that special instruction, assistance, and/or equipment are required. Children may be classified as exceptional because of intellectual, physical and/or behavioral, and/or sensory reasons. The term also is used in referring to gifted children.

Experience chart. A story or narrative statement developed by students and recorded on large charts or the blackboard, which is used to develop a variety of academic and social skills.

Free Appropriate Public Education (FAPE). Used in P.L. 94-142 to mean special education and related services that are provided at public expense, which meet requirements of the state educational agency, and which conform to the individualized education program (IEP) requirement of P.L. 94-142.

Handicapped (see also exceptional children). The term handicapped is more restrictive than the term exceptional, in that it does not include the gifted. When the gifted are to be included in referring to a population of students requiring special instruction, assistance, or equipment, the term exceptional is generally applied.

Individualized Education Program (IEP). A requirement of P.L. 94-142, which specifies that an educational plan must be developed in writing and maintained for each handicapped child. The IEP must include a statement of the child's current level of educational performance, annual goals, short-term instructional objectives, specific services to be provided, information and dates services are to be provided, and criteria for evaluation.

Instructional objectives. A specification of (1) performance outcomes as a result of instruction, (2) conditions under which the performance can be expected, and (3) criterion for evaluation of successful performance.

Integration. Used in the context of special education, this term refers to the placement of handicapped children in educational programs also serving nonhandicapped children.

Least restrictive environment. When applied to the education of exceptional children, the term refers to the principle that handicapped children should be educated with nonhandicapped peers in regular educational setting whenever possible. Allowances are made for placement in special classes or other settings when they are the least restrictive based on needs of the individual involved.

Lesson plan. A description of the basic information concepts and skills emphasized in each lesson.

Mainstreaming. The practice of educating children in regular educational settings. This generally involves the placement of handicapped children in regular classrooms and the provisions of support services when necessary. The practice is gaining wide popularity in meeting educational needs of the mildly handicapped.

Public Law 94-142. The education for all Handicapped Children Act of 1975. (See the *Federal Register*, August 23, 1977, Vol. 42, No. 163, for details on the rules governing this Act.)

Resource unit. Reservoirs of ideas for activities varied in type usually generated by committees of teachers.

Scope of lesson statement. A statement of general content of a specific lesson, which relates to the total lesson.

Seatwork. Independent activities for students designed to extend instruction.

Special class. A program option for exceptional children involving the assignment of children with similar instructional needs to a class taught by a certified special teacher. Special classes sometimes are referred to as self-contained classes.

Support services. Special services provided to exceptional children beyond their basic educational program. Such services may include speech therapy, occupational therapy, physical therapy, music therapy, tutoring, and psychological services.

Task analysis. The process of specifying the steps or components of a task for the purpose of delineating manageable instructional objectives.

Teaching unit. Units designed by teachers with a specific group of children in mind using the subject matter as a vehicle for teaching knowledge.

Unit evaluation inventory. A survey of all the objectives taught to students as a result of units of instruction used to evaluate the effectiveness of instruction.

Unit of instruction. Sequential plan of instruction designed by instructional staff, which integrates the teaching of academic and social skills within the context of a theme, which builds on the previous experiences of the students.